Test Driven

D1570144

Test Driven

HIGH-STAKES ACCOUNTABILITY
IN ELEMENTARY SCHOOLS

Linda Valli
Robert G. Croninger
Marilyn J. Chambliss
Anna O. Graeber
Daria Buese

Teachers College, Columbia University
New York and London

Published by Teachers College Press, 1234 Amsterdam Avenue, New York, NY 10027

Library of Congress Cataloging-in-Publication Data

Test driven : high-stakes accountability in elementary schools / Linda Valli . . . [et al.].
    p. cm.
  Includes bibliographical references and index.
  ISBN 978-0-8077-4894-7 (pbk : alk. paper) — ISBN 978-0-8077-4895-4 (cloth : alk. paper)
  1. Educational tests and measurements—United States. 2. Elementary schools—United States—Examinations. I. Valli, Linda, 1947–

  LB3051.T415 2008
  372.126—dc22

                                          2008004591

ISBN: 978-0-8077-4894-7 (paper)
ISBN: 978-0-8077-4895-4 (cloth)

Printed on acid-free paper
Manufactured in the United States of America

15 14 13 12 11 10 09 08   8 7 6 5 4 3 2 1

Contents

Preface

The 2001 reauthorization of the Elementary and Secondary Education Act, No Child Left Behind (NCLB), greatly expanded the federal role in education and established a new regime of high-stakes testing. Although standardized testing, even required testing, is not new to public schools, the 2001 reauthorization radically increased testing requirements and consequences for all schools. Not only were states required to test annually all third- through eighth-grade students in reading and mathematics, states were also required to establish proficiency standards and guarantee that students attain these standards by 2014. Schools that failed to make progress toward compliance with the federal timetable were to face progressively severe sanctions, including the possibility of major restructuring and state takeover. Whereas prior reauthorizations encouraged states to create performance-based accountability frameworks, NCLB required states to do so with high-stakes consequences.

Although there is strong public support for using standardized testing to hold schools accountable for student learning, there is little agreement about how best to do so. The framework promoted by NCLB emphasizes frequent testing, clear timelines, and serious consequences for schools that fail to meet annual yearly progress. A central assumption of the policy is that a stronger emphasis on school outputs will focus students, teachers, and principals on what students need to know and how best to teach them. Frequent test results will provide information to parents and teachers about how well schools are doing and sanctions will motivate principals and teachers to do better. But how tenable is this assumption—that is, how are schools actually responding to the challenges of high-stakes testing? Are schools improving their educational programs and enhancing the educational opportunities afforded students? Is the heightened emphasis on testing and sanctions promoting desirable forms of teaching and learning in schools or "quick fixes" to raise test scores? This book grew out of a desire to address these questions.

The schools that we describe in this book participated in a larger 4-year study of reading and mathematics instruction that we began in 2001, just before NCLB became law. Our initial focus was on understanding fourth- and fifth-grade teachers' notions of quality instruction, documenting their actual classroom practices, and relating those practices to students' achievement records. Because of our interest in struggling learners, we situated the study in moderate- to high-poverty elementary schools in a large metropolitan school district. As our involvement with principals, teachers, and their schools moved into the 3rd year, 2 years into NCLB, we began to observe how the challenges of high-stakes testing were reshaping and driving much of what occurred in schools, from discussions at staff meetings to instruction in classrooms to interactions between students and teachers. Testing was beginning to dominate every aspect of daily life in these schools, often in ways that raised fundamental questions about the effects of high-stakes testing on teaching and learning.

During the 4th year of the study (2004–05), we selected three elementary schools to conduct in-depth case studies. Each school served a diverse and largely low-income population of families. Although all three schools were affected by the challenges posed by high-stakes testing, the schools varied in their ability to redirect resources, adapt to new policies, and sustain professional conceptions of teaching and learning. One school approached the challenges posed by new policies as a series of crises to be managed (or mismanaged) as state-mandated testing approached. Another school realigned priorities, when necessary, and adapted practices while managing to sustain its primary identity as a strong, professional community. The third school standardized new requirements and strengthened the school's bureaucratic structures, all in an attempt to meet its primary goal of getting off the state's list of failing schools. This is the story of these three schools, their teachers, and their principals.

We would like to thank the National Science Foundation for supporting the research (Grant No. 0115389) that made this book possible. Over the years, our thinking was enriched by interactions with other members of the research team, Patricia Alexander, Jeremy Price, John Larson, and with our advisory board members, Susan Addington, Richard Allington, Robert Calfee, and Aaron Pallas. Smart and hardworking graduate assistants, who always maintained a sense of humor, kept us going and made the work enjoyable. We appreciate each of them, but thank those by name who contributed directly to this manuscript by collecting, coding, archiving, or analyzing data on these three schools—Lorraine Adkins, Min-Tun Chuang, Carolyn Eick, Pragati Godbole, Jane Hall, Yen Hui Lu, Kristie Jones Newton, Dawn Little, Nat Malkus, Jessica Palladino, Carol Rinke, and Addy Salvo. We also benefited greatly from the hard work and diligence of our project manager, Rose Savitsky Schmidt, who kept *us* accountable as we conducted these case studies and the larger study of which they are a part.

Moving a manuscript to publication is always a challenge, but the anonymous reviewers and the editors at Teachers College Press skillfully guided us through the process and offered invaluable insights about the ideas and organization of the book. Finally, we thank the personnel at Stevenson School District, particularly the staff at Brookfield, Cherry Ridge, and Hawthorne elementary schools, for allowing us into their work lives. As readers will see in the following chapters, life in these schools was not easy, and our intrusions did not help. Yet, to a person, school staff members made us feel welcomed and trusted. We hope that we have done justice to their efforts.

We use pseudonyms throughout the book to identify individuals and the schools and district that participated in the study.

Overview

Holding schools, local educational agencies, and States accountable for
improving the academic achievement of all students . . .
                                                    —No Child Left Behind Act

SINCE 1983, when the National Commission on Excellence in Education
published *A Nation at Risk,* federal and state policymakers have sought
ways to increase student achievement and reform a deeply fragmented
education system (Croninger, Valli, & Price, 2003). In the decade that followed, federal and state education policies shifted from a focus on inputs,
on providing schools with additional resources to address educational inequalities, to a focus on outputs and performance-based accountability
(Goetz, 2001). The 1994 reauthorization of the Elementary and Secondary Education Act (ESEA), Goals 2000, provided the basic framework for
systemic, standards-based reform. By aligning clear content standards for
subjects, performance standards that indicate mastery of content, and
assessment standards to measure what students actually know and can
do, states would facilitate the development of rigorous academic standards,
effective pedagogy, and greater learning in schools (O'Day & Smith, 1993).

While Goals 2000 established standards-based reform as the framework
for federal education policy, it was the 2001 reauthorization of ESEA, No
Child Left Behind (NCLB), that transformed it into a potent performance-
based accountability system. States were to establish performance goals (i.e.,
acceptable proficiency levels) in reading and mathematics and then ensure that students meet those goals by the 2013–14 school year. To determine progress toward meeting goals, NCLB required states to test student
performance in Grades 3 through 8 and penalize schools that failed to make
progress in achieving the federal timetable. Unlike prior legislation that
addressed equity by targeting specific populations of students for compen-
satory services or funding, NCLB required schools to disaggregate testing
results and achieve the same proficiency goals for all students.

Although NCLB has been characterized as more evolutionary than revolutionary (McDonnell, 2005), it deviates radically from prior legislation in important ways (McGuinn, 2006; Sunderman, Kim, & Orfield, 2005). First, it dramatically expands federal control over schools by requiring that states hold all schools accountable for achieving state-designated proficiency levels in reading and mathematics. Prior to NCLB many states exempted schools not receiving Title I funds from testing and reporting requirements. Second, NCLB more than doubled the amount of testing required in schools. The 1994 reauthorization called for three testing points between Grades 3 and 12; NCLB, however, requires six testing points between Grades 3 and 8 and at least one testing point in high school (Rudalevige, 2003). Finally, NCLB requires states to sanction schools that fail to meet annual yearly progress (AYP) for all students, including special education students and English Language Learners (ELL). While prior legislation was vague about timelines and sanctions, NCLB "ratchets up" the pressure on principals and teachers to raise test scores to levels that are historically unprecedented.[1]

For those who believe that the failure of American schools rests with an absence of will, mostly on the part of principals, teachers, and their students, NCLB is a welcome departure from prior legislation that did little to hold schools accountable for student performance or taxpayer dollars. Others, however, worry about the demands being placed on principals, teachers, and students and question the wisdom of relying so heavily on testing to determine what constitutes a quality education (Noddings, 2007). Although the merits of NCLB may be debated in terms of its effects on achievement scores (e.g., Center on Education Policy, 2007a; Fuller, Wright, Gesicki, & Kang, 2007), there is growing interest in understanding how NCLB, and reforms like it, affect everyday life in schools (Sunderman, Kim, & Orfield, 2005; Sunderman, Tracey, Kim, & Orfield, 2004). Does an emphasis on standards, testing, and sanctions motivate principals and teachers to create more desirable educational experiences for their students? Are teachers more engaged in their jobs, more collaborative in their work, and more focused on improving instruction? Or, as some have argued, does the emphasis on high-stakes testing narrow the educational experiences of children (Center on Education Policy, 2007b; Noddings, 2007); undermine professional standards (Sleeter & Stillman, 2007); and create disturbingly stressful environments for principals, teachers, and their students (Perlstein, 2007)?

This book grew out of a desire to understand how high-stakes testing affects daily life in schools. It tells the story of how three elementary schools—Hawthorne, Brookfield, and Cherry Ridge—responded to the challenges of high-stakes testing. Beyond the increased pressures to make

AYP for specific populations of students, these schools also addressed a series of school district policy enactments meant to further promote standards-based reforms, including substantial changes to the district's curriculum, intensified professional development activities, and additional student assessments. These schools shed light on the ways in which principals and teachers respond to the multiple and sometimes conflicting mix of policy initiatives associated with reform, and they provide evidence that high-stakes accountability policies—in both subtle and not so subtle ways—are reshaping life in schools. We argue that the direction of these changes, even in the best of schools, is not very encouraging. More specifically, the current emphasis on high-stakes testing, at least as manifested in the three high-poverty schools that we studied, creates a test-driven culture that narrows the curriculum, weakens student-teacher relationships, and undermines professional standards for teaching and learning.

Four connected themes weave their way through the book. First, high-stakes accountability policies dominated local policies and practices in all three schools, particularly in Cherry Ridge, the school most "at risk" of not meeting AYP. As each school approached the month when students were to take the state-mandated assessments, concerns about testing increased and influenced almost every aspect of school life. Second, the need to meet AYP became the main concern when making daily decisions about school programs and the allocation of school resources. Professional development activities, staff meetings, and instructional decisions became focused on achieving this goal. Third, schools varied in their capacity to adapt to external mandates and create or sustain positive educational environments for teaching and learning. More specifically, the schools differed in the organizational and relational resources that could be called upon to sustain professional standards for practice and create positive educational experiences for students. Finally, even in the most "capable" school, there was a general trend toward transforming teaching into test preparation and learning into improvement in test scores. High-stakes testing, along with the practices promoted by it, created powerful incentives to focus exclusively on the "bottom line"—raising test scores to make AYP.

Together, these themes highlight a central paradox of NCLB: as more emphasis is placed on assessment results, particularly in the form of higher standardized-test scores, less emphasis is placed on professional standards for teaching and learning. As others have found (Darling-Hammond, 2007; Sunderman, Kim, & Orfield, 2005) and these chapters reveal, this happens for a variety of reasons. Because the scope of knowledge assessed by state testing is relatively small, schools narrow their own curriculum so that teachers do not "waste time" on content that may not be tested.

Moreover, a common strategy is to pull out or constantly regroup students at risk of failure, even though this strategy has been found to fragment students' learning experiences and disrupt lessons. Yet another strategy is for teachers to focus on borderline students—those with the greatest likelihood of being nudged into the proficient level on state tests. Although "student" triage may boost test scores in the short term, it also raises serious questions about professional standards and the equitable treatment of children. Finally, schools differ, sometimes radically, in their capacity to transform external policy mandates into successful local enactments and positive learning environments for students. In the pages that follow, we explore these themes and their consequences for teaching and learning.

CASE STUDY CONTEXT

This case study is part of a longitudinal research project that examined teaching and learning in moderate- to high-poverty elementary schools. The primary goal of the larger study was to examine how teachers help students acquire foundational skills in reading and mathematics. A secondary goal was to understand how aspects of the organizational and policy context facilitate (or hinder) the ability of teachers to scale up and sustain positive forms of teaching and learning in these elementary schools. We focused on the fourth and fifth grades because these grades represent an important transition for students in terms of curricular demands and an important challenge for teachers in terms of dealing with widening gaps in student knowledge. Prior research (Balfanz, 2006; Chall & Jacobs, 2003; Chall, Jacobs, & Baldwin, 1991) indicated that students who fall behind in core subject areas in these grades are at considerable risk of failure in subsequent grades.

We grounded the study in conceptions of good teaching derived from cognitive psychology, reading instruction, and mathematics education. Because we believe that teaching should be closely guided by understandings of how people learn (Bransford, Brown, & Cocking, 1999), we drew on five research domains that were central to the development of the American Psychological Association's (APA) Learner-Centered Psychological Principles (Alexander & Murphy, 1998). While the manifestations of exemplary teaching may differ somewhat in reading and mathematics, those domains indicate that good teaching, regardless of content area, promotes deep, principled learning of content; encourages the development of cognitive and metacognitive skills; motivates students to engage deeply in subject matter; addresses individual and developmental differences among students; and creates inclusive, affirming, and successful learning environments. We then developed a series of instruments and research protocols to capture the occurrence and consequences of these pedagogical practices, including classroom observations, daily curriculum logs, individual interviews, focus-group interviews, and student records.[2]

We situated the study in Stevenson, a large and diverse school district that was facing a wide range of educational challenges associated with significant demographic changes and heightened expectations for student performance. In the past 2 decades, the enrollment of low-income students had doubled at Stevenson. At the time of our study, the district enrolled nearly 140,000 students and had roughly 19,000 employees, making Stevenson one of the largest school districts in the nation. Approximately 30% of the students in Stevenson participated in free and reduced-price meals services (FARMS), and 12% participated in English for Speakers of Other Languages (ESOL) programs. We selected the school district because of its racial and economic diversity, its reputation for collecting reliable data about students and schools, and its considerable investments in standards-based reforms to address a growing achievement gap.

The study design called for identifying a group of moderate- to high-poverty elementary schools with greater-than-expected achievement gains and then following these schools and their fourth- and fifth-grade teachers for 3 to 4 years. When a school agreed to participate in the study, we attempted to recruit all the fourth- and fifth-grade teachers, focusing especially on the teachers who taught reading and mathematics in regular classrooms. When identified schools declined to participate or withdrew from the study, we replaced them with schools in the district that had similar demographics and, when possible, reputations for good teaching and learning. During the 4-year period in which we collected data, approximately 30 elementary schools and 125 teachers participated. As a group, participating schools had higher-than-average achievement levels in reading and mathematics on the state's mandated fourth- and fifth-grade assessments than schools with comparable FARMS enrollments, although the range in achievement levels varied substantially across the study's schools.

In the 4th year of data collection, we selected Hawthorne, Brookfield, and Cherry Ridge for in-depth case studies. Although not an original component of our research design, it became increasingly evident that we would need to develop a new set of protocols and collect additional data if we were to understand how changes in the policy environment, particularly the implementation of NCLB, were influencing what was happening (and not happening) in these schools. The three schools selected for case studies served large numbers of students who participated in FARMS (half or more of their students) and substantial populations of English Language Learners (ELL) (one fifth or more). Each also had a racially and ethnically diverse student population, which included African American, Hispanic, White, and Asian students.[3] Beyond being representative of the types of schools we targeted for study, we also chose these schools because they were at varying degrees of risk for meeting 2004–05 AYP requirements.

The case studies represented an intensification of data collection rather than a change in research design. We continued to observe reading and mathematics lessons using time-sampling protocols, visiting fourth- and fifth-grade classrooms roughly 16 times during the year (eight times to observe a teacher's reading lessons and eight times to observe mathematics lessons). These observations provided us with detailed information about lessons, including the nature of teacher and student interactions. Teachers also continued to complete daily logs that identified the curriculum topics covered during a day's lesson. These logs provided insights into curriculum coverage, particularly as schools approached the month designated for the state assessments. We examined the observation and log data for possible themes and insights about how high-stakes testing was influencing instructional practices, classroom interactions, and curriculum decisions in fourth- and fifth-grade classrooms at all participating schools. We augmented these data with interviews, on-site observations, and the collection of relevant artifacts.

Throughout the 2004–05 school year, a seven-member research team collected additional data in the three case-study schools. We conducted more than 30 individual and group interviews with school administrators, specialists, and classroom teachers. Because of our research focus, we also attended meetings that related, either directly or indirectly, to the teaching of reading and mathematics in fourth- and fifth-grade classrooms. To that end, we took detailed field notes on well over 100 meetings: whole-school staff meetings, leadership meetings, grade-level meetings, and staff development meetings. We also collected whatever documents were distributed or created at these meetings. In each of these data-gathering opportunities, our intent was to develop a better sense of how policies were interpreted and enacted, as well as the consequences of these responses for teaching and learning.

The distinctive cultures and organizational structures of the three schools determined, in part, which and how many meetings we attended. Hawthorne, for example, frequently cancelled, then rescheduled, meetings at the last minute, making our participation more difficult. Brookfield did much of its work in whole-school meetings before the official start of the day. Cherry Ridge had a tradition of grade-level, after-school planning meetings. Although team members were assigned primarily to one school, several spent time in two or all three of the schools. This helped bring into relief similarities and differences across schools and refocus data collection to ensure consistency. Whenever feasible, two team members attended interviews or large meetings in order to compare notes, clarify understandings, and identify further data-gathering needs.

The research team also met as a whole group more than a dozen times before and throughout the school year to develop our goals and protocols, to assess and refine our data collection strategies, and to discuss emerging themes and patterns. All audiotapes of interviews were transcribed and, with field notes of meetings, entered into NVivo and coded to facilitate analysis. We paid particular attention to the way schools compared across such dimensions as school organization and culture, meeting agendas, policy influences, curriculum, assessment, professional development, and the teaching of reading and mathematics. We also asked school principals to review the "Policy and Organizational Context" papers we wrote about their school's organizational structure, operational plan, instructional programs, and policy context to confirm the accuracy and interpretation of data. Through comparative analyses, these data sources captured different school capacities and varied responses to a range of external mandates, including NCLB and district-initiated reforms. Our analysis focused on understanding how an increasingly high-stakes, test-driven policy environment is reshaping school life, especially the teaching and learning of reading and mathematics.

POLICY CONTEXT

Although NCLB comprises a broad range of provisions, including those designed to guarantee that teachers are "highly qualified" to teach their subject matter, the legislation's immediate effect was to require states to develop testing regimes consistent with the newly articulated federal mandates (McGuinn, 2006; Rudalevige, 2003). So even though the state in which Stevenson is located already had a well-articulated set of curriculum, performance, and assessment standards, a state-appointed panel decided to overhaul the state's assessment program to better align curriculum, instruction, and testing with the provisions of NCLB. The state's prior curriculum standards had encouraged teachers to help students read critically, apply skills and knowledge to solve problems, integrate knowledge across different content areas, and work effectively on problems individually and in groups. In contrast, the new standards focused on basic knowledge and skills that could be more easily assessed using traditional standardized achievement tests. Providing broad, measurable expectations for subjects by grade, these newly developed standards were followed by more specific indicators of the knowledge, skills, and abilities (KSAs) to be tested by state assessments.

Changes in the state's assessment practices were even more dramatic. Rather than assess students in reading, mathematics, writing, language usage, and social studies, the state narrowed the focus of assessments to reading and mathematics, in part to cover the expenses associated with conducting the assessments in additional grades. Whereas the prior assessment practices required students to answer a set of questions about 8–12 complex tasks over the course of a week, sometimes individually and sometimes in groups, the new assessments required students to complete a standardized achievement test over 4 days with 90 minutes of testing per day. Almost every question on the prior assessment required students to answer in writing, while the format for the new assessment was multiple choice and short constructed response (SCR). Moreover, the new assessment practices required that testing be done in March, as opposed to at the end of the year, so that the state had enough time to report the results to parents before the beginning of the new school year (a requirement of NCLB).

William Barnes, Stevenson's superintendent, endorsed many of these changes in the state's curriculum standards and assessment practices. But unlike many school districts that adopted the state's newly articulated curriculum as their own, Stevenson passed a policy in 2001 that called for the district to develop a rigorous curriculum "derived from *local, state, national, and international* standards" (emphasis added). The district's curriculum was to be more comprehensive than the state's, a reflection of Stevenson's commitment to previous reforms, local school-improvement initiatives, and a long-standing desire to be first among the state's public school systems. The district launched its new mathematics curriculum in every grade in the fall of 2002 and phased in the new reading curriculum, implementing it in the grades that we studied, in the fall of 2004.

Along with implementing the new curriculum frameworks, the district also made substantial investments in full-day kindergarten programs, reductions in class size, and the hiring of professional development and curriculum specialists in schools. As part of its overall goals to improve student achievement and narrow the achievement gap, Stevenson implemented targeted reading programs for low-achieving students, diagnostic reading assessments, a new grading and reporting system, a school performance management system, and a plan for greater inclusion of special education students in regular classrooms. In the fall of 2003, the year before our case studies began, Stevenson mandated reading intervention programs in the 18 Title I schools with the highest FARMS enrollments and "highly recommended" that other high-poverty schools adopt these programs. All three of the schools in our study implemented some form of reading intervention, such as Corrective Reading.

Stevenson also changed its own assessment practices to align them better with NCLB and to provide more timely information to teachers about student performance. The district continued to administer the Comprehensive Test of Basic Skills (CTBS) in reading and mathematics in the second grade to provide information about student performance prior to the federally mandated assessments in the third through eighth grades. In addition to the CTBS, the district mandated a series of diagnostic assessments in reading. Schools were required to administer the Stanford Diagnostic Reading Test (SDRT) twice a year for selected third- through fifth-grade students at risk of failing the state assessments and the Measures of Academic Progress in Reading (MAP-R) twice a year for all students in the same grades. The year of the case studies was the first year for these assessments. In subsequent years, the school district planned to increase the frequency of assessments to provide schools with more timely information about what students could and could not do in reading. It also planned to begin similar diagnostic assessments in mathematics.

In keeping with the spirit of performance assessments, Stevenson also sought to implement a new grading and reporting system. The overall goal for the new system was to provide students and parents with more accurate information about individual student performance. Using a somewhat elaborate system for grading, teachers were to report academic achievement (actual competencies) and learning skills (orientations toward academic work) separately. This meant that grades were to reflect only academic achievement or competencies in subject areas, while effort and behavior were to be reported separately as learning skills. Although the new system of grading and reporting was not as fully implemented in 2004–05 as originally planned, each school had to begin using the new system.

The performance management system implemented in the school district, the Baldrige plan, had been originally designed for American businesses and industries. A version of the system was adopted by Stevenson in the mid-1990s to improve school performance, primarily through establishing schoolwide monitoring and problem-solving processes that emphasized the importance of maximizing student learning. Stevenson phased in implementation of the system across the district. At the time of the case studies, Brookfield and Cherry Ridge were in their first year of implementation. Although neither school fully implemented the system during the year of the case studies, Brookfield used the Baldrige system more extensively in its goal-setting efforts. Hawthorne was scheduled to implement the system the year after we completed the case studies.

An additional district policy that affected at least one of the schools in the study was inclusion. Under pressure from the state to increase the number of students with disabilities educated in general education settings, Stevenson began a major initiative to evaluate and redesign the district's inclusion policies in 2003. The goal of the initiative was to enable more students to be served in their home schools and to spend more time in general education classrooms. Although schools were not yet forced to meet an inclusion deadline, Cherry Ridge responded to the initiative the year of the case studies by eliminating all self-contained special education classes. As explained in the subsequent chapters, the principal at Cherry Ridge believed that accelerating the mainstreaming of students with disabilities would help the school achieve AYP for this population of students.

THE SCHOOLS

Hawthorne, Brookfield, and Cherry Ridge are pre-K through fifth grade elementary schools located within 10 miles of one another. The schools served similar student populations, benefited from being a part of a well-resourced school district, and reported similar organizational structures. Nonetheless, there were important differences among the schools, especially in their capacity to address external mandates and sustain reforms. We present two profiles of the schools in the paragraphs that follow—a composite profile and an individual one. The composite profile emphasizes similarities among the three schools, while the individual profiles emphasize the differences, especially in each school's capacity to respond to external policy demands.

Composite Profile

The size of the student enrollment at each school was about average for the district, where elementary schools ranged from about 225 to more than 900 students. Hawthorne was the largest school in the study, with roughly 575 students, followed by Cherry Ridge, with approximately 500 students, and Brookfield, with 400 students (see Table 1.1).[4] However, with at least three quarters of their students classified as African American, Asian, or Hispanic, each school was considerably more diverse than the district's elementary schools as a whole, where White students rep-

Table 1.1. School demographics.

	Hawthorne	Brookfield	Cherry Ridge	District Average (125 schools)
AYP risk	Medium-High	Medium	High	Low
Number of students	575	400	500	500
Race/ethnicity				
Hispanic	42%	40%	48%	21%
White	25%	25%	11%	41%
African American	17%	22%	32%	23%
Asian	16%	13%	9%	15%
Free and reduced-price meals services	60%	55%	75%	30%
ESOL	20%	25%	25%	10%
Special education	15%	15%	10%	10%
Student mobility	20%	15%	30%	15%
Staff-student ratio	8:1	8:1	8:1	10:1
Average class size, grades 3–5	20	20	15	25
Staff experience				
< 5 years	45%	25%	30%	20%
5–15 years	30%	50%	50%	40%
> 15 years	25%	25%	20%	40%

Notes: AYP = Adequate Yearly Progress. ESOL = English for Speakers of Other Languages.

resented about 41% of the student population. Compared with district averages, the three schools had substantially larger numbers of students classified as ESOL (one fifth or more vs. 10%) and FARMS (one half or more vs. 30%). Hawthorne and Brookfield also had somewhat larger special education populations (15%) than the populations in the district (10%), and Hawthorne and Cherry Ridge had somewhat higher mobility rates (20% and 30%, respectively) than the average rate in the district (15%). Although there were differences in the enrollments among the three schools, when compared with district averages, the schools served similarly disadvantaged student populations.

As part of a well-resourced school district, each school also had an extended professional staff to assist in the operation of the school and the implementation of education programs. As part of its commitment to school improvement and standards-based reforms, Stevenson funded a full-time staff developer, a full-time reading specialist, and a half-time math content coach at each school. Each school had an 8-to-1 student/instructional staff ratio compared to a 10-to-1 student/instructional staff ratio for the district. Moreover, the average class size for reading and mathematics in the third through fifth grades was 15 students in Cherry Ridge and 20 students in Brookfield and Hawthorne. The average class size in the school district was 25 students. These lower class sizes were a result of a district-wide commitment to lower class sizes in high-need schools and local investments in acquiring additional staff.

Following district guidelines, all three schools used Title I or local funds to support new positions and academic support programs for their students. Hawthorne and Cherry Ridge used Title I funds to add staff positions beyond those provided by the district: for example, a gifted and talented teacher, an additional mathematics specialist, Reading Recovery/ESOL teachers, as well as classroom teachers. Hawthorne also had partnerships with the city and private agencies to provide after-school care, summer programs, and mentoring opportunities for students. Brookfield had an ESOL Club that provided an hour of homework support twice a week for students in Grades 3–5 and a strong outreach program for Hispanic families with a coordinator position funded by a city government grant. Cherry Ridge used Title I funds to identify and nurture students for gifted programs and to support a school-based health center that offered comprehensive care: physical examinations; hearing and vision screening; first aid; and emergency, mental health, and social services.

At a formal organizational level, Brookfield, Hawthorne, and Cherry Ridge had much in common with each other and many other elementary schools in the Stevenson School District. A visitor would find annual goals developed through a school improvement process, a decision-making structure that involved professional staff, the same curriculum frameworks, and scheduled on-site professional development opportunities for teachers, all of which reflected district policies and administrative expectations for schools. If a formal organizational chart was made of the decision-making structures in each of the schools, they could be collapsed into one without losing much of their individual uniqueness. Hawthorne, Brookfield, and Cherry Ridge all had some form of leadership council composed of specialists and team leaders. Councils were scheduled to meet approximately once a month and were charged with assisting in the operation of the school, ranging from making administrative decisions about school priorities to implementing specific activities and new programs. Each school was organized into grade-level teams, and each school relied on whole-school and team meetings to coordinate activities.

Individual Profiles

Although the schools were similarly organized, at least on paper, and bene-fited substantially from being in a well-resourced school district, there were important differences among these schools, especially in their capacity to address the demands of a high-stakes policy environment. Capacity has been described as the "collective power" of the school staff to accomplish its goals (Newmann, King, & Youngs, 2000). In these three schools, two types of capacity—organizational and relational—affected how each school responded to external policy pressures (see Figure 1.1). By *organizational capacity* we mean the human and material resources a school has at its disposal and the productive use of those resources (Malen & Rice, 2004). We consider the effective use of time, staff expertise, and curriculum materials to be important indicators of a school's organizational capacity (Gamoran, Secada, & Marrett, 2000; Malen & Rice, 2004; Newmann, King, & Youngs, 2000). By *relational capacity* we mean those formal and infor-mal relationships among staff that develop not just shared understand-ings but collective commitments and high levels of motivation for achieving organizational goals (Bidwell, 2001; Bryk & Schneider, 2002; Spillane, 2005). We consider the trust that faculty have in each other and in ad-ministration, the openness of communications among staff, and the will-ingness to work collaboratively to address school problems to be important indicators of a school's relational capacity.

We describe these capacities in each of the schools and discuss in the following chapters how these capacities mediated the ways in which a high-stakes policy environment reshaped life in each school. As indicated in Figure 1.1, Hawthorne, Brookfield, and Cherry Ridge differed on these dimensions of capacity. Hawthorne had the least capacity to productively respond to external pressures, with little evidence of the effective use of existing resources or collaboration. Unless faced with a crisis, responses to external policy mandates were largely laissez-faire. The principal had a hands-off approach, leaving faculty to develop and maintain an individu-alistic approach to teaching and school improvement. Little attention was paid to developing systematically either the organizational or the relational capacities of the school (see lower left-hand corner of Figure 1.1).

Brookfield, on the other hand, had the greatest capacity to accom-plish its goals and respond to the challenges of high-stakes policies. Orga-nized as a professional community, Brookfield was strong on both

Figure 1.1. Organizational and relational capacities.

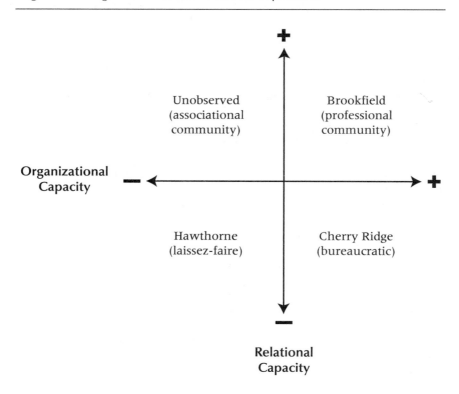

organizational and relational capacity. Leadership was distributed and the principal encouraged a collaborative approach to setting school goals and solving emergent problems. The school was efficiently run and staff members were highly motivated to succeed, even when they questioned the logic and additional demands made by external mandates and reforms. Organizational and relational capacity building was a high priority and fundamental strategy for addressing the challenges of a high-stakes policy environment (see upper right-hand corner of Figure 1.1).

Cherry Ridge provides yet a different profile of capacity. Strong on organizational but weak on relational capacity, Cherry Ridge functioned as an efficient bureaucracy with a top-down, hierarchical approach to external pressures and school problems. The principal was actively engaged and focused on developing organizational plans and strategies for addressing the challenges posed by high-stakes policies, especially given that the school was on the state and district "watch list" for failing to achieve AYP. There was less evidence of the type of professional, collaborative community that we saw at Brookfield. Although small pockets of collaborative relations could be found, as an organization, Cherry Ridge focused on increasing its organizational capacity but often at the expense of the school's relational capacity (see lower right-hand corner of Figure 1.1).

The final profile of capacity was unobserved in our study—a school with strong relational capacity but weak organizational practices (see upper left-hand corner of Figure 1.1). It is not difficult to imagine schools that emphasize strong associational ties and personal relationships but at the expense of diminished expectations for organizational performance (see Sedlak, Wheeler, Pullin, & Cusick, 1986, for a classic example in the literature). Such schools have substantial relational capacity but its use is limited to strengthening interpersonal ties and avoiding conflicts among administrators, teachers, and students.

Hawthorne. Located within a few blocks of a major commercial thoroughfare, Hawthorne sits on more than 10 acres in a residential neighborhood of single-family homes. Approaching the school, a visitor does not have a sense of its size because of its sprawling design and the placement of its four portable classrooms at the back of the building. The rather dated appearance of the school, which opened in the early 1950s and was renovated in mid-1980s, was brightened by colorful and abundant student work posted along the hallways. With long, meandering halls, Hawthorne seemed like a maze. Walking through hallways, a visitor felt as though the school was divided into clusters of teachers and classrooms, an impression consistent with the school's relatively weak relational capacity and organizational efficiency.

Elaine Everett, Hawthorne's principal for the past 6 years, was the only one of the three principals who had children living at home. As a single parent of two teenagers, she also had major responsibility for an aging parent. These responsibilities took their toll on Ms. Everett, who was frequently out of the building, and then on personal leave for the last 6 weeks of the school year, when her daughter had major surgery. During her absences, the school's assistant principal, Adam Fox, was in charge of the school. Although these disruptions in leadership contributed to the school's weak relational capacity and organizational efficiency, there was also evidence that these weaknesses had persisted for some time. Nearly half the staff (45%) had fewer than 5 years of experience, a proportion lower than those of the other two schools and far below the district's average of 20% (see Table 1.1).

At Hawthorne, Elaine Everett met with her assistant principal, staff development teacher, reading specialist, and math content coach for administrative matters. Formally called the Task Team, this group came together periodically to plan staff meetings, discuss district directives around curriculum and testing, and consider a number of other issues such as teacher and student scheduling and the monitoring of student progress. The larger Leadership Team comprised the Task Team, grade-level team leaders, and ESOL and special education teachers. According to the school's organizational plan, decisions and information from the Task Team meetings were to be disseminated to the Leadership Team, who, in turn, disseminated them to their grade-level teams. Members of the Leadership Team were also to represent the concerns of individual teachers to members of the Task Team, sharing teachers' questions and ideas regarding administrative decisions.

In actuality, however, these teams failed to function very effectively. At a Task Team meeting in early September, for example, the principal, assistant principal, reading specialist, math content coach, and staff developer engaged in lengthy discussions about the new curriculum reading guides and working with grade-level teams to focus more on instruction and not just on curriculum coverage. But members of the team also brought up, for agenda setting, a wide array of additional topics to be covered at the subsequent Leadership Team meetings, including blood-borne pathogens; abuse and neglect training; the school handbook; procedures for academic intervention and special education referrals; deadlines for the school improvement plan; and the scheduling for testing. Although any one of these topics might be worthy of including in the school agenda, the Task Team seemed unable to establish a clear set of priorities for the year. As noted by the observer, "There were so many demands and competing agendas, it was difficult for the team to prioritize topics for the staff meetings and the leadership team" (September 9, 2004).

This sense of "too many demands" and the absence of direction persisted throughout the year. Field notes capture the tone of the various leadership meetings, as well as the weak relational capacity and organizational efficiency that characterized the school:

Meeting meandered: Discussion about the topics for future staff meetings was overshadowed by other concerns of team members. The wide range of issues and concerns of team members quickly became lengthy conversations (September 9, 2004).

The meeting seemed hurried and although it was designed to be organized, it wasn't. The expectations of the principal regarding what could be accomplished in an hour were unrealistic (September 27, 2004).

The goal of this meeting seemed to be how to manipulate the teachers into accepting the changes that Elaine thought were necessary (October 25, 2006).

Throughout the year, meetings of the Task Team and of the Leadership Team, as well as whole-staff meetings, were frequently canceled or scheduled on an ad hoc basis. Directives seemed to be top-down rather than mutually decided and focused on crisis management rather than capacity building or priority setting. There was a noticeable distance, both physically and psychologically, between the principal's office and teachers' classrooms. Although Hawthorne had met AYP standards in each of its previous years, it was in danger of failing to meet AYP in reading for ESOL and special education students. In the previous year, Hawthorne had only met AYP for these students through the state's "safe harbor" exception.[5] As the school calendar approached March, Hawthorne became even more hierarchic and chaotic, as it lacked the capacity to address the additional educational challenges posed by NCLB and the state's high-stakes assessments.

Brookfield. Although only a few miles from a busy thoroughfare, Brookfield's setting seems almost pastoral. Visitors drive through a neighborhood of single-family houses set on large lots with abundant old trees before turning into the school's entrance. As one of the oldest elementary schools in the district, dating back to the late 1800s, Brookfield has undergone many changes. The current structure is a large red-brick, split-level building constructed in the mid-1950s and renovated 30 years later. Proud of its history, the school displayed pictures of the original school building and a brief history in the foyer. Brightly colored banners and posters in English and Spanish welcomed visitors and announced the importance of character building. Student assignments and artwork were neatly hung in every hallway, and student achievement data, by grade level, were posted close to the main entrance. Nine portable classrooms eased overcrowding. Brookfield's overall physical appearance conveyed school pride and a strong sense of community.

By the year of our study, Liz Moore had been the school's principal for 15 years. Although the school was too small to qualify for an assistant principal, Ms. Moore was given a principal intern, Luke Comer, who assumed the principal's role as part of his internship program during most of the spring semester. Because principals were not allowed to be in the building during the culminating part of internships, Ms. Moore was given assignments in the central office. But collaborative processes were so well established at Brookfield that Ms. Moore's absence was hardly noticed. This stability was created, at least in part, by Brookfield's experienced staff. Roughly three quarters (75%) had 5 or more years of experience, a figure comparable to the district average (see Table 1.1). Widely considered to be a desirable place to teach, many staff members remained rather than move to schools with fewer educational challenges.

Although Ms. Moore and Mr. Comer had the last word in decision making at the school, they relied heavily on the counsel and expertise of the reading specialist, staff development teacher, and math content coach for decisions involving instruction. These specialists were part of the Instructional Council, which included professional support staff, grade-level team leaders, and a representative of the Parent Teacher Association (PTA). This group enabled administrators and professional support staff to disseminate information to the faculty and staff and to receive feedback from them in return. Brookfield's Instructional Council met approximately once a month in the Media Center before the school day began. In efficiently run, hour-long meetings, the group set the school agenda, marked progress toward achieving goals, and solicited guidance from staff about the school's direction.

Meetings were highly collaborative, with the administrative leaders preparing agendas that invited input from teachers. Team members were forthcoming with alternative suggestions and concerns, and teachers volunteered to be on committees. Reflections at the end of field notes capture the collegial and efficient organizational character of the school:

> The principal is cognizant of demands on teachers and is trying not to overwhelm them with new processes and demands. Liz told the teachers that she didn't want them to leave this meeting thinking they had another assignment to do. She also softened a deadline on formalizing the mission statement and conducting a walk through (November 4, 2004).

> Although the specialists and principal led the meeting, the teachers were very comfortable voicing their opinions and providing information. The atmosphere was businesslike but gentle. For example, Liz was not defensive about the teachers' concern that they were out of the classroom too much (December 2, 2004).

Brookfield had the feeling of being a tight-knit family. Disagreements occurred, but they were voiced openly, in a respectful atmosphere. Even with its relatively large Hispanic, ESOL, FARMS, and special education populations, Brookfield had made AYP every year since the passage of NCLB. Although the stress of sustaining proficiency increased as the school calendar approached March, the administrators, teachers, and support staff had access to stronger collegial relations and organizational efficiencies to address these challenges and sustain a sense of professional community.

Cherry Ridge. Tucked into a residential neighborhood, Cherry Ridge is surrounded by detached, single-family houses. Most of these houses, however, were not owner occupied, but rentals, often shared by several families. In addition, many students came from neighboring apartment complexes, helping to explain why, of the three schools, Cherry Ridge had the highest FARMS enrollment (75%). Although the building was more than 50 years old, it was modernized in the late 1990s and had a fresh, new and inviting feel to it. The front lobby was spacious and colorful with modern lights, a vaulted ceiling, and open balcony. A bilingual (Spanish/English) staff member was always on call in the main office where a PTA bulletin board had messages in English and Spanish. Like Brookfield, the main school building was supplemented by nine portable classrooms.

Julia Hancock had been the principal at Cherry Ridge for more than 20 years and was supported by an assistant principal, Bonnie Strauss, who was in her first year as a school administrator. With her limited experience and music education background, Ms. Strauss exerted little leadership at the school, focusing instead on implementing Ms. Hancock's various directives. Cherry Ridge was run as an efficient, tightly controlled bureaucracy. There was never a sense of chaos, but rarely a sense of family. Each staff member clearly knew what he or she was expected to do and approached the school year with mixed amounts of anxiety and determination. In measures of years of experience, Cherry Ridge's professional staff had less than average for the district and less than Brookfield's, but more than the staff at Hawthorne. Although 70% of the Cherry Ridge staff had 5 or more years of experience, the fourth- and fifth-grade teachers in our study had substantially less.

Of the three schools, Cherry Ridge had the largest Instructional Leadership Team, composed of administrators (principal, assistant principal and a district school performance director), professional staff (staff developer, reading specialist, math content coach, new teacher mentor, teachers' union representative who was also the technology support person, and the Title I academic support specialist), and the grade-level team leaders. This group met once a month for 1½ hours. The principal often presided over these meetings, especially at the beginning of the year, when she communicated her expectations on issues such as district mandates, school activities, parental involvement, professional development, and budget. Midway through the year, other school leaders, including the assistant principal and the staff developer, assumed more responsibility for running the meetings and the principal became one of the participants. Members of the team provided routine reports about their areas of concerns or updates about the progress made toward achieving annual goals.

Although organizationally Cherry Ridge was run as efficiently as or perhaps even more so than Brookfield, collegial relationships at Cherry Ridge were weak. Instructional Leadership Team meetings were highly organized and ran like clockwork, but tension and discontent were palpable among members, with Ms. Hancock candidly acknowledging that interpersonal relations were not her strength. Field notes leading up to the state assessments in March illustrate a general deterioration in these relationships across the school year:

> The principal ran a tight ship. . . . While the principal dominated the meeting, everyone seemed to provide input equally. . . . All participants seemed involved and eager to get their school off the improvement list (September 27, 2004).

> [The principal] on one side, and staff on the other side. . . . Things are much tenser than first impressions might reveal (October 11, 2004).

> Demands on teachers' time continue to be an issue (November 8, 2004).

> There is constant panic and furious "rushing" to integrate yet another tool for helping kids score proficient on AYP. Teachers are complaining, off the record, of low morale (December 13, 2004).

Of the three schools, Cherry Ridge was under the most pressure to meet AYP. Although the school had satisfied its AYP requirements the previous year, it was the first year that the school had done so (and only by slim margins in reading for ESOL and special education students). Because of its earlier failures, the school had been placed on the state's school improvement or watch list; parents were allowed to send their children to other, more successful schools; and outside vendors were providing tutoring and after-school academic support services to FARMS students. The principal at Cherry Ridge left no uncertainty about the school's number one priority—to achieve AYP for a 2nd year in a row and to get the school off the district and state watch lists. Building relational capacity would have to take a backseat to implementing organizational efficiencies designed to meet that singular goal.

THEMATIC CHAPTERS

In the book's organization and chapter titles, we try to capture the continuous dynamic that characterizes policy at the school level. Focusing on the school as the analytic unit enabled us to see the complex local enactments of high-stakes accountability. It also brought into relief commonalities and differences within and across schools. While policymakers tried to influence schools through external mandates, local actors were responsible for implementing those mandates. These actors had various degrees of power within their schools to determine agendas, different levels of agreement and engagement with policies, and different capacities for action.

Each of the following chapters describes a critical site in which school-level responses to the policy press occur. The chapters progress from a broad cultural view of the schools to a close look inside classrooms. In Chapter 2, we explain how the three schools became test-taking cultures. Core aspects of school culture such as the use of time and space, setting priorities, and defining students' relationships with the school were all driven by the high-stakes climate in which the schools functioned. In Chapter 3, we see how these test-taking cultures affect roles and responsibilities within the schools, with professional staff increasingly taking on the roles of test managers. As Chapter 3 illustrates, using assessment data to inform instruction was far more difficult than policymakers envisioned.

Chapter 4 focuses on curriculum. Stevenson School District had its own curriculum frameworks and newly distributed instructional guides. The state had its recommended curriculum that linked its content standards to state assessments. In this chapter, we examine how teachers used these curricula to guide their planning and how high-stakes accountability affected the enacted curriculum. Chapter 5 then turns to teachers' opportunities to learn the new curriculum as well as numerous other district initiatives. Although teachers' professional development opportunities were plentiful, they were often narrowly aligned with state test-taking expectations and proficiency goals.

The themes explored in the chapters on school culture, roles and responsibilities, curriculum, and professional development foreshadow the erosion that occurred in the quality of classroom teaching. Chapter 6 shows how teachers began to regard and enact teaching, and how they thought about themselves as teachers, in these high-stakes contexts. In the concluding chapter, we make recommendations for school personnel, school district leaders, and policymakers. School accountability is unlikely to disappear, although, as evidenced by public debates and the criticisms of NCLB, it will inevitably change. The challenge we discuss in Chapter 7 is how to safeguard legitimate concerns about accountability while keeping schools from becoming barren landscapes of teaching and learning.

CHAPTER 2

Creating Test-Taking Cultures

To ensure that all children have a fair, equal, and significant opportunity to obtain a high-quality education . . .
— No Child Left Behind Act

We're putting so much pressure on them here at school . . . "Read this, bubble in your answer here, write a SCR." . . . I feel like elementary schools, or this elementary school, has lost the title *elementary school.*
— Barry Mott, fourth-grade teacher

I don't always know them by face; I know them by data.
— Heather Nichols, reading specialist

THE NO CHILD LEFT BEHIND (NCLB) ACT of 2001 is a significant milestone in U.S. educational history. Prior to its passage, the question "What has America expected of its schools?" could be answered in three words: attendance, access, and achievement (Graham, 1993). These three "A" words capture the nation's heightened aspirations for schooling over the 20th century. First came the push for compulsory attendance. Second was the demand for increased access to high-quality programs and institutions regardless of race, gender, or disability. And third was the expectation of higher academic achievement for all students. With the passage of NCLB, a fourth "A" could be added to that list of expectations: accountability. Not satisfied that schools have done everything possible to give all children the opportunity to obtain a high-quality education, federal legislation now holds "schools, local educational agencies, and States accountable for improving the academic achievement of all students, and identifying and turning around low-performing schools" (NCLB, 2001).

But what do schools look and feel like when they strive to meet the accountability requirements of NCLB? That question of broad impact on daily life in schools seems to be rarely considered in the legislative process. While these broader, reshaping consequences might be overlooked by policymakers, they are experienced firsthand by teachers. For fourth-grade teacher Barry Mott, accountability pressures so transformed his elementary school, Cherry Ridge, that it bore little resemblance to the elementary school of his experience and memory. For Heather Nichols, the reading specialist at Hawthorne, accountability meant that she spent her days looking at test data, not working with students. As a result, her knowledge of students was limited to test scores. She was unable to put faces to names. The experiences of these teachers signify a deep, fundamental shift in school culture. As we describe in this chapter, in responding to accountability messages from the policy environment, Hawthorne, Brookfield, and Cherry Ridge became particular types of schools—schools characterized by test-taking cultures.

Culture is often thought of as a characteristic of individuals or groups. But culture characterizes organizations as well. While individuals bring their home cultures to the institutions in which they participate, collective life in institutions produces cultures of their own. By school culture, we mean the commonsense way of life that members of a school community establish for themselves. It is evident in the words they speak, the actions they take, and the materials they produce. At the heart of a school's culture are institutional definitions of students and modes of operation that shape roles, priorities, and use of time (Page, 1991; Waller, 1932). Far from being stable, institutional cultures are dynamic processes negotiated by group members with various degrees of power in interaction with often more powerful social and political contexts (Valli, 1986). Because culture is often tacit, it is most noticeable in everyday behavior, language, and routines (Hamilton & Richardson, 1995; Sarason, 1971).

Those who study school culture have noted marked differences across schools, describing them, for example, as isolating or collaborative (Lortie, 1975; Rosenholtz, 1991); healthy or toxic (Deal & Peterson, 2003); and heavenly places, diseased institutions, or intellectual think tanks (Page, 1990). The cultures of Hawthorne, Brookfield, and Cherry Ridge were also dissimilar. With its limited capacity for change and laissez-faire management style, Hawthorne had the most traditionally individualistic culture. Relying on internal expertise and collaborative working relations, Brookfield had a strong professional learning culture. And with its strong top-down management but weak relational capacity, Cherry Ridge functioned as an efficiently-run, but dispiriting bureaucracy. These differences in school culture were deeply rooted and persisted throughout the school year. Nonetheless, each school also became, in its own way, a test-taking culture. While most apparent in Cherry Ridge, the "watch list" school, norms of accountability and measurement were prominent in the other two schools as well.

By *test-taking culture* we mean something quite different from assessment-centered learning environments that "provide students with opportunities to revise and improve the quality of their thinking and under-standing" (Bransford, Brown, & Cocking, 1999, p. xvii). There is ample evidence to suggest the benefits of teachers giving their students on-going formative evaluation and feedback (Black & Wiliam, 1998a; Shepard, 2001). In contrast, we mean school cultures in which "test performance is imposed as the ultimate goal of instruction" (Alexander & Riconscente, 2005, p. 30). In test-taking cultures, learning is supplanted rather than supported by assessments. Schools participate in gaming strategies to avoid adverse consequences, and teachers reshape instructional activities to mirror standardized tests. As a result, students often learn less than when learning, not testing, is the explicit goal (Alexander & Riconscente, 2005; Popham, 2003; Shepard, 2001; Valli & Chambliss, 2007).

In this chapter, we describe the ways in which school personnel at Hawthorne, Brookfield, and Cherry Ridge actively engaged in creating test-taking cultures. This was evident in beginning-of-the-year rituals, such as writing the school improvement plan and establishing the school schedule; in school routines, such as determining meeting agendas and monitoring teacher work; and in the language used to discuss students. Teachers and school administrators may not have always liked what they were doing, agreed with the goals they were asked to accomplish, or even realized the impact of their actions. In some cases they may have lacked the power or capacity to do things differently. Nonetheless, testing-oriented norms, expectations, and relationships pervaded the school year. We focus below on three core aspects of school culture: scheduling time, setting priorities, and defining students' relationships to the school. In subsequent chapters we track this test-taking culture as it affected the staffs' roles and responsibilities, the reading and mathematics curricula, professional development, and teaching and learning.

SCHEDULING TIME

In *How Schools Work*, Barr and Dreeben (1983) describe four central administrative functions. One of them is "the arrangement of a schedule so that all children in the school can be allotted an appropriate amount of time to spend on subjects in the curriculum" (p. 6). But how does one decide "appropriate amount of time"? Tom (1984) argues that this is a moral, not a technical, decision, because it involves deciding for others what is a desirable end: what is worth knowing. How a school schedules time is a normative expression of cultural values. The schedule establishes what could arguably be called the most central pattern of daily life in schools. While the use of time during a lesson expresses classroom culture (Valli & Chambliss, 2007), the scheduling of time during the school day and across the school year expresses the culture of the school. How time was scheduled in the study's three schools privileged tested content and literally redefined the meaning of *school year*.

The School Day

Because Hawthorne, Brookfield, and Cherry Ridge were part of a school district that had clear content standards and curriculum frameworks, similar schedules would be expected in all three. The school district required all fourth- and fifth-grade students to have at least 1 hour of mathematics and 1½ hours of reading/language arts per day, approximately half the instructional time available. For Title I schools, it recommended 2 hours for reading. The three schools not only complied with but, in a number of instances, exceeded the district's demands, with students spending between 60 and 90 minutes a day in mathematics and between 110 and 205 minutes in reading. As explained below, this time allotment represented 60–100% of the instructional day in these schools.

Figure 2.1 presents the percentage of time spent on subjects at each school. At Hawthorne, fourth and fifth graders had a full 2 hours of reading and fifth graders had almost 1½ hours of mathematics (60–70% of the instructional day). In addition, students below grade level in reading or mathematics were pulled out of social studies or science classes for additional instruction. For these students, as well as ESOL pullouts, instructional time in social studies or science was minimal to nonexistent. Fourth graders would have less than ½ hour of science or social studies a day; fifth graders in need of remedial reading, mathematics, or ESOL would miss out on social studies and science entirely. The only time not spent on tested subjects for these students was the roughly 20% of the day allocated to specials (e.g., art, music, physical education, and so on).

At Brookfield, the only non–Title I school, the "official" schedule followed the district's directive of 1 hour of mathematics and 1½ hours for reading. However, students also had an additional 20 minutes of DEAR (Drop Everything and Read) a day, increasing reading time to nearly 2 hours, just 10 minutes shy of the recommendation for Title I schools. Fourth and fifth graders also received "test prep," primarily in reading, 2 days a week as part of either their science or social studies block. This

Figure 2.1. Percentage of time spent on school subjects.

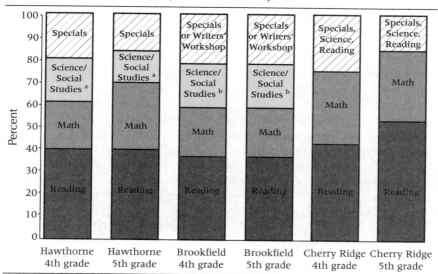

^a A small number of students are pulled for 30 minutes to attend Reading, Math, and ESOL (English for Speakers of Other Languages) intervention.

^b Prior to the state test, test prep occurs two days per week. In addition, a small number of students attend chorus.

was part of the school's response to the district's reading intervention program. As a non–Title I school, Brookfield was not required to implement reading intervention. But the principal did not want to risk rejecting a district recommendation and missing AYP. Far better to miss AYP while complying. In addition to this reading time, fourth and fifth graders with severe grade-level deficiencies were pulled from other classes for extra remedial help—causing some teachers to feel as though their classrooms were revolving doors. The remaining 20% of the instructional day was devoted to either specials or writers workshop.

At Cherry Ridge, the most at-risk school, the only time for learning something other than reading and mathematics was a 1¼-hour block of time in the fourth grade and a ¾-hour block in fifth grade. When these blocks of time involved specials, they were rarely changed. Because specials were taught by art, music, or physical education teachers, that block of time provided valuable joint planning time for the regular classroom teachers. However, when these blocks involved science, which was taught by the regular classroom teachers, they could be (and often were) used for more reading instruction. Social studies is missing from the school's "official" schedule entirely. If the district's new grading and reporting system had not required quarterly grades for science and social studies, one wonders if they would have been taught at all. To produce quarterly grades, teachers were told to embed social studies and science in reading and to base grades in those subjects on the writing they were doing to practice for the state test. Classroom observations of reading classes confirmed that teachers followed through on this directive. In addition to writing assignments, discussion of social studies text was organized around reading comprehension strategies such as finding the main idea and recognizing cause and effect.

We can see from these schedules that the claim "what gets tested gets taught" accurately described the use of instructional time at these schools. At the low end of assigned instructional time for tested subjects was Brookfield, with 60% of the instructional day scheduled for mathematics and reading. But on the 2 days a week when "test preparation" replaced social studies, science or chorus, that percentage increased to more than 70% of the day. Unlike Brookfield, Hawthorne's daily schedule for reading and mathematics stayed the same throughout the week. Fourth graders spent more than 60% of their instructional day in reading and mathematics and fifth graders slightly less than 70%. For students pulled out of classes for remedial reading or mathematics, these percentages could be as high as 80%.

Of the three schools, Cherry Ridge assigned the most time to reading and mathematics. With no social studies on the schedule, reading and mathematics accounted for 75% and 85% of the instructional day for fourth and fifth graders, respectively. However, as at Brookfield, the daily schedule could vary. For both grade levels, the time block designated for "Specials and Science" could also be used for reading. When that happened, students spent a full 100% of the school day in the two tested subjects, with reading alone filling 60–65% of the day.

These figures correspond to those of other studies of the impact of high-stakes tests, which indicate reduced time for social studies and less time than was state-mandated (Bailey, Shaw, & Hollifield, 2006; Jones & Thomas, 2006). Teachers from North Carolina reported spending 75% of their time on reading and mathematics (Cawelti, 2006). On a nationally representative survey of 299 schools across all 50 states, the Center on Education Policy (CEP) specifically asked about use of instructional time. More than 70% of the districts reported that they had "reduced instructional time in at least one other subject to make more time for reading and mathematics—the subjects tested for NCLB" (CEP, 2006, p. vii). As in our three schools, some districts reported double periods of these subjects, with below-grade-level students totally missing instruction in other subject areas. Mirroring the pattern of Hawthorne, Brookfield, and Cherry Ridge, districts with schools in improvement status took the most time from other subject areas in order to maximize instructional time for reading and mathematics (CEP, 2007b). While reading and mathematics have long overshadowed other elementary school subjects (Goodlad, 1984), their dominance seems to be increasing at the expense of other valued knowledge domains.

The School Year

In addition to the daily instructional schedule, the schools' yearly schedules were also strongly influenced by a test orientation. Early in the year, Stevenson's central office had mailed every school an official test calendar indicating the window dates for the administration of each type of test for each grade level. With the exception of June, no month was free of state- or district-imposed tests. Hawthorne's principal, Ms. Everett, was stunned when she saw the calendar. Realizing the number of days that would be given over to diagnostic-test administration, she asked her leadership team rhetorically, "When are teachers expected to teach?" (September 9, 2004).

   A few weeks later, at a whole-school staff meeting, Ms. Everett tried to put a positive spin on the testing requirements. Members of the Leadership Team had just finished a PowerPoint presentation, which listed all the school's "Initiatives and Programs." Ms. Everett wanted teachers to see how much was going on in the school and what would be required of them. Overshadowing other items on the list were a host of diagnostic assessments and initiatives that required diagnostic tests: primary grades reading assessment, ESOL assessment, running records on PalmPilots, Horizons, Dynamic Indicators of Basic Early Literacy Skills (DIBELS), Diagnostic Reading Assessment (DRA), data meetings, CTBS, Measures of Academic Progress in Reading (MAP-R), Stanford Diagnostic Reading Test (SDRT), Corrective Reading, and the state test. Sensing, and possibly feeling a need to justify, this imbalance, Ms. Everett quickly interjected that ultimately the district wanted to "maximize instructional time and minimize assessment time." But, she added, this was a transition year, so they first had to put the programs in place (October 25, 2004). By the end of the school year, having experienced the full weight of the assessments, Hawthorne's assistant principal, Adam Fox, complained, "We have 180 days with students and we have all of these assessments. . . . The district is killing us with all these tests" (May 24, 2005). Figure 2.2 depicts the percentage of students required to take district or state tests across the school year.

   Not included on the district-issued calendar were the mandated unit tests in mathematics (five–six per grade level) or school-mandated diagnostic tests such as DIBELS to identify students for intervention in early grades at

Figure 2.2. Estimated proportion of students taking district- or state-mandated tests by month, 2004–05.

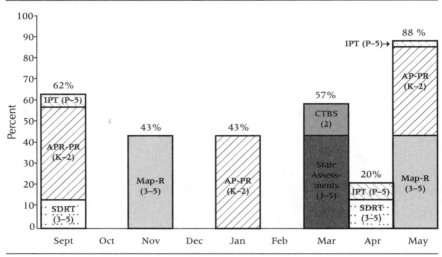

Notes: IPT = IDEA Proficiency Test of Reading and Writing; AP-PR = Assessment Program for Primary Reading; SDRT = Stanford Diagnostic Reading Test; Map-R = Measures of Academic Progress in Reading; CTBS = Comprehensive Test of Basic Skills. Each bar represents the estimated proportion of students taking district- or state-mandated tests in that month. Parentheses indicate the grades affected by testing. In addition to the tests shown here, during the months of October through February, exempt special education students take the Alternative-State Test on an individual basis; this test affects roughly 0.1% of the student population.

all three schools, and DRAs for all grade levels at Hawthorne. Because the school district was late in mandating the MAP-R and SDRT, schools had already begun administering the diagnostic tests they had decided upon at the school level: Images, Test Ready, DRA, DIBELS, and so forth. For the following year, Stevenson planned to increase the number of times MAP-R was given and to add MAP-M (Measures of Academic Progress in Mathematics) to the list of required tests. Selected to be part of the National Assessment of Educational Progress (NAEP) sample for 2004–05, Cherry Ridge had yet another—federally mandated—test to add to their schedule. Also missing from the calendar were teacher-made assessments, given in some reading and mathematics classes at least once a week.

Among the numerous tests on Figure 2.2 is the most important assessment of the year: the state test, given at the beginning of March. Although in past years the test had been given in May, testing dates had been moved up to early March. This ensured that test results would arrive in time to inform decision making for the following year, as required by NCLB. It also created what came to be known as the "March to March" school year, with the entire fourth quarter literally falling into the following school year. On the monthly calendar handed us by Ms. Hancock, the Cherry Ridge principal, there was a large, handwritten notation for March 14: "FY 06 School Year Starts!!" At a meeting in late April, Ms. Hancock reminded the Leadership team that they were already in the first marking period of the following year. This theme literally resounded throughout the school building through intercom announcements. The day after the state tests were finished, Ms. Hancock welcomed students and staff to the "first day of the new school year."

Although not as pronounced at the other two schools, we regularly heard informal talk of the March–March school year. At a September whole-staff meeting at Brookfield, for example, the principal interjected with a reminder that the school year was March–March when the staff developer was helping teachers develop plans to monitor student performance in tested areas. At a December planning meeting with fourth- and fifth-grade teachers, the reading specialist expressed frustration with accommodating the district's new reading curriculum with the March–March year. She complained that this testing cycle was the result of NCLB and not a response to concerns about student achievement. Other teachers were less certain about the rationale behind the testing cycle, but just as frustrated about not knowing and trying to accommodate curriculum coverage: "Time is what they continuously complain about—that there are just not enough hours to get it all done. And the assessment comes in March" (Heather Nichols, September 22, 2005). In the laissez-faire climate of Hawthorne, teachers complained that, to accommodate the earlier testing time, planning should have been from March to March. But because leadership did not encourage adjustment to that testing cycle, they ended up having an intense test preparation period in January and February when everything else "went by the wayside. It was all geared to [state-test] prep" (Joy Karlsen, June 8, 2007).

SETTING PRIORITIES

In addition to setting the daily and yearly calendar, two common opening rituals of schools are writing a school improvement plan (SIP) and setting staff meeting times and agendas. In these activities, a school sets out its priorities for the year, declaring either what it values or what it knows it must accomplish. These activities do not occur in a vacuum, but in interactions with the broader educational context. In their plans and agendas, the schools announced and enacted three priorities that further signified a test-taking culture. First, they used SIPs and meetings to keep their agendas narrowly focused on AYP and testing requirements. Second, they monitored teachers' work to ensure a unified focus. And third, they used time and space, originally intended for other purposes, for testing needs. These priorities guided the schools' organizational behavior throughout the year. In examining these priorities, we can see how school personnel "notice or select information from the environment, make meaning of that information, and then act on these interpretations, developing culture, social structures, and routines over time" (Coburn, 2006, p. 345).

Narrowing the Academic Focus

The primary requirement for SIPs in Stevenson School District was a listing of all school improvement objectives. Although all schools were directed to list at least one objective for pupil services and one for gifted and talented programs, academic objectives were the main expectation, in keeping with the district's first guiding principle: "Improve the education design and delivery of instruction and curriculum by utilization of proven best practices." Another influential guiding principle was related to the district's goal of closing the achievement gap: "providing students with a strong foundation in reading, writing, mathematics, and technology so that they can excel in all areas of the curriculum." Title I schools had additional SIP requirements, including a needs assessment, monitoring student achievement, and a plan for parental involvement. In following these requirements and guiding principles, school leaders had the AYP goals of the state test firmly in mind.

School SIPs. Each school's improvement plan followed the district's directive to have objectives in the required areas of gifted and talented programs; pupil services; and for Title I schools, parental involvement. However, these were generally given cursory attention. For example, one pupil services' objective was simply a vague claim: "Staff will work on new ways to collaborate to better meet the needs of our students: academically, physically, and emotionally." In contrast, the academic objectives were highly specific and notably limited to the tested areas of the curriculum: reading and mathematics. Writing was mentioned only as a means to demonstrate reading comprehension.

For each school, the first academic objective focused on the improvement of reading—the AYP problem area. For Hawthorne, reading was the only academic objective. It was specified by grade level and included ways of monitoring progress. For example, increase in Grades 3–5 reading skills was to be "measured by running records, Developmental Reading Assessment (DRA) and formative assessments. Additionally we will be gathering and monitoring data received from SDRT, MAP-R and DIBELS testing." Brookfield and Cherry Ridge did not mention specific ways of monitoring with their objectives, but they did specify the amount of improvement they hoped to see, which corresponded exactly to the state's annual measurable objectives.[1] This is a typical example: "To achieve the 2005 Annual Measurable Objective (AMO) of 57.8% in reading (53.6% in mathematics) for all students and in the eight subgroups."

Using the district's specified format, all three schools then delineated the tasks they would undertake to accomplish these objectives. In reading, Hawthorne said they would monitor the success of instructional strategies, especially for English Language Learners (ELL), special education, Hispanic, African American and "double-dip" students through administrative observations, writing assessments, and data meetings.[2] These data meetings were times when key administrators and support staff met with a classroom teacher to discuss below-grade-level students. Brookfield's plan emphasized the importance of monitoring student learning and making instructional change based on assessments, walk-throughs, and data analysis. And, having missed AYP in the special education reading category, Cherry Ridge emphasized the inclusion of both special needs and ELL students in general education classes with intensive supplemental support.

Interviews with principals about their schools' priorities confirmed our reading of these documents. In response to a question about Hawthorne's goals and priorities, Ms. Everett talked about making teachers aware of the school's academic focus (reading) so that students would master the curriculum standards and demonstrate that in their writing. She went on:

> The other part that was uppermost in my mind was AYP, of course, and how we are going to achieve it. We made it, kind of made it, by the . . . safe harbor . . . making everyone aware of our data and where we were looking good and strong and where we seemed to have some issues. . . . But how are we going to achieve AYP? Where do we need to focus? Looking at our data we truly needed to be very aware of our English second language cell and our special education cell because that's where we were approaching trouble if we really didn't make an impact. So, I wanted to share with them [the staff] what other successful schools were doing. (April 28, 2005)

And although Brookfield had been making AYP without the safe harbor, the principal, Ms. Moore, still called adequate yearly progress the school's highest priority: "You know, the highest priority is [the state test]. I mean, I have to meet each of the cells for AYP for the [state test]. . . . . One of the things that the teachers need to be doing is monitoring so that they know where the kids are in meeting the [state's learning outcome] goals. . . . I have to have them successful on [the state tests]" (September 28, 2004). To achieve this goal, Ms. Moore had grade-level teams spending substantial time looking at indicators and talking about "what proficiency looks like for that indicator."

But of all the principal interviews, the one with Ms. Hancock unearthed the pressure experienced by a school leader for whom AYP was a dire necessity. As we did for each principal, we handed Ms. Hancock a summary of the interview questions. After a quick glance, she set them aside and, for 1½ hours, described how the school goals were driven by external policies:

> The goals and priorities really are influenced nationally, state and local and very little—there's very little autonomy within the school building because of the school being in need of improvement based on No Child Left Behind. So, No Child Left Behind is really driving our school improvement plan and our instructional design, our organizational design and how we spend our Title 1 money . . . end of sentence. (September 16, 2004)

Ms. Hancock explained that prior to NCLB, SIPs emphasized reading and writing goals. But with NCLB, those goals "changed dramatically. . . . Writing is gone for all practical purposes because there aren't enough hours in a day." Explaining how NCLB gave states the responsibility to set standards and that "school districts have the authority to write the curriculums," Ms. Hancock described how that authority was being subverted as schools paid increased attention to the "recommended" state curriculum and the assessed KSAs (knowledge, skills, and abilities). Like Elaine Everett, Ms. Hancock said that although some schools replaced Stevenson's curriculum frameworks with the state curriculum, Cherry Ridge did not do that:

> No. We can't. Stevenson requires us to use the Stevenson curriculum. It's very rich and it's very good. What I'm going to ask them [teachers] to do is make sure they know, if they're teaching fractions, what will be assessed. . . . Those teachers need to know what the state expects fourth graders to know and be able to do about

fractions and what fifth graders need to do and be able to do about fractions. They're not going to use the curriculum; they're going to use our curriculum. But they're going to look and see what's tested. (September 16, 2004)

Whether using the state's recommended curriculum directly or employing Ms. Hancock's more sophisticated approach, all three schools fostered a narrow view of the school curriculum. Inscribed in the SIPs, this view was repeatedly expressed through meeting agendas that focused on testing in the targeted curriculum areas.

Meeting agendas. To obtain an overall picture of meeting agendas, we prepared a chart listing the meeting date, type (whole school, leadership team, grade level, and so forth), and agenda items for each school. We then determined the percentage of meetings that dealt with testing issues. Counted as testing topics would be items such as the new diagnostic testing requirements, student achievement monitoring tools, test accommodations, state test preparation and practice, short constructed response (SCR) scoring, and test preparation materials.[3] Not counted as testing topics were agenda items such as the new grading and reporting system, parent involvement, instructional strategies, English Language Learners, child abuse, and inclusion. At least half the meeting agendas at each school had test-related topics that occupied much of the meeting.

At Brookfield 50% of meetings devoted substantial time to one or more of these topics; at Cherry Ridge, 63%; and at Hawthorne, 70%. When we looked at the meetings held in January and February, the weeks just before the state test in which schools seemed particularly affected by the high-stakes testing environment, we saw a slight increase in the test focus at Brookfield (up from 50% to 58%), the same 70% at Hawthorne, but a substantial increase at Cherry Ridge from 63% to 100% of meetings. Even though Cherry Ridge had suspended School Improvement, Leadership, and whole-staff meetings during that time, all 15 of the grade-level and curriculum implementation meetings we attended during those 8 weeks concentrated almost exclusively on assessment topics. Furthermore, these agendas made apparent that the SCR test format was the assessment topic of greatest concern in all the schools. SCRs were discussed at almost half the meetings at Hawthorne and Brookfield; at Cherry Ridge they were on nearly two thirds of the meeting agendas. As seen in later chapters, they became foundational to what it meant to teach and learn in these schools.

Although the testing agendas of the three schools were similar, each school enacted these agendas differently. The approach that school leaders promoted reflected organizational and relational capacities. With its weak capacity, Hawthorne's agenda was to borrow a successful test-preparation strategy from a neighboring school. With a strong professional capacity, Brookfield's agenda was tapping into staff expertise and developing consensus about proficiency expectations on the state test. Drawing on its organizational capacity, Cherry Ridge used a bureaucratic strategy to maintain a test focus: keeping teachers accountable by requiring them to document their work. In the following paragraphs we explain how these three different approaches helped each school further develop a test-taking culture.

At Hawthorne, one of the most significant test-related topics was a neighboring school's notoriously successful strategy of making AYP after they had failed the previous year. The widely held perception of that school's success was teaching directly from the recommended state curriculum, which embodied the writing expectations and assessed KSAs of the state test. A Task Team meeting in late October foreshadows how this emphasis unfolded at Hawthorne. The meeting was called to plan the agenda for a whole-staff meeting later that day: to examine student achievement monitoring tools, which the mathematics and reading specialists had brought with them as requested. But the Task Team never looked at the monitoring tools, and more than 1½ hours elapsed before the principal said, "Can we quickly plan what we're going to present this afternoon?" (October 25, 2005). Instead of planning that agenda earlier in the meeting, Ms. Everett had been preoccupied with how Canterbury Elementary School had gotten itself out of AYP danger. Regarded as somewhat of a miraculous success story, Canterbury was a model that Ms. Everett wanted her teachers to follow. As she reported to her Task Team, Canterbury teachers were not following the Stevenson curricula; they accessed the state's recommended curriculum and taught only those indicators that were marked for testing. Teachers had one planning day a quarter and a 2-hour team-planning block a week. Ms. Everett ended her remarks by contrasting Hawthorne's teachers to Canterbury's as less dedicated and said she would like the team to visit Canterbury to see what they were doing.

This presentation evoked considerable discussion, which eventually turned to the upcoming staff meeting: How would they get teachers to implement this model? The Task Team began by deciding to give the staff one planning day a quarter and left it to the staff developer to plan. What had begun as a nonagenda item—commenting about a neighboring school—had suddenly become school policy that would require, as we will see later, major changes in the school schedule and expectations. Curiously, no one seemed to note the 180-degree shift in the goal for team planning. In their September meeting, aspirations had been expressed for team meetings to focus on instructional strategies rather than merely curriculum coverage. Now, at this October meeting, coverage clearly dominated. Ms. Everett expected her team to help her convince teachers to use the state's recommended curriculum, but without telling them to stop using the district's new instructional guides.

Instead of imitating another school's practices, Brookfield's meeting agendas had a different, though still test-related, focus. At numerous whole-school, Leadership Council, and grade-level meetings throughout the year, teachers tried to reach consensus on what proficiency would look like for key curriculum indicators. To reach agreement, staff used the Baldrige system as an organizational tool. Early in the school year, the Instructional Council received training in creating "linkages charts," named for a graphic that visually connects the Baldrige process components: leadership, strategic planning, student/stakeholder focus, information and analysis, faculty/staff focus, process management, and results. The group first used these charts for their SIP priority on writing in response to reading and later for their mathematics objective. This process lasted throughout the year. Brookfield staff kept returning to the question: What would proficiency look like in writing in response to both reading and mathematics?

As they worked through this process together, the Brookfield staff was often led by the school's staff developer, reading specialist, or math content coach, who jointly planned, and revised, with teacher input. For example, the leadership team had proposed that, to achieve their SIP goal for mathematics, students would need to "demonstrate complete understanding of concepts taught through use of words, numbers or pictures" (January 6, 2005). In this statement, the leadership team was trying to emphasis the distinction between giving the correct answer and demonstrating understanding of the answer. This was particularly important because the state test required not just the answer, but a written explanation of student thinking. Students would not receive a proficient answer unless they demonstrated understanding through their SCRs, which could comprise words, numbers, or pictures. To clarify the intent of that goal, teachers suggested adding the terms "explaining or modeling" and offered a number of ways that students could do this. Once the goal statement was rewritten, grade-level teams wrote action plans describing how they would reach common understandings of proficiency as well as how they would help students demonstrate proficiency. Ways to develop consensus included grade-level data discussions, team scoring, and developing a store of "benchmark" papers.

Cherry Ridge established a test-taking orientation in their meeting agendas with yet another approach: documentation of their work.

Documenting their data-based decision making was a centerpiece of Cherry Ridge meetings—particularly with respect to scoring students' SCRs to determine the tested areas that needed further practice. This description of a fifth-grade meeting was typical: Teachers would share samples of best, middle, and lowest SCRs that students had written; discuss what the student knew and needed to know; then generate possible instructional strategies to advance the student. Teachers were required to complete "capture sheets" that were submitted to the administration every week, documenting the school's ongoing diagnostic assessment. These capture sheets indicated the student's level (e.g., "middle"), what the student knew (e.g., "a fact from the text"), what the student needed to know (e.g., "to provide evidence"), and what the teacher would do next with the student (e.g., "talk through the text"). This SCR documentation process was part of the school's reliance on data-gathering protocols to target a narrow band of academic indicators. Having attended district data-analysis training, the principal was committed to data protocols and action plans, particularly for special education and ELL students. She saw this as a way of tracking reading performance and preventing students from falling through the cracks. Like their counterparts at Brookfield, Cherry Ridge teachers were examining student work and trying to reach agreement on proficiency. But the requirement for documentation almost always overshadowed this more substantive agenda.

At all three schools, a test-taking focus dominated SIP goals and staff meetings. At Hawthorne this occurred largely by promoting an imitation or mimicking strategy characteristic of a low-capacity institution dealing with uncertainty (Rowan & Miskel, 1999; Scott, 2001). Rather than develop their school's capacity, Hawthorne simply used a strategy that had been found to be effective elsewhere. In sharp contrast, Brookfield reshaped the school culture toward test taking by tapping into teacher expertise and involving staff in decision making. At different levels of staff meetings throughout the year, teachers not only revisited their understandings of proficiency in students' SCRs, but also were productively involved in suggesting improvements in their collaborative work.

Brookfield's approach, so distinct from Hawthorne's, characterizes a high-capacity institution. But even there, the requirements of the performance management system sometimes became just another exercise, another chart, another action plan which staff members approached halfheartedly. Comments were made by staff that they had long been doing many of the recommendations coming from the Baldrige system and that they wanted "credit" for sharing their plans at staff meetings (February 3, 2005). These comments seemed a not-so-subtle way of teachers letting the administration know that they were being asked to do a lot of extra planning and documentation because of external, assessment-oriented mandates. With a professional learning community well in place, this bureaucratic requirement seemed to interfere with their work as much as it facilitated it. Different still in how they embedded a test-taking orientation in their daily routines was Cherry Ridge. Lacking Brookfield's professional capacity, Cherry Ridge relied on a strategy characteristic of bureaucratic institutions: having employees create an auditable paper trail of their work.

But none of the school leaders, not even Brookfield's Liz Moore, simply trusted that follow-through on school priorities would occur just because information was disseminated and teachers had written action plans. The stakes of failure were simply too high. The school-level goals and agendas that were established and communicated publicly, in group sessions, had to be enacted privately by individual teachers in individual, and sometimes isolated, classrooms (O'Day, 2002). Therefore, principals, as well as the school district, felt obliged to monitor these test-oriented priorities with formal walk-throughs and informal classroom observations. This monitoring, described below, reflected and deepened the schools' test-taking cultures.

Monitoring Teaching and Learning

The district's policy of "walk-throughs" was a way of making sure that teachers attended to desired practices and content standards. The school principal was generally involved in helping establish the focus. Combined teams of district and school representatives, often twelve at a time, literally "walked through" classrooms with standardized protocols and criteria. These walk-throughs were billed as a nonevaluative feedback resource that would provide insight into the type of support needed by a local school. However, minutes from the Board of Education described them as providing "direct monitoring and supervision" and were often described by teachers as intimidating—even when their own colleagues were part of the group. After visiting classrooms, team members would meet for debriefings that were structured around the stated outcomes of the visit. Communication back to the school was to provide support for staff on what was working and to identify "opportunities for continuous improvement."

At Hawthorne, district-led walk-throughs were scheduled to take place in February, just a month prior to the state test. This timing put teachers in a quandary. Ms. Everett had explicitly directed them to use commercially produced test preparation materials recommended by neighboring Canterbury during this time. Canterbury's principal found these materials to be more tightly aligned with the state's tested content than the district's curriculum was. Believing this strategy would enhance the school's chances of making AYP, Ms. Everett had no qualms about putting Stevenson's instructional guides temporarily to the side. Although teachers did not want the district's walk-through team to see students working out of commercially produced workbooks, neither did they want to fake a lesson. The teachers resolved their dilemma by resequencing their test prep calendar so they would be actively teaching the lesson's objective, also found in the district's instructional guides, on the walk-through day. That way, their practice of having students do independent work out of test prep booklets would not be so evident. This situation reflects the confusing messages that Hawthorne teachers often received. At a fall staff meeting, they had been told that walk-throughs would evaluate their fidelity to and quality implementation of the district's instructional programs. Then they were asked to set aside the district's instructional guides and teach from commercially produced materials as though there was no contradictions in those messages.

Wanting her school to be prepared, Brookfield's Ms. Moore conducted informal observations in preparation for the formal district walk-throughs. At the end of September, she announced at a whole-staff meeting that she was concerned that some of the teachers were not posting specific agendas in their classrooms that listed what students should know and be able to do by the end of reading and mathematics lessons. She was adamant that the agendas should be "fine-tuned" to what the teacher was doing that day and that these should reflect curriculum indicators. Clearly dissatisfied with the agenda statements she had seen in some classrooms, she said that she should see more on a math agenda than "The students will subtract." Once the official walk-throughs occurred, Ms. Moore organized feedback from the district team at whole-staff meetings. Receiving generally positive feedback, Brookfield teachers were asked to discuss in teams: "What would be the next logical step for your grade level in the next month and a half?" (December 14, 2004). This type of group question was typical of the way Brookfield teachers' professional judgment was respected and their collaborative work encouraged.

Rather than use district walk-throughs for general instructional observations, the principal at Cherry Ridge used them for feedback on the school's new classroom inclusion approach: How well was it targeting their ELL and special needs students? In addition, Ms. Hancock and her leadership team regularly monitored classrooms for compliance with school-level directives. One was the "60/30" mathematics lesson format in which teachers were expected to keep pace with the district curriculum during the first 60 minutes and review problem areas in the last 30 minutes. Another school directive that was closely monitored through these informal walk-throughs was "test simulations." These simulations were periods in which students practiced taking tests under the exact conditions and using the exact format of the state test. Teachers did not like the simulations, saying that students were so "burnt out" from test preparation that "they couldn't handle it anymore." However, they felt as though they had little choice but to comply. As Ms. Clemson, a fifth-grade teacher, said to us, "It was being looked for, you know. It was being looked for" (May 26, 2005).

Even though principals were aware of the anxiety these walk-throughs generated and called them nonevaluative, teachers still felt "under the gun" (Valli & Buese, 2007). Told that a large team would be conducting a walk-through of his classroom, one particularly candid fifth-grade teacher said to his teammates, "This scares the [expletive] out of me" (February 10, 2005). He wondered when any of the visitors had last taught, and his teammates expressed concern that they would be singled out for doing something wrong. A fourth-grade teacher similarly expressed her opinion that the walk-through team would be looking for something to criticize so it would not matter how prepared or well planned teachers were, and a special education teacher called the dreaded experience "horrible." She felt as though she was faking her lesson. While some teachers no doubt benefited from the feedback, this form of monitoring created a more intense experience of surveillance than teachers had heretofore experienced or has been reported in the literature (Firestone, Monfils, Hayes, et al., 2004). With the burden of accountability for student achievement resting primarily with principals it is not surprising that walk-throughs became as much pressure to comply as they were feedback for support.

Repurposing Time and Space

So far, we have argued that official school calendars, SIPs, meeting agendas, and walk-throughs oriented these three schools around testing. In addition to these planned events, testing demands increasingly usurped the use of time and space that was originally set for other priorities. Other studies have found that once time allocations have been made for the school year, they are rarely changed (Firestone et al., 2004). But in the test-taking cultures we observed, that was not the case—at least not for teachers' use of out-of-class time. Making time, as well as space, to support testing was a high priority. As early as September 8, field notes record the significance of the March testing and its impact on time. At a professional development meeting with Brookfield's fourth- and fifth-grade teams, Ms. Breman, the staff developer, wrote on the posted schedule, "No March meeting due to testing" (September 8, 2004). Ms. Moore later told the Instructional Council to "block off March," as they were planning the spring calendar (December 2, 2004). And at Cherry Ridge, Ms. Hancock closed the January School Improvement Team (SIT) meeting by reminding the group that the next SIT was scheduled for February 28, the day before the state test began. As noted by the observer, "Everyone agreed that they should delay this meeting until March 14" (January 31, 2005).

Ms. Hancock also regularly had a "countdown" to the state test days. This began as early as mid-December, with field notes indicating that "everyone has the number 9 on their mind—9 weeks until [the state test]" (December 13, 2004). Closer to the beginning of the testing dates, Ms. Hancock lost track of time, believing there were 20 days left until the start of the state testing period. When her assistant principal pointed out at a SIT meeting that there were only 19 days left, Ms. Hancock "gasped, nonverbally expressing her anxiety" (January 31, 2005). School days, and weeks, mattered only in terms of their proximity to the test—how many days were left to prepare.

Competing pressures on teacher time also became more and more obvious as the high-stakes state test date approached. Invariably, test priorities won out. Administrators delayed a visit to a school that was a high implementer of the Baldrige system and canceled a Math Night for parents. Professional development time was canceled, even though substitutes had already been hired. A "mathathon" fund-raiser assembly was postponed because teachers were "cramming" for the test. Teachers were pulled out of their classes to receive instructions on testing booklets, procedures, and confidentiality and to sign a statement that they would not discuss test contents with anyone. As Hawthorne's reading specialist told us, "There will be meetings. . . . There will be security training, which is mandatory. I mean, nobody can step foot in the rooms until they're trained. And there will be walk-throughs of the whole testing process" (December 22, 2005). Paraeducators and staff members also were pulled from regular assignments to administer the test and give accommodations. ESOL classes were suspended as necessary and substitutes covered classes while regular classroom teachers gave individual accommodations to their own students. This use of teachers for individual test accommodations rather than classroom instruction was done because of a strong belief that ESOL and special needs students would perform better on the state test if they received accommodations by people they knew and who had practiced the test with them.

The symbolic and functional use of space also privileged testing. As a fifth-grade teacher at Hawthorne pointed out, "You walk into the school [and] the first thing you see is that bulletin board that shows [state test] scores and where we were last year and where we're expected to be for the next year. So, I mean that's . . . the mindset" (May 31, 2005). That was the mindset at the other two schools as well. Brookfield, for example, had a "Data Wall" in the entry hallway of the school. When the report from the 2003–04 state test showed that Brookfield students were above the state average, the administrators congratulated the teachers on their work and prominently posted the results on the Data Wall. At Cherry Ridge, an assessment orientation was also obvious in the school hallways. Early in the year, an observer's field notes capture her reaction to the student work that typically adorns school walls: "Obsession with indicators and standards flows over even into school projects—displays are accompanied by indicators! Wow" (September 28, 2004). As the school began to use the Baldrige system more fully, teachers began thinking about Data Walls in their own classrooms: "Kids are gonna . . . be more aware of their own progress. . . . That'll kind of light a flame under some of them" (May 25, 2005).

Testing also won out over other school functions in claims for space. Because classrooms did not have computers for every student, tests that were computer based, such as the MAP-R, had to be administered in computer labs. In Hawthorne and Cherry Ridge, this meant closing the computer lab for instructional, training, or other purposes whenever these tests had to be given. Because classes were regularly scheduled in the labs, some students would necessarily miss their computer instruction, which was often related to writing, mathematics, or social studies, during that testing period. So, for example, Hawthorne, which had to administer the MAP-R twice a year to four classes each of third, fourth, and fifth graders, would need to close the computer lab for at least 24 class periods to accommodate that test alone.

The situation was worse at Brookfield, and schools like it, which did not have a dedicated computer lab. As the principal told us, "We do not have a computer lab, so we have to do it in our media center, where we have 15 computers. . . . So, that means . . . our media center is going to be closed down for quite a long time to get all that assessment done" (September 28, 2004). With an average class size of 21 and two classes at each grade level, Brookfield had to close the media center for at least 18 class periods. Twice the number of lessons would be disrupted as well, because some students from one classroom went for the test during one time period, and other students went at another time. In the following year, Stevenson School District planned to double the number of MAP-R administrations and add two administrations of MAP-M (Measures of Academic Progress in Mathematics). This would double and triple the amount of time that the schools' computer labs or media centers would be unavailable for instructional purposes.

RELATING TO STUDENTS

In the previous sections of this chapter we have described how Hawthorne, Brookfield, and Cherry Ridge created test-taking cultures by the way they scheduled time and set school priorities. Implicit in those sections—made explicit here—is the role of the student in these types of schools. Numerous concerns have been raised in both the popular press and the scholarly literature about the impact of high-stakes testing on students, particularly poor and minority students (Valenzuela, 2005). Among these concerns are increases in drop-out rates (Darling-Hammond, 2004), exposure to less curriculum content (CEP, 2006), and excessive pressure on students to pass tests (Firestone, Monfils, Schorr, Hicks, & Martinez, 2004). Overlooked in these analyses are the fundamental ways in which test-taking cultures reconstruct relationships with students. Who is the student in the life of the school? How is it that, in a high-stakes accountability environment, students come to be known by data rather than by face? In the examples below, we describe the powerful pressures on school personnel to construct relations with students in ways that benefited the school more than the student. This includes shuffling students from school to school to avoid having them on their AYP rolls, publicly ranking students by proficiency, and influencing school attendance.

Hawthorne's principal, Elaine Everett, complained to us about principals at neighboring schools. As the elementary school in its geographic area with the most comprehensive special education services, Hawthorne was obliged to receive students with Individualized Education Programs (IEPs) who could not receive adequate services from its "sister" schools. When she was sent students just weeks before the state test, Ms. Everett questioned the motives of the other principals. During our interview she asked rhetorically:

> What are you doing? How can you transfer in this fifth grader? Why are you transferring in a fifth grader to me in March? You know—so that their scores don't count for your school. That's mean. You can't do that; it's a fifth grader. They've been in your school their whole little life. So why are you going to give them to me now? I know why you're giving them to me now—and you're not going to do that. (April 28, 2005)

Even though these students would not be in her school long enough to be included in its Annual Measurable Objectives (AMO), Ms. Everett was alarmed about moving a student from a general education class in one school to a learning and academic disabilities (LAD) class in another:

And now their kid is in a LAD program. Did the kid really need to be in a LAD program? You know and did they really need to be in a LAD program 2 or 3 months before the school year ended? Come on, that's mean.

Understanding that these principals were trying "to get out of the whole AYP nightmare by getting the kid the heck out of their school," she worried that the high-stakes testing environment was fostering an "I don't care" attitude toward children: "It's not a healthy environment."

But Ms. Everett herself inadvertently fell victim to that unhealthy environment. During the September Leadership Team meeting, she had given teachers a handout for the improvement of teaching and learning. Describing the handout as an official document of what they were "supposed to do" as a school, she apologized for not having paid more attention to it in previous years when the quality of teaching was the district's priority. Calling their attention to the "evidence of student learning" throughout their school improvement plan, Ms. Everett then stated that the district's emphasis was now on student learning. She wanted her teachers to understand why they were concentrating so heavily on various types of student data to monitor: that they were indeed adhering to the district's directive to shift their attention from teaching to student learning.

To help teachers make that shift, Ms. Everett asked them to write down the reading level of each of their students. Teachers put this information on large chart paper that Ms. Everett had hung on the media center walls during a whole-school staff meeting. Students were listed by name in the following categories: high (above grade level), middle (on grade level), low (below grade level), and IEP students. Linking this task to the SIP reading goal, Ms. Everett said this information was essential to document because the school was attending to the learning of each individual student. She then posted these charts on the walls of her office throughout the rest of the year and brought them to data meetings. Not only were they in her field of vision when she worked in her office, they were easily seen by visitors—including students. One fifth grader who spotted her name in the "low" category cried out, "You think I'm stupid" (January 20, 2005). After that incident, Ms. Everett kept the chart paper folded to hide student names and classifications.

This public identification, classification, and discussion of students according to grade-level reading scores is what prompted Hawthorne's reading specialist, Heather Nichols, to say that she knew students by data rather than by name. Her primary knowledge of students came from all the "data points" that teachers collected on students and brought with them to data meetings. How school staff thought about students was intimately wrapped up in the data points they collected on them. It was also connected to how they thought about school attendance, with principals issuing frequent reminders about the importance of students not missing school—or testing days. Even at a school like Brookfield, with its collegiality and family-like atmosphere, teachers were told to encourage their students to "be here" for the state test, and to provide incentives if necessary (February 3, 2005). Although there were make-up days, schools were responsible for the percent of students who took the state test, and make-up tests were more time consuming to administer.

There being much at stake, student attendance was a near obsession at Cherry Ridge. First, the state's targeted attendance rate was 94% for schools to make AYP. Second, Ms. Hancock, the school's principal, believed there was a vital connection between attendance and achievement scores. At staff meetings, she would lead her teachers in reciting the mantra "One day of absence is equal to 3 days of lost instruction." She also asked the leadership team to analyze data to determine which families had children with high absences. She specifically mentioned Hispanic parents who took their children out of school to visit family in Central America. Referring to the demographic reporting categories for AYP, she said, "This kid is poverty, ESOL, Hispanic—everything" and labeled parents' actions "unconscionable." The reference was clearly about jeopardizing the school's ability to make AYP, not about the child's well-being.

These comments were reminiscent of earlier comments made by Ms. Hancock about the benefits of Cherry Ridge having a full-service health clinic. Although she discussed the physical well-being of her students, especially those without health insurance, she was focused on the instructional, and AYP, implications:

> We had a little girl who was crying out here on Friday—a third grader who didn't want to come into school because she had a headache. I walked out there, helped her separate from her father, brought her in; she's registered in the health center, so they could give her Tylenol, right here. She went back to class. So, when you're looking at things like attendance, school participation, and learning, can't teach them if they're not here. (September 16, 2004)

Discussing the health center at a leadership meeting, Ms. Hancock again mentioned its advantage in terms of attendance: no need to send students home for a low-grade fever or cough when you can give them an aspirin.

Fenstermacher (1979) and Biesta (2004) have argued that high-stakes accountability climates can shift educators' sense of personal responsibility for students to an impersonal contractual relation. By having their attention drawn outward, to the accountability demands of the state, educators seem to lose sight of the individuals for whom they are responsible. Rather than feeling entrusted, in loco parentis, with the well-being of their students, educators can develop the restricted, amoral relationship of a service provider. When that happens, students become a means to an end—achieving AYP—not an end in themselves. Bryk and Schneider (2002), echoing Dewey, make the case that schools should be judged not just by their outcomes, but by the quality of life within them: "The social relations of schooling are not just a mechanism of production but are a valued outcome in their own right. . . . The quality of social exchanges that occur here, and how various parties understand and interpret them, are of great human significance" (p. 19).

CONCLUSION

Accountability, the fourth "A" in America's expectations for its schools, brought considerable change to Hawthorne, Brookfield, and Cherry Ridge. But it was not the change envisioned in NCLB for all students to have a high-quality education. By focusing school goals and meeting agendas on AYP requirements, the schools restricted their academic focus, developed their calendars around testing, and used teacher time and school space for testing rather than instruction. The schools' relationships to teachers and students were also transformed. Teachers' work was under heavier surveillance and students often became little more than "data points." By enacting these changes, the schools became places of test-taking cultures, places in which measures of progress limited the quality of education and quality of life in school. In the following chapter we see how entire role responsibilities began to revolve around testing and test schedules.

CHAPTER 3

Becoming Test Managers

Annual testing provides teachers with a great deal of information.
—Reauthorization of No Child Left Behind Act

I don't think that, in general, the teachers have enough knowledge and analysis of the assessments to move forward.
—Liz Moore, school principal

A<small>CCORDING TO</small> the U.S. Department of Education in the quote above, outcomes from the state test administered once a year will give teachers "a great deal of information" that they presumably can feed back into their instruction the following year. This description of annual testing portrays it as formative assessment whereby information from the test can be used to adapt teaching to meet student needs (Black & Wiliam, 1998a). If the primary purpose of the annual assessment were to provide information about students that schools could use formatively, we doubt that any school would feel compelled to create a test-taking culture similar to the ones that we described in Chapter 2. Schools would focus their attention on designing effective classroom instruction, use the annual test to determine the success of the instruction, and subsequently refine their instruction accordingly. However, the annual state test, whose outcomes can affect a school profoundly, is summative rather than formative, more analogous to assigning grades to the students in a school than providing information to guide instruction. Schools have felt compelled to prepare students for this annual test as well as to administer additional types of testing to collect information on student performance that they then could use to influence instruction.

The tasks of preparing students to be assessed summatively are clearly different from monitoring student learning to improve instruction. Others have observed that administrators, specialists, and teachers can face difficult problems in reconciling these two roles and that confusion between them can impede improvement of practice (Black & Wiliam, 1998a).

School personnel at Hawthorne, Brookfield, and Cherry Ridge had no choice. Fulfilling both these roles profoundly affected how schools scheduled their time, set priorities, and related to students.

Adding to the complexity is that ways of preparing students for summative assessment are by no means obvious. The positive effects of providing test practice have not been well established (Valli & Chambliss, 2007), even though such practice is an entrenched strategy for improving student performance on summative assessments. Publishers have produced test practice materials designed to meet each state's annual test complete with sample items organized according to topic. Indeed, it is possible to take courses that provide practice for the Scholastic Aptitude Test, the Graduate Record Exam, the Law School Admissions Test, and so on. The businesses that have developed these courses make strong claims for their effectiveness. But independent evaluations that have been made available to the public are harder to locate. Having students practice on sample items and holding practice testing sessions may do little to improve student performance beyond helping students feel more comfortable in a test-taking environment.

In contrast, the positive effects of formative assessment on student performance have been well established over age groups from young children to young adults, across several subjects, and including several countries (see Black & Wiliam, 1998a, for a review). Improving formative assessment has enhanced student performance, particularly for low achievers. But in the numerous studies, both the assessment and the resulting instruction have been carefully designed to facilitate feedback between students and teacher. The assessment has been innovative, and the resulting instruction has required substantial adjustment in teaching and classroom practice. Developing a program of effective formative assessment has proved to be a complex task in these research studies.

To respond to the dual roles of preparing children for a summative assessment and collecting test data to inform instruction, Stevenson School District relied on multiple ways of targeting students' instructional needs: commercial tests (e.g., MAP-R, SDRT), district-created tests (e.g., mathematics unit assessments), school-selected diagnostic tests (e.g., DRA), and assessments developed by individual teachers and grade-level teams. The district intended that data from these assessments be vital components in its planning process aimed at continuous improvement, a concept that emphasizes data use as a means to support standards and accountability policies (Ingram, Louis, & Schroeder, 2004). With this goal in mind, formative assessment data were to be used to make instructional decisions about individual students and to align curriculum and instruction. Studies show that districts predict that an increased focus on data use produces favorable intermediate outcomes such as greater use of student data and an increase in positive teacher beliefs on the value of data to inform instructional decisions (Kerr, Marsh, Ikemoto, Darilek, & Barney, 2006). Less is known about the actual process of data use and its relation to teaching and learning.

At Hawthorne, Brookfield, and Cherry Ridge, the principals, specialists, and teachers approved the intent of the district's plan, but the heavy implementation burden it placed on the schools interfered with reaching the goal. The cumulative number of tests required considerable coordination of resources and time for test administration and data management. In this chapter, we look at the ways in which the administrative requirements of the tests, the training needed to understand the tests, and the management and analysis of test data turned staff members, particularly staff developers, reading specialists, and math content coaches, into test managers. As we shall see, these roles often detracted from rather than supported core instructional roles.

GEARING UP FOR A YEAR OF TESTING

Before discussing how test management affected the roles and work of specialists and teachers, we describe how and to whom testing responsibilities were delegated. One of the greatest barriers to data use in schools is the lack of human capacity to support data-driven inquiry (Kerr et al., 2006). Although research points to teachers' lack of data analysis skill, human capacity inevitably falls short when the testing agenda itself is complex, voluminous, and rushed. Stevenson was aware that the volume of testing and the demands associated with data analysis would require designated personnel to shepherd school staffs through the interrelated requirements of test administration and data use. However, it did not fund or have an official listing for the position of *test coordinator*. So at each of the three schools this responsibility was assigned to the reading specialist. But the test coordinator job was too much for one person. In each case, the responsibilities were so time consuming that the position was jointly held or supported by other staff members.

While Hawthorne and Brookfield had informal data teams, Cherry Ridge constituted a formal data team that began to meet for 45 minutes with the principal every Monday morning to analyze student data. At Hawthorne, although the reading specialist was the official test coordinator, the principal, Elaine Everett, asked her assistant principal to cocoordinate when she saw the testing schedule for the year. In previous years, Ms. Everett had already put in place a larger data team to help with testing responsibilities. As Heather Nichols, the reading specialist, told us, "Two years ago, Ms. Everett said, 'This is consuming you, and you are not able to function. This is nuts, let's make a committee.' So Greta [math content coach] helps out and Melodie [staff developer] helps out, and our resource teachers provide the accommodation piece that I need" (December 14, 2004). At Brookfield, the reading specialist, Karen McNeil, and the staff developer, Lottie Breman, were "co-testing coordinators." At Cherry Ridge, the first-year reading specialist, Opal Kladowski, was asked to fill the role of test coordinator, assisted by Carmen Ledwich, the technical support staff member, and a larger data team (instructional data assistant, math content coach, staff developer, and academic support specialist), which Ms. Ledwich chaired.

The role of the test coordinator comprised a number of functions. Chief among them were learning and communicating the nature and purpose of the tests; overseeing the administration of the tests, including accommodations; analyzing test results; and determining instructional implications. To assist the test coordinators and data teams, Stevenson funded a part-time instructional data assistant (IDA) for each school who helped with "the collection, analysis, and dissemination of instructional data" by entering data into and extracting them from systemwide databases, developing spreadsheets, and preparing reports for use by teachers and administrators that would be useful in evaluating and improving instruction.

Although we focus on test management for Grades 4 and 5, test coordinators managed testing at all grade levels, pre–K through 5. In addition to the state-mandated test administered to every third–fifth grader in reading and mathematics, Stevenson used the Comprehensive Test of Basic Skills (CTBS) for second graders to ascertain areas of weakness that could be addressed by primary grade teachers. As described in Chapter 2, Stevenson also used numerous tests for diagnostic purposes, including the SDRT and MAP-R, and had implemented a new software program on PalmPilots so primary-grade teachers could keep running records on their students. Because most of the test coordinators were unfamiliar with these tests and programs at the start of the year, they were required to attend district training. Along with these test and assessment responsibilities, Opal Kladowski, the new reading specialist at Cherry Ridge, had the additional task of overseeing the administration of the National Assessment of Educational Progress (NAEP) when her school was chosen to be sampled that year.

In the following sections, we describe what happened in the schools as the professional support staff worked with the administration and teachers to fulfill test coordinator functions and respond to multiple initiatives and mandates. School capacity and principal preference interacted with external pressures to reshape roles and responsibilities in unique ways. However, certain commonalities were evident. As experienced personnel, they remembered when teachers had little instructional guidance or feedback and contrasted the present situation as preferable. But they also regretted the lack of time to work with teachers on instruction and resented the amount of time testing requirements took from the schools' core mission: teaching and learning.

New Forms of Testing

In Chapter 2 we presented the extensive testing agenda for the 2004–05 school year. The schools were accustomed to giving the state achievement test, the mathematics unit tests, and more informal formative and summative assessments, but the recently added diagnostic reading tests (SDRT and MAP-R) were a new responsibility. Principals, test coordinators, and teachers worried about the nature of the tests, the basics of administering them, the amount of time the tests would take away from instruction, and the stress that testing would place on physical and human resources.

The SDRT was designated for students with reading difficulties. But simply deciding who would take the test became a new, complex task that test coordinators and, at some schools, teachers took on. A September staff meeting at Hawthorne exemplifies the problem. Ms. Nichols, the school's reading specialist, conducted the meeting. Lamenting that she had "to order the tests before I knew what they were" and approximate the number to order, she was clearly annoyed that the district would expect test coordinators to estimate eligibility prior to the start of school. Telling teachers that they were the final decision makers, Ms. Nichols presented the teachers with a "decision tree" prepared by the district that would help them determine which students would take the test. This decision tree displayed an intricate process of examining the state achievement scores and two forms of diagnostic data for incoming fourth-grade students, and diagnostic and formative assessment data for fifth-grade students. Decisions about who would take the SDRT had to be made within the next 6 calendar days.

Ms. Nichols further informed teachers that she thought there were four or five subtests per grade. No more than two subtests were to be given in one day. As the tests had yet to arrive and she had not seen them, she could not give teachers concrete information about the number of sessions for which they would have to prepare. Unable to answer teachers' questions, Ms. Nichols admitted that she had little information about either the administration or the usefulness of the test. Stating that she had only received the information that she was discussing 3 days earlier, she acknowledged that much had to be worked out for students receiving accommodations and English Language Learner (ELL) students. She did, however, tell the group that two teachers from each grade level would administer the assessments while the other two would instruct the exempt students according to district provided suggestions.

Brookfield also had to cope with the late introduction of these diagnostic tests. But, characteristically, Brookfield's principal, Ms. Moore, thought about the impact these mandates would have on her students. Talking specifically about the SDRT, she said, "We didn't find out until a few weeks before school that we were going to have to give the Stanford Diagnostic Reading Test to, again, selective students at third, fourth, and fifth grade. Now, the selected students we're giving it to are most probably the same selected students that we're giving the Horizons and the Corrective Reading to. So, those poor babies are going to be tested out" (September 28, 2004). However, believing the SDRT would provide valuable information, she decided to test a broader rather than a narrower range of students. Although she had to comply with the district's mandate to administer the tests, Ms. Moore expressed determination in helping teachers make sense of the results.

Teacher Responses to Testing

Test management pervaded nearly every aspect of teachers' work. It was unusual to hear teachers talk about instruction without it being linked to some form of testing, and conversations around testing revealed unwavering concern about meeting AYP. At grade-level, whole-school, and leadership team meetings, agendas reminded teachers to be cognizant of the alignment of "what was taught" to "what would be tested." Although teachers and administrators voiced concern about the holistic needs of students, rarely did their conversations stray far from testing. At Hawthorne, teachers were pressed to do additional diagnostic testing throughout the year. At Brookfield, teachers tried to squeeze in test practice while still meeting the district's curriculum expectations. And at Cherry Ridge, teachers struggled to create test questions that matched both the district and the state formats.

In addition to Stevenson's required diagnostic tests, Hawthorne's administration had decided that teachers would have an additional test to administer: the Diagnostic Reading Assessment (DRA), which was a test that had been used by the district in previous years. This test was developed to diagnose reading problems in low-performing students, but there was some confusion at Hawthorne about who was to be tested and how to administer the DRA. At a professional development meeting in January, the principal told the fourth-grade teachers that DRA scores were to be recorded on students' report cards. Teachers were certain that they had these scores only for their low-performing students. When the teachers challenged the principal about the situation, she responded that, of course, they had this information on all their students. How could they know their students' reading levels if they did not? Ms. Everett falsely assumed that the lists teachers had produced for her at a meeting earlier that year—of high, middle, and low readers—were based on DRA data. In fact, teachers had arrived at that fall meeting unprepared for that assignment and without any data. They simply had used their best spur-of-the-moment judgment to categorize their students. When the principal left the January meeting, teachers sat worrying how they would test the higher-performing students for whom they did not have DRA scores in time to prepare report cards.

Teachers saw this additional administering of the DRA as an imposition, but more important, they felt inadequately prepared to administer it. They had only one DRA training session, the previous year, and they believed the test to be too subjective. They thought a well-trained teacher who did not have a close relationship with the students would be a better choice. The teachers also complained that giving the DRA tests was a significant imposition on their teaching time. The test was administered individually and took 20 minutes per pupil. Ms. Everett was clearly out of touch with her teachers' opinions about the test. From her perspective, the teachers were well prepared as test administrators and were given sufficient time for testing. She said in an interview, "So, we actually brought them the DRA training, and then we actually gave them the substitutes to release them so that they could then have a day of giving their kids a DRA. So they should feel good about all of that" (April 28, 2005). For the teachers, having a substitute take over while they attended to testing was more work for them, and of greater concern was their belief that the testing "impacts the children on grade level and above grade level, because you're taking teaching time away from them" (Joy Karlsen, June 8, 2005).

Over the course of the year, the combination of diagnostic reading tests, mathematics unit tests, and the state test challenged the management skills of Hawthorne's staff, as classes were suspended, students were pulled for testing while others remained in their classrooms, personnel was taken from other duties to provide accommodations, and computer labs and instructional spaces were taken over for testing. Mr. Swindell, a motivated team player and organized fifth-grade teacher at Hawthorne, indicated the degree to which testing affected his school:

> It would be interesting if we could sit down and figure out how much of our teaching and administrative time is taken up with testing, because if you look at the state assessment and all the state

assessment prep, the data meetings . . . Before a teacher goes to the data meetings they have to do DRAs, the MAP-R, the SDRT. . . . If we put all of that together, plus the fact that teachers are pulled out of the classroom to attend some of these meetings. And the support staff, the academic support staff, sits [in data meetings] for 4 days, 5 days in a room instead of delivering services to children. (May 31, 2005)

The teachers at Brookfield echoed Mr. Swindell's concern about too much testing and its effect on students. In September, the fourth- and fifth-grade teams met in half-day meetings to start test preparation plans. They completed a calendar that would guide the 2 days a week that they would meet with all of their students from November to March to work on the assessed knowledge, skills, and abilities (KSAs). In these planning meetings the teachers were introduced to the latest test prep materials and discussed the importance of teaching students the correct way to fill in the answer sheets so they would be comfortable with the format when the test rolled around in March. They were also instructed to prepare a list of "monitoring tools" they would use over the course of the test prep sequence. The previous year their primary monitoring tools were quarterly assessments: tests that were aligned to the school district's curriculum and instructional guides. The year of the study, the monitoring tools became more closely linked to the state's testing expectations, and the closer these tools matched the state test format, the better.

In addition to deciding what skills they would teach when, and how they would assess student progress, teachers also had to consider the logistics of setting up practice sessions. Class time would need to be carefully scheduled, and extra adults would need to provide accommodations. But because there were not enough practice test booklets or accommodators for all the teachers to give practice assessments at once, teachers made their instructional decisions around test booklet and accommodator availability. After more than an hour of planning around testing, Ms. Hinton, a fourth-grade teacher, started to joke about the number of tests the students were getting that year. She asked, "How many times do we need to test these kids?" (September 29, 2004). But her humor did not mask her worry that too much effort was going into testing.

At Cherry Ridge, testing with one eye on the district's unit tests and the other on the state test became a routine part of instructional planning. During grade-level team meetings, teachers planned for weekly testing to make sure students were prepared for the mathematics unit tests. The teachers regularly struggled with matching teacher-made tests to the differing formats of the two required tests. A review of weekly test scores at a fourth-grade meeting reveals the type of conflict teachers experienced around routine testing. Ms. Ledwich, the head of the data team, probed to determine if student errors resulted from instructional weaknesses or the format of particular questions. A quick consultation between two teachers indicated that the same test questions were difficult for both classes. But when one teacher said that she thought students were not used to seeing questions written in this manner, the teacher who had written the questions responded in an exasperated tone, "This is exactly how it will be on the test. I used word for word from the unit test" (November 12, 2004). Trying to repair relationships, Ms. Ledwich brought up the added difficulties of preparing students for the state test, which had a slightly different format and, at times, used different vocabulary. Although teachers have always given students regular tests to check their progress, these tests now became exercises in aligning test formats. Weekly assessments became as much a tool to help students become familiar with district and state test formats as they were a way to check on their understanding of content.

These examples are illustrative of a common dilemma that occurred in each of the three schools. The mechanics of testing overwhelmed the diagnostic purposes of the assessments. At Hawthorne, the principal's insistence that every child be tested in reading clouded her perspective of the DRA's utility and the amount of support teachers needed. This lack of support resulted in limited teacher buy-in. At Brookfield, teachers initially focused on the alignment of formative assessments with the district's curriculum. However, testing pressures turned their alignment focus increasingly to logistical preparations, such as scheduling accommodators. Similarly, at Cherry Ridge alignment to the state test became a key feature of designing weekly formative assessments. What started out as using the tests to assess student progress reverted to familiarizing students with district and state test formats.

LEARNING ABOUT TESTS

Stevenson's strategic plan for school improvement stressed the use of data to identify and address opportunities for improvement systemwide. District personnel saw assessment as a systemic device to improve the performance of the organization, which, in turn, would produce positive achievement outcomes for students. Given the number of assessments and their purported benefit for targeting instruction for students, one assumes that teachers would receive focused and ongoing training in the interpretation and use of test data. But the professional development around testing was uneven in the three schools. At Hawthorne, training around testing, if it existed at all, was well hidden from our research team. At Brookfield, focused and well-planned training was provided when test results from the SDRT and MAP-R first surfaced, but there was little follow-up. And at Cherry Ridge, test training was restricted to the professional support staff.

Using its "trainer of trainers" model for test interpretation, the district had each school send representatives, usually the designated test coordinator and one or two others, to training sessions. The school leaders at each of the schools described the value of these sessions. Hawthorne's reading specialist told us that the MAP-R training she and the principal received was "phenomenal" and she recalled the enthusiasm that she and Ms. Everett experienced at the training:

> Elaine and I had so many ideas. You're not supposed to be talking during [the training presentation], and we couldn't stop. They're like, "If you have something to say, write it down." And we were constantly back and forth with instructional implications and where to go and, you know, we had the teacher data right in front of us, and I'm like, "I want to run back and tell this teacher this, because this makes sense." (December 14, 2004)

Ms. Nichols then expressed the sober reality of disseminating information from the training in a busy school schedule: "The reality of it is, when you get back here, there's not any time to do it." She explained that the teachers never received the information needed to interpret the MAP-R because they could not find time for a meeting:

> If we couldn't pull them together and do it the right way there's no point in giving them all these little bits and pieces. They're so overwhelmed as it is. . . . Elaine's trying to respect the teachers' time, and she tells me not to have meetings. . . . We still have not had a formal SDRT and MAP-R data analysis meeting, and I know we need it. (December 14, 2004)

But this approach to safeguarding teachers' time created frustration. Time had already been taken for the testing. To then do nothing with these data seemed to be a greater waste of time. As one of the special education teachers explained:

> They [her students] took the test [MAP-R] at the beginning of the year, and then they just took it again a couple weeks ago. . . . And you go onto the Web site, and you get all the data, but they weren't standardized numbers. . . . So we got all this information, but we

never got any feedback from anybody as [to] what does this mean? You know, what does a score of a 167 on this test mean? So, we took the time, they did the testing, but then it was difficult to really use any of the data because we didn't have any frame of reference. . . . The same thing with the [state test]. . . . They're taking so many tests, but what do we actually see from any of that? Not enough. (June 6, 2005)

Learning to interpret and use data was taken seriously at Brookfield. Just a few days before the winter holiday the principal, principal intern, staff developer, reading specialist, and guidance counselor had a 90-minute meeting with the fourth-grade classroom, special education, and ESOL teachers. Having received the results of the MAP-R and SDRT reading tests, the Leadership Team prepared materials for the fourth-grade teachers to learn to interpret. There were four stated objectives on the agenda:

- How do data from MAP-R and SDRT help us prepare students for the MSA?
- How to read individual student reports from the SDRT.
- Develop breakdowns for students in individual teachers' classes.
- Identify trends and patterns on the SDRT.

After stating the objectives, Ms. Moore, the principal, began the meeting by asking teachers what questions they had when they looked at data and encouraging them to think about instructional implications. Not wanting teachers to be overwhelmed, she emphasized that she did not expect them to change their instruction dramatically, but to rethink student placements and to use the curriculum guide to target specific areas of need based on the test scores. She then handed out class summaries of the SDRT data and, assisted by the reading specialist, explained how to interpret various aspects of the report, such as stanine scores and the progress indicator cut score table.

Teachers were then given data grids to fill in for their classes by transferring SDRT scores from students' individual reports to a comprehensive report for their classes that had the following columns: Student Name, Race, ESOL, Special Ed, Phonetic Awareness Stanine, Areas of Concern, Comprehension Stanine, Areas of Concern, Vocabulary Stanine, Areas of Concern. As teachers filled out the grid, Ms. Moore encouraged them to look for patterns and they talked about their personal knowledge of students as it related to the data. The teachers only had time to fill in data on one or two of their students, but this led to a discussion of whether the test format could be a reason why phonetic awareness emerged as a problem area, whether the fourth-grade groups were too heterogeneous, and whether patterns indicated the need for any particular interventions. Comments such as "This data point reinforces what we previously knew about this kid" were heard throughout this conversation. Only one concrete suggestion was made: that the special education teacher pull lessons on vowels and diphthongs for the fourth-grade teachers to use. However, since she herself had not yet covered those areas with her students, she did not have materials readily available.

The principal intern and staff developer then presented information about the MAP-R through a PowerPoint presentation and distributed another packet to teachers with MAP-R results for all the students in their classes. Norm-referenced and aligned to the state tests, the MAP-R data included mean scores and standard deviations for various types of comprehension (literal, interpretative, evaluative) on various types of texts (informational and literary) as well as a general reading process score. This presentation and discussion opened up a host of questions and concerns about the scoring structure of MAP-R matching the state test, the misalignment of the district's curriculum guides with the state test, and general concerns about the "massive amounts of data being accumulated on students." Nonetheless, the teachers continued to seriously look at their students' scores, trying to identify patterns that would inform instruction. The meeting ended with the suggestion that focusing on implications for just one student might have better aided the teachers in learning to read and use the data. It was unclear at this point if any of the meeting objectives other than "how to read individual reports" was accomplished, but if teachers were to take the tests and analyze them as presented in the training, they would have hours of work ahead of them.

The leaders at Cherry Ridge took yet a different tack in helping teachers learn how to use the data from the various tests. Teachers were not given training on interpreting the diagnostic tests. Rather, Cherry Ridge had a system in place by early October, developed by their data team, that was intended to streamline the way test data were presented to teachers and to help them use the data to inform instruction. As one of the district's highest-poverty Title I schools, Cherry Ridge had extra resources and, as a school on the state's improvement list, the incentive to hire a technology support teacher, Carmen Ledwich. As the head of the data team, Ms. Ledwich accompanied the principal to Stevenson's Data-Driven Decision Making classes. She had learned enough by early October to show faculty what kinds of tools were available on the Internet. In mid-December she reported the work of the data team to classroom teachers. Explaining that data teams were expected to create action plans for data-based decision making, Ms. Ledwich said that their team decided to focus on special education, since that was the school's AYP target population. Starting with reading, they asked themselves questions about curriculum, accommodations, and the data sources that would provide answers. From these discussions, the data team created a template, already distributed to team leaders, to track information about individual students.

The template had five columns in a landscape format and numerous rows for individual student names. In addition to teacher and student names, the other three main columns were Data Sources, Interventions, and Parental Involvement. Under Data Sources were cells to record mostly test scores: from the CTBS, state test, informal reading inventories (IRI), SDRT, MAP-R, and Learning Styles. Test score information would be filled in for teachers, but the learning-styles cells would be left blank, since teachers were the ones who would know if their students were auditory or visual learners and so forth. The Interventions column included both in-school supplemental assistance (e.g., Horizons, Corrective Reading) and after-school programs (e.g., Math Achievers, ESOL Theater). Ms. Ledwich explained that the purpose of these data was to help teachers decide if they should try to get a student into a particular after-school program that might be beneficial. The third column, Parental Involvement, included Math Night, Conferences, IEP Meetings, and Family Technology Night. Ms. Ledwich emphasized the importance of parental involvement, saying that this information would help them determine if that area of student support needed attention.

Once this system was in place, the data team planned to replicate it for special education mathematics and then for ESOL students. Teachers were encouraged to let the data team know if they thought any other data sources would be helpful. The principal and another member of the data team emphasized the importance of working closely with the special education population, since some of these students counted multiple times in the AYP report (e.g., IEP, FARMS, minority, and ESOL). Ms. Ledwich closed the meeting by saying that these data were most useful in determining the types of extra support students needed, apart from the regular classroom instruction.

In addition to the reading assessments, teachers had the district mathematics unit test data to examine. Brookfield's math content coach, Laura Seibert, articulated how these data were presented to teachers and told us that the most important part of her job was "the state test and the data piece," in other words, helping teachers understand data reports on the mathematics unit assessments. Ms. Seibert stressed their connection to state test preparation:

> We're looking at those [state test] scores to start the year off and they kind of drive us through the year. And we're looking at our AYP and with our superintendent, I mean, data has really influenced my job—trying to help teachers look at that data and where do we

go with it. . . . The teachers have these summary reports that come out and so it's taken us a while to really look at those and really take that and where can we go with this . . . to really look at instructionally how did we teach it, what can we do differently, how can we embed it and go back and reteach those skills. (May 17, 2005)

Ms. Seibert described the complicated color-coded summary reports the teachers received about their students. The color coding, which was intended to be a quick visual reference for teachers, had to be interpreted carefully to fully understand a student's achievement. The colored stripes on the reports included numeric scales indicating the specific level a student was operating on for different skills:

But these summary reports, it's very difficult. . . . The reds are minimal understanding. And minimal is zero to 50% of that concept area. But the yellow, the developing, is from 50 to 90 and that's a huge band. So we always, when we look at those, you know, learning and experiencing this, you can't just look at the colors. . . . So, when I look at this I just see data and the state test. I feel like that's my job in a nutshell almost, having teachers be aware of that. (May 17, 2005)

If learning to interpret test data is a precursor to using test data effectively, teachers in all three schools had a long way to go. One difficulty was that these tests required teachers to increase statistical understanding in order to interpret the tests accurately. Hawthorne's teachers did not have the opportunity to learn about new test data because the school lacked the human capacity and time to organize training. Although teachers at Brookfield received some training, they encountered an emerging problem with commercially produced formative assessments. The tests were not well aligned to the sequencing of topics in the school curriculum. If formative assessments were to evaluate student learning of curricular content, these tests were missing the mark. In addition, the district mathematics assessments, although aligned to the curriculum, did not produce user-friendly reports. The math content coach feared teacher misinterpretation of the reports, complicating their use in determining instructional responses. At Cherry Ridge, the data team attempted to use commercial tests and school-designed assessment data broadly, to identify students' learning needs in a way unconnected to the delivery of the curriculum. They were more attuned to the district's plan of using test data for organizational improvement by refocusing resources such as interventions, after-school programs, and parent involvement.

In terms of informing instruction, much of this formative assessment was seen as rich in potential, but hard to make sense of. Researchers point to a number of obstacles for teachers in using assessments in ways that inform them conceptually about their students' learning and the effectiveness of their instruction. They stress that along with the alignment issues we noted, conceptual use of multiple data sets requires a *gradual* process of problem reconceptualization as data are collected, brainstorming explanations for data patterns, and developing strategies to address the most compelling explanations (Sharkey & Murnane, 2006). We saw bits and pieces of these ideas in the work of teachers at Brookfield and Cherry Ridge, but the use of formative assessment data to conceptualize authentic instructional improvement seemed an impossibility as teachers themselves were only peripherally exposed to the data, reducing their opportunity to become knowledgeable about it.

WORKING WITH TEST DATA

Administering the tests, attending district training sessions about the tests, and bringing that information back to teachers were, on their own, major endeavors. However, the biggest question for principals and test coordinators was how to put test data to work. Generally it was used for student grouping and intervention decisions, rather than to inform classroom instruction. Hawthorne's size and laissez-faire organization did little to help teachers use the available data for instructional decision making, while Brookfield, with its smaller population and professional organization, was better able to follow through on implications from data. Cherry Ridge, with its greater human resources and bureaucratic organization, strove to analyze data for teachers and guide them in using it. But regardless of how school leaders promoted data use, the sheer amount of testing and the effort associated with the management of resulting data interfered with the best-laid plans for data-driven instructional improvement and had unintended consequences for those who were responsible for orchestrating it.

Struggles to Organize Data

Teachers had an abundance of test data about their students' skill levels, particularly in reading. Most of the data was processed by the district, which sent reports back to the schools. As found elsewhere (Wayman & Stringfield, 2006), a major challenge for schools is to create a systematic way of organizing data so it is useable for teachers. Although the schools had data teams of one form or another to help manage and analyze data, over the course of the year this responsibility fell heavily on the shoulders of the specialists. Try as they did to efficiently organize data, the specialists at the three schools were overwhelmed with this task. As a result, the information the data promised was not well realized to inform instruction even though talk of using data for that purpose was widespread.

For example, Hawthorne's Instructional Data Assistant (IDA) compiled data from mandated tests, but the administration could not find a systematic way of presenting it to teachers. Surprisingly, despite her talk about the importance of data, the principal relied on a makeshift system, teachers' handwritten "data charts," which she kept on her office wall as her primary source on students' reading levels. As explained earlier, those charts were produced spontaneously, from teacher memory—not from systematic data analysis. Ms. Everett referred to these charts as "living documents" to inform instruction and encouraged teachers to use them. But doing so required a trip to the principal's office, a place many teachers preferred not to visit.

For reading, DRA data were the most readily available to Hawthorne teachers because they administered the tests, but the teachers had as much confidence in their own knowledge of students as they did in those scores, a condition that is common when teachers are faced with data that are not rooted in their daily instruction (Coburn & Talbert, 2006; Ingram et al., 2004). Teachers also had access to MAP-R and SDRT data through the district database, but because they had no training on how to interpret the results, they made no effort to look at the data. Data access then, became restricted to the specialists and principal. Because these school leaders were preoccupied with other matters, however, data analysis with teachers rarely occurred.

Brookfield's reading specialist and staff developer shared responsibility for managing reading test data, and they quickly realized that teachers did not have time to organize and analyze individual student reports from the various data sets. Also, because of the statistical nature of the reports, there was concern that teachers might misinterpret the data, given the inadequacy of their training. Ms. Seibert's concern about teachers' misinterpretation of the summary reports from the mathematics unit tests resulted in the discontinuation of their use by the teachers. She told us: "About middle of the year, January or February, we kind of put a halt to [grade-level meetings to review mathematics unit assessment reports]. . . . I was finding that they were not becoming productive discussions" (May 17, 2005).

To provide teachers with students' reading data in a useful form, Ms. McNeil created classroom-level databases from the multiple assessments so Brookfield teachers could look at trends and patterns. Reflecting on the amount of time that assessment responsibilities required of support staff and teachers, Ms. McNeil empathized:

> When we say "looking at data," first of all you have to plan and test and keep data. It all takes time. No matter what way anybody tries to have you do it in a better form, it still takes a lot of time. And then to analyze data, and then [administrators] also talk about, "It's good to have conversations about data and meet and discuss," and that's all great but it takes up time. And . . . yet education in the elementary school hasn't changed. You're still with your kids almost every minute of the day and yet you need time to meet, and you need time to plan, and you need time to look at data. There's no time. . . . And [teachers are] tired. I see that greatly. (May 17, 2005)

The reports Ms. McNeil developed were kept on hand to review with teachers when they voiced concern about a student's progress. Teachers could have access to this information but did not have the burden of tracking its constant flow into the school. Teachers were responsible for tracking data from classroom assessments and observations of individual students. These data were kept in data notebooks and those, along with data compiled by the professional support staff, were used by teachers, counselors, and specialists to determine interventions for students who were performing poorly. However, plans were being made to shift more data management responsibility to teachers the following school year. In an end-of-year interview, Ms. Breman, the staff developer, told us that she, the math content coach, and the reading specialist had begun surveying teachers about the kinds of data they used so they could help them keep more of their own data the following year.

> We're trying to get . . . some input, some data as to where teachers are in the use of quality tools and what kind of data they're monitoring already and what's the most important kind of data to look at because you can't monitor everything. . . . We're trying to work on having the data organized so it's usable . . . when they want to make instructional decisions on children. So, we're working with data notebooks for teachers. We want to move into data notebooks with students as well. So, that's probably the big push for next year that we're starting with right now. (June 7, 2005)

This statement foreshadows another change in teachers' instructional responsibilities that accompanies the test-taking culture of the schools.

Teachers would instruct students in managing their own scores on class-room assessments, a districtwide initiative that was on the horizon. Although there are benefits to students monitoring information about their learning, this practice also demonstrates that the district was raising test management to a concern not only of adults, but of children as well.

Testing took time from other responsibilities, but the specialists at Cherry Ridge were positive about assessment data giving them valuable information for reteaching. Ms. Kladowski, the reading specialist, contrasted the current situation from the years she spent as a second-grade teacher and did not even keep a grade book: "None of us did." Ms. Ledwich, the technology support teacher, spoke with passion about the benefits of having "authentic" assessments that had the school district's stamp of approval rather than just teacher judgments on teacher-made tests. Ms. Odett, the math content coach, believed that major inroads had been made that year in having data inform instruction. In describing the 60/30 mathematics lesson format she had introduced to the school, she commented that "it requires having looked at your data to know what you want to be reviewing" (June 7, 2005).

But the amount of time that test management took was a source of constant frustration. Although Ms. Kladowski's expertise as the reading specialist was helping teachers make instructional adaptations, she was so busy managing all the tests that this expertise was left untapped: "By the time we get done with one test then we're on to a new one. So then I'm organizing and trying to implement this next test. . . . That's the frustrating part. . . . There's a lot of questions, like . . . when are we actually going to teach?" (January 26, 2005).

Despite the general optimism that the various tests would support improved teaching, few pedagogical decisions were made about how to improve instruction using the information that was being collected about students. In the following section we examine how test data were actually used in the three schools. Test data did not help teachers tailor their instruction for individual students. They were used for student-grouping decisions and assigning students to intervention programs. But these programs, most of which were prepackaged, did not support teachers' development of alternative methods for improving students' understanding of curricular topics or developing student skills within the regular classroom.

Weak Links to Practice

The main reason for giving the state test in March, in compliance with requirements of NCLB, was to have data available for decision making the following year. Those decisions included sanctions (e.g., removing staff) and other consequences, such as allowing parents to transfer students out of low-performing schools. However, the March–March calendar also enabled schools to treat the state test as a formative evaluation, providing information for instructional adjustments the following year. In that respect, its function was similar to that of the other diagnostic tests and data gathering that schools were doing throughout the year. These data were used in two ways: to inform grouping decisions and to inform instructional decisions. At each of the schools, grouping and regrouping decisions were more evident than instructional decisions. Decisions were made in different ways, but each school used some combination of data team and grade-level meetings to facilitate the process.

The schools used test information to make initial classroom assignments at the beginning of the school year and to regroup or reassign students during the year. Assignments to accelerated mathematics and reading classes were usually made first. Then test data were analyzed to determine which low-achieving students would receive supplemental instruction. All three schools assigned students with reading difficulties to additional classes: ESOL, Soar to Success, Corrective Reading, Adventures in Reading, Horizons, and so forth. In addition, Hawthorne provided regular "double-dip" classes in mathematics for students who needed extra assistance (Valli, Croninger, & Walters, 2007).

While fairly stable, class compositions would change as suggested by ongoing diagnostic testing. Staff developers, reading specialists, and math content coaches worked with ESOL, special education, regular classroom teachers, and administration to make these decisions. Instructional decisions were most often discussed at grade-level meetings, which specialists often attended. Hawthorne held regularly scheduled data meetings about borderline students with individual teachers, while Brookfield did this work in their small grade-level teams.

Data meetings were held at Hawthorne approximately every 6 weeks to monitor students who were receiving supplemental instruction. At the beginning of the year, teachers were told to fill out referral sheets on students who were not already receiving sufficient academic support. To help the data team make decisions, teachers were to include the instructional strategies they were already using with students. While these meetings most often dealt with reading concerns, students' mathematics achievement could be discussed as well. At the data meetings, a classroom teacher would be scheduled for a 45-minute block of time to discuss students who were underperforming. At meetings in early October with the reading specialist, staff developer, math content coach, and ESOL specialists, teachers discussed how students were progressing in their classes, their reading level according to their DRAs, what strategies the specialists were using with students receiving interventions, and whether the student should be referred for further screening or an Educational Management Team (EMT) meeting.

By the end of January, data meetings became larger and more formal. The reading specialist previously had asked teachers to keep her up to date on students' reading levels. That would enable her to update data files in advance so the meetings themselves could focus on instructional strategies. On a day we attended, eight consulting teachers and specialists, the principal, and the IDA crowded into a small, dark room to meet with individual classroom teachers. As each teacher came into the room, the IDA projected a data table about the student to be discussed. The table included, for each quarter, the students' reading level, their reading report card grade, the reading intervention they were assigned to, their mathematics intervention, and the next steps that would be used to help the student improve. But developing strategies requires time and reflection and only a few minutes were allotted for the discussion of an individual student. Often, arriving at decisions such as determining a student's eligibility for test accommodations consumed the allotted time. Afterward, fourth-grade teachers complained that the meetings were little more than "reporting out" sessions and that their professional opinions were not valued.

Brookfield's principal, Ms. Moore, did value teacher judgment and succeeded in conveying that message to her teachers. She also emphasized the importance of looking at multiple measures to ensure that good decisions were being made about students. With a student population of less than 400 and a strong commitment to knowing their students and families well, the Brookfield staff had, and was expected to have, an understanding of their students that included but went beyond test data. Even with training, teachers remained skeptical about the value of additional diagnostic test information. Accustomed as they were to keeping data on their students, the special education teachers had the most doubts. In their joint interview, Ms. Grant and Ms. Keller explained how they had documentation "this thick" about student reading levels, but still had to administer the SDRT:

> Ms. GRANT: It was very frustrating for me that we had to spend 2 mornings taking this, when I already know, could tell you very specifically, what their reading level is. "What, they're below grade level?" Shocking!
> Ms. KELLER: To have to test and retest and test and retest. It takes so much time away from instruction. . . . We want to monitor children's reading. We want to know their level. We want to see

their progress. But do we have to . . . give them a MAP-R, and an
SDRT, and [a state test]?

Ms. GRANT: But we already—for the children we're talking about—
have so much documentation.

Ms. KELLER: They don't need that much testing. . . . Pick your
instrument, stick with your instrument, make sure it's reliable,
and everyone understands it.

In contrast, the regular classroom teachers, who tend to have considerably less diagnostic data on their students, seemed somewhat more
convinced that the new assessments were helpful—especially the com-
puter-based MAP-R, which was relatively short and provided immediate
feedback on all their students. Emma Hinton, a fourth-grade teacher, complained that there was too much to learn about these tests in too short a
period of time, making the use of data difficult. But as a teacher, she found
having something other than her subjective impression reassuring:

I think the testing is necessary. A lot of people don't, but today we
had a MAP-R and I'm looking at these scores and I'm like, wow,
this is such a great tool. It's one more piece of information that I
have versus someone coming up to me, "So what level are they
really at?" Before it was, "I feel they're at this [level]," but I didn't
have a test that I could give them in a reasonable amount of time
and find out, OK, they're progressing. (May 17, 2005)

Karen McNeil, the reading specialist, also reported on the benefits of
having these test scores when individual students were discussed at grade-
level or data meetings. Apparently following up on a suggestion made at
the fourth-grade team meeting, she created databases that compiled diagnostic information about individual students. Counselors and other
members of the Leadership Team also worked on data management issues so that teachers did not have to fill out the kind of forms themselves
that were first introduced at their December data meeting. This sense of
learning from each other, listening to each other, and making helpful
adjustments pervaded working relationships at Brookfield. The math content coach also described ways that she and grade-level teachers looked
at the previous year's unit assessments and preassessments as a way of
anticipating problem areas: "We talk about, OK, instructionally what can
we do differently to make it clearer this year? And we go through the unit
and try to hit on areas where, you know, this was a hard topic or we don't
want to teach it this way again" (May 17, 2005).

With the support of the reading specialist and staff developer, the fourth-grade team made adjustments in their reading intervention program. Both fourth-grade teachers had a wide range of reading levels in their classes. So many of their students missed part of the reading period for more targeted Corrective Reading that they were frequently left with only about one third of their class. In addition, the supplemental test preparation sessions were originally designed for homogeneous groups, so Emma Hinton and Pat Kim had only some of their original reading classes for those sessions. Feeling as though they were not spending enough time with the reading students for whom they were the teacher of record, Ms. Hinton and Ms. Kim suggested a different model: keeping their own reading students for the test preparation period so they could better align that supplemental instruction with the district curriculum and work more closely with the same students. Mr. Comer, the principal intern, transmitted this request to the principal, who approved the change. Interestingly, this was one of the biggest changes made midyear, and it was made solely on the basis of teacher judgment, not assessment data.

At Cherry Ridge, test data, rather than teacher judgment, had privileged status. Although teachers did have input on grouping decisions based on their knowledge of students, the last word about student placement came from test data. Several grade-level meetings at the beginning of the year were used to place students in remedial reading groups. The initial fourth-grade meeting turned into one-on-one sessions between the reading specialist and the two classroom teachers, even though the entire group of teachers and support staff was present. As other members of the group occupied themselves with e-mail and perusing resources, the classroom teacher helped the reading specialist decide whether to place students in decoding, comprehension I, or comprehension II groups, or whether the student was advanced enough to be in the William and Mary group. Because not all students had diagnostic test scores, the reading specialist relied on the teachers' judgment.

At the fifth-grade meeting that same day, the four teachers who taught reading used the results of the SRA Corrective Reading Placement Test to divide students into low, middle, and high groups. Lisa Franklin, the experienced team leader, expressed surprise that so many fifth graders needed decoding help—as evidenced by the 23 who were placed in the low group. Cecilia Kelley, who had attended the Corrective Reading training and knew the students, said that many of them were ESOL or had IEPs and that the problem was fluency, not decoding per se. The students simply did not have time to finish the entire test. Taking this knowledge of the students and tests into consideration, the group created five reading intervention groups.

The three lowest groups would use Corrective Reading, although the balance between decoding and comprehension would vary. Since the other two groups did not need assistance with decoding, their reading intervention would focus on comprehension strategies. The teachers agreed that the groupings were the best they could do at the time, based on the information they had, but that they could switch during the year as they got more clarity about both the students and the intervention materials, which they were using for the first time. When the fifth-grade team met 2 weeks later, they voiced disapproval of the data team's changing some of their assignments. As the team leader told her teachers, "I had no idea they were going to give you these groups for the reading intervention. . . . We have to use teacher judgment here. . . . It's important for them to not just hand you a list" (October 20, 2004).

This issue of teacher judgment arose again when the fifth-grade team thought they should return to a writing block after the state testing was finished in March. As a team, they believed that, for most students, reading comprehension could be well taken care of during the 90-minute balanced reading block. They agreed to retain reading intervention for students with decoding needs and then spent most of their reading meeting creating the reading and writing groups and figuring out the logistics. With considerable disappointment, the team heard the following week that the principal, Ms. Hancock, denied their request. Her reasoning was that because the school district had determined that their students needed reading intervention, it would have to determine that they no longer needed it. Ms. Franklin told the team that they would need to work with Ms. Kladowski, the reading specialist, to identify a formal way to submit their request to the district. As Bonnie Strauss, the assistant principal, told them—quoting the superintendent—when she stopped by their meeting: "I'm going to tell you what to do until your results tell me I don't have to tell you." Clearly, teachers in at-risk schools had less autonomy—even in making data-driven decisions—than teachers at other schools.

These examples illustrate that instructional decision making based on test data was often marginalized in favor of using the tests to group and regroup students. Considerable time that could have been used discussing what was learned from the tests about students' abilities was lost to shuffling students. Although grouping decisions are an important component in designing instruction, pedagogical discussions that could have been enriched by test information were frequently absent. Ms. Winchester, a fourth-grade teacher who accepted a position at a different district school at the end of the year, raised questions about her team's focus throughout the school year: Grouping was not her issue, instruction was. She did not feel as though the instruction she was giving her guiding reading groups was working well. The problem was not the groups or the size of the groups, which Ms. Ledwich had suggested as the problem, but the lessons themselves. When, she wondered, would they talk about those?

Also evident was the ongoing interplay between teacher judgment about students and information from the tests. Teachers acknowledged the value of testing, but in all three schools teachers pressed their principals for some level of autonomous decision making. In their abiding belief that they had valuable knowledge about students that was undetectable by standardized tests, these teachers resembled their high school counterparts. In a recent study of nine high schools involved in continuous improvement efforts that emphasized data-based decision making, researchers found that "teachers and administrators often rely on anecdotal information, their experience, and intuition rather than on information they have collected in a systematic manner" (Ingram et al., 2004, p. 1273). However, this did not mean that teachers rejected information from other data sources, such as diagnostic tests. As we saw in examples above, teachers tried to make sense of multiple sources of data. They were frustrated when data seemed redundant or when it conflicted with other supposedly "valid" data. They also rejected data that did not seem well aligned with valued learning outcomes. Data were most valued when they confirmed their own professional judgments.

CONCLUSION

Stevenson School District's strategic plan aimed at continuous improvement through testing and data-based decision making had payoffs, but not in the ways that the district intended. Ultimately, the promises of data-based decision making were an illusion in terms of real instructional improvement. Test data are most useful when they are used "directly as an integral part of each pupil's learning work" (Black & Wiliam, 1998b, p. 146). At Hawthorne, Brookfield, and Cherry Ridge, this was not the case. Most testing was isolated from student work and, thus, failed to inform instructional decisions. Yet it permeated teacher work, turning classroom teachers and, particularly, content area specialists into test managers. Making AYP was a matter of such urgency in the district that consideration of how the testing regime would affect the teachers' work was given inadequate forethought. Furthermore, as the district added testing, it did not prepare a satisfactory system to help schools disseminate test results to teachers. Leaders at each school were left to their own devices to find ways to make the data comprehensible to and useable by the teachers.

In this chapter we saw that training around testing was key to both its implementation and the analysis of results. The schools managed the implementation of the new SDRT and MAP-R tests well, despite their strain on physical space, human resources, and test coordinators' lack of advanced information. The district had confidence that its trainer-of-trainers model would facilitate the analysis of test data. However, it failed to realize how complex and unfamiliar these data would be to teachers, or that, as others have found, they required significant time to organize, analyze, and integrate into decision making (Coburn & Talbert, 2006; Ingram et al., 2004; Young, 2006). As a result, the potential of the tests to drive instructional improvement was diluted, or in some cases nonexistent, leaving school personnel to question whether the returns from the tests were worth the investment of resources.

Two resources suffered most—time and expertise. Throughout our year in the schools, teachers worried about the time the tests took from instruction. Additionally, as they were constantly reminded to develop monitoring tools, perform diagnostic testing, administer unit assessments, and practice accommodations, teachers' psychic space was affected as well. Intellectual energy was devoted to matching testing formats rather than using test data to better understand and act on students' learning needs. As reflected in complaints of test management consuming their time, the disciplinary skills and knowledge of content area specialists were vastly underused.

We would like to be able to say that by becoming test managers teachers made better instructional decisions. But with the exception of a few teachers noting that the diagnostic testing confirmed what they already knew about their students, test data were not well used to make decisions beyond student grouping. Although teachers attempted to use the data for instructional planning, the assumption that testing would provide teachers with useful information was simply wrong. Obstacles were not merely logistical, but were in the assumption itself. The distance between test data and instructional decisions is further and less direct than acknowledged by policy directives. In the following chapter, we turn to another problematic policy assumption: that curriculum, academic standards, and assessments are easily and well aligned.

CHAPTER 4

Subordinating the Official Curriculum

Ensuring that high-quality . . . curriculum, and instructional materials are aligned with challenging State academic standards so that students, teachers, parents, and administrators can measure progress against common expectations . . .

—No Child Left Behind Act

The [state's curriculum] . . . aligns the [state] Content Standards and the [state] Assessment Program and will be available in a number of formats for teachers, central office staff, students, parents, and the other stakeholders. [It] defines what students should know and be able to do.

—The state's Department of Education

The taught curriculum shall be aligned with the [district's] written curriculum and the [state's] assessed curriculum to bring about a high degree of consistency.

—Stevenson School District

Everyone was concerned about the alignment of the curriculum with the [state test]. They aren't convinced that it will work as intended.

—Fourth-grade Brookfield teacher

THE FIRST THREE quotations above suggest a seamless alignment of curriculum and assessment at the state and local levels as recommended by many advocates of coherence (e.g., Newmann, Smith, Allensworth, & Byrk, 2001). In its published statement of goals, Stevenson School District indicated a desire to achieve just such an alignment. In this chapter we look at how the alignment of district curriculum, the enacted curriculum, and the state assessment actually unfolded during the year of our study and why "everyone was concerned" that alignment would not work as intended.

In the years prior to our study, Stevenson School District had some form of published learning expectations for reading, mathematics, social studies and science for Grades Pre-K through high school. Among the district's stated beliefs about curriculum was that it be well "balanced across" the disciplines. In Chapter 2, we indicated how each of the three schools allocated time in the school day to each of these disciplines, a factor that influenced what curriculum could be delivered. In that chapter we also noted, as have other researchers (Au, 2007; Bailey et al., 2006; Center on Education Policy, 2007b), the extent to which the high-stakes testing environment of NCLB resulted in allocations of school time that marginalized science, social studies, and the arts.

In this chapter we describe Stevenson's curricular frameworks for mathematics and reading and how high-stakes testing policies pressured school personnel to substantively alter or supplement the district curriculum. We also report on other ways in which school administrators and teachers found themselves subordinating the district curriculum to the state curriculum. Some might argue that these changes are exactly what the standards-based reform movement was intended to do: align the taught curriculum with state standards. But, as we shall see, alignment pressures made a rich and coherent curricular experience even more difficult for teachers to achieve.

As teachers struggled to maintain curricular coherence and build on student knowledge and interests, what counted as valued knowledge in these two subject areas was often limited to what was on the state assessment. So although policies and resources tended to "cohere" around this crucial assessment, the most important site for coherence—the school curriculum—became more distorted or restricted, process and skill oriented, and fragmented. These transformations occurred despite the school district's substantial investment in guides and teacher workshops that supported a broader curriculum and, in mathematics, was organized around carefully sequenced core concepts.

With the growing urgency of making AYP, teachers began to align the curriculum content and teacher-made test questions to the assessed knowledge, skills, and abilities (KSAs) of the state curriculum and to use sample test questions to model and practice for the test. Especially at Cherry Ridge, but at the other two schools as well, teachers felt compelled to match closely the content they taught to what would be tested, and they worried about how well aligned the district curriculum was with the state tests' content, language, and format. In both subject areas, and across all three schools, state assessments help explain differences between the official school district curriculum and the curriculum that was enacted.

STEVENSON'S OFFICIAL CURRICULUM FRAMEWORKS

At the time No Child Left Behind was implemented, Stevenson school district was "rolling out" its new instructional guides for mathematics. Two years later, Stevenson introduced its new fourth- and fifth-grade instructional guides for reading. These guides were the most comprehensive statement of what the district believed students should learn and teachers should teach in these subject areas at each grade level. Embodying what the district valued as knowledge and how it represented reading and mathematics, the guides were the district's answer to one of the most basic curriculum questions: "What knowledge is most worthwhile?" (Schubert, 1986, p. 1).

In keeping with the long-held tradition and current practice of local educational authority in the United States, we call the school district's curriculum "official" and the state's curriculum "recommended." As Julia Hancock, the principal at Cherry Ridge, explained,

> The school districts have the authority to write the curriculums. Some curriculum departments in this state are using the [recommended] curriculum exclusively. Stevenson, you know, chooses to have their own curriculum, and it's a beautiful curriculum. . . . But at the state level, the state sets the standards and the state says, "This is what we'll be testing. We want all third graders to know and be able to do this." So, very clearly our teachers have to be knowledgeable about that [recommended] curriculum. (September 16, 2004)

Prior to the rollout of Stevenson's new instructional guides, teachers had been using an assortment of textbooks, materials, and programs. For reading, teachers used core books, but never basal readers; they used reading programs such as William and Mary, Junior Great Books, Soar to Success, and the Wilson Reading System. In mathematics, a set of objectives guided instruction at each grade level. However, there was general agreement that the mathematics objectives placed too much emphasis on discrete tasks and that the scope and sequence were "off" (Board of Education Minutes, September 25, 2000).

Those who had been teaching in the school system for a number of years remembered the days when teachers had very little to guide them. As Opal Kladowski, the reading specialist at Cherry Ridge, recalled about her first years of teaching:

> I started as a second-grade teacher and . . . we literally had nothing. . . . We had no guides. We didn't use a reading series. . . .

What we had was basically on those shelves right there. . . . We had the core books and that's what we used. And it was very difficult because most of our kids could not read the core books. . . . We didn't have the beginning-reader type books and the leveled books. . . . We all just kind of did our own things. (December 1, 2004)

Mathematics classes were similar. The math content coach at Hawthorne, Greta Shephard, had previously taught in a school district where everything "was very structured, and you could move a child from school to school to school, and everybody would be on the same page. I came here, and I was amazed that nothing was the same within the classrooms in the grade level" (June 6, 2005).

School personnel credited the current superintendent, William Barnes, for putting in place what Cohen and Spillane (1992) would consider a more comprehensive and systematic instructional guidance system. The initial impetus seems to have been the high rate of student mobility within the district, making consistency in curriculum coverage and sequencing desirable across schools: "If students switch schools, they don't want them to experience a different curriculum, miss things, or repeat things" (Cherry Ridge, Franklin, February 23, 2005). Stevenson gave three reasons for curricular revision across subject areas: to establish a coherent and measurable curriculum with consistent expectations across grade levels and subject areas, to provide a means to monitor student progress toward meeting curriculum standards, and to align the district curriculum with the state curriculum and assessment measures.

For administrators who were feeling the pressure of No Child Left Behind, Dr. Barnes's actions in calling for the development of an instructional guidance system were almost prescient. Brookfield's principal, Liz Moore, complimented Dr. Barnes for being proactive with regard to No Child Left Behind in establishing a sense of urgency about curriculum frameworks and support for teachers. Julia Hancock, the principal at Cherry Ridge, was even more profuse in her praise, explaining how, before Dr. Barnes became superintendent, "schools had complete autonomy":

The teachers did the scope and sequence. That's very different. That's not No Child Left Behind. That's the leadership of this particular superintendent, which happened to be, thank goodness, visionary, in terms of what happened with No Child Left Behind. You cannot be successful unless you are aligned with

the . . . state standards. . . . You're never gonna make it.
(June 20, 2005)

Beginning in 2001, then, central office personnel devoted considerable resources to establishing curriculum frameworks for mathematics,
reading/language arts, science, and social studies consistent with state
content standards and learning outcomes, as well as national and international standards. Board approval of these frameworks brought about the
development of "blueprints" that organized curriculum expectations into
units of instruction and included some brief teaching and assessment suggestions. These blueprints were followed, in subsequent years, with the
"rollout" of comprehensive instructional guides, delivered in three-ring
binders for each quarter of the school year.

Mathematics Curriculum

Mathematics was the first content area to roll out its instructional guides,
with fourth- and fifth-grade teachers receiving them in the 2002–03 school
year. The overall goal of the school district's mathematics curriculum was
to help students achieve both conceptual understanding and procedural
fluency: to be able to reason mathematically and to solve authentic mathematical problems. Emphasis was placed on curricular coherence and vertical articulation across grade levels. To accompany the guides, schools had
to select one of two textbooks approved by the school district.

The guides used unit and lesson plan formats to organize the content,
instruction, and assessments for the mathematics curriculum at each grade
level. Each teaching unit (e.g., measurement, statistics, geometry) contained
a content map, instructional focus, time frame and sequence, vocabulary,
resource references, preassessment samples, review and enrichment suggestions, and a listing of the relevant pages in the two approved textbooks.
In those instances where the textbook treatment of a learning objective was
missing or deemed insufficient, there were sample lesson plans. The content maps identified core ideas central to the discipline, critical questions
related to each core idea and specific learning objectives. Unit assessments,
developed by the district's curriculum division, had to be given within a
specified time period.

The organization of units and core ideas were closely aligned with the
National Council of Teachers of Mathematics (NCTM) document *Principles
and Standards for School Mathematics* (NCTM, 2000). By most measures, the
fourth- and fifth-grade mathematics curriculum would be considered rich
and challenging. Indeed, an external review conducted by the Educational

Testing Service described the Grades 4–8 mathematics curriculum as providing high standards and allowing for innovative teaching (district newsletter, 2002).

Reading Curriculum

The instructional guides for reading were rolled out 2 years after the mathematics guides (2004–05) and a few months after the state published its recommended curriculum with clear indicators of what content would be tested in the state assessments. The instructional guides were written with a balanced literacy program in mind, in keeping with the standards developed by the International Reading Association (IRA) and the National Council of Teachers of English (NCTE) (IRA & NCTE, 1996).

The reading program was to include a writing program, listening and speaking were to be integrated throughout, and students were to be working with substantive texts from both narrative and expository genres. For the first time, fourth- and fifth-grade teachers were expected to limit whole-group instruction to a "mini-lesson" in order to meet regularly with small reading groups. The recommended delivery was in an extended class period with this sequence: a whole-group reading lesson (15–30 minutes), small-group or buddy reading and independent seat work (60–75 minutes), writing (40 minutes). The guides were organized into corresponding whole-group reading, small-group reading, independent seat work to practice literacy processes while the teacher was meeting with a small group, and writing sections, with sample lesson plans and a wide range of titles of suggested materials.

By the year of our study (2004–05), teachers had become generally familiar and comfortable with the mathematics guides, but this was less true of their familiarity with the just-released reading guides. As had happened with the mathematics rollout 2 years earlier, teachers often received the instructional guide for the following quarter just days before they were supposed to teach from it. In addition to the short preparation time, teachers felt overwhelmed by the scope of the reading guides, which contained far more than they could possibly cover. And, unlike the mathematics curriculum, no materials or assessments were included in the frameworks, except as examples. In schools with more limited resources or more challenged to make AYP, the time devoted to finding appropriate materials and writing assessments was a source of real annoyance. As the fifth-grade teachers at Cherry Ridge complained, "Shouldn't someone else have done that for us?" (May 25, 2005). Depending on their perspective and the schools' resources, teachers felt free or forced to select their own texts and create their own assessments.

Teacher Response to the Frameworks

Although teachers found the first year of each curriculum's implementation difficult, they generally praised the work of the central office staff. Hawthorne's math content coach, Greta Shephard, talked about seeing a shift away from only teaching algorithms: "Everything was add, subtract, multiply, and divide, and never a reason why you did that, just learning how to do it, and I see more of a shift now where that's not the only part of math. And I think one reason for that is that the units force you to do that" (December 16, 2004). Eddie Wilson, a teacher at Brookfield, affirmed that perspective: "What I like about the math is that I think it is rigorous and I think that it does challenge the kids to really think about what they're doing and it's no longer, for the most part, it's no longer the drill and kill. And I enjoy the fact that . . . they gain an understanding of . . . the reasons why you do certain things and why certain things happen" (June 2, 2005). Teachers were similarly pleased to receive the reading curriculum. As Anita Sanchez, a fourth-grade teacher at Hawthorne, said:

> It was nice to have it finally, so that there's some order to what we were doing. We weren't just pulling things out, and, oh, we know we need to go over character traits. . . . We could all be on the same page, following the same types of things, knowing where we're going from day to day or week to week. (June 8, 2005)

But as teachers began using the instructional guides, concerns about alignment with the state's curriculum surfaced. In mathematics, for example, a math content coach was so upset about the perceived differences in state and district terminology (e.g., faces versus bases in geometry) that she planned to contact the district's mathematics curriculum supervisor, whom she knew personally, to suggest better alignment with the vocabulary used on the state test. In reading, a group of fifth-grade teachers realized that the definition of *compare* they had been using was inconsistent with the one used by the state. Rather than using the word *compare* to mean "same" and the word *contrast* to mean "different," the teachers had taught their students that to compare meant to find similarities and differences, a commonly accepted definition. This discovery, which would require corrective teaching, caused them to double check their operational definitions of other key terms, such as *text features* and *text structure*.

During their collaborative planning time, grade-level teams worked hard to write test questions that were parallel to the structure of the state's test questions. This was particularly challenging in mathematics, where teachers tried to align the format of their questions with both the district's unit tests and the state test. In reading, teachers, such as the two fifth-grade teachers quoted below, also began to notice that the state test emphasized reading strategies whereas the district's curriculum focused more on literary genres:

> SIMPSON: A lot of times we would have these [state] standards
> you'd want to make sure that we met, but then we'd have a
> hard time finding it in the reading curriculum, so that took a
> lot of time.
> KELLEY: [The instructional guide] wasn't always ideal for teaching
> . . . the key reading strategies. And although we've been told
> that it matches up with the state curriculum and [assessed
> KSAs] I don't think we always found that to be completely
> evident to us [group laughter]. . . . We spent many, many
> team meetings trying to match things up and figure out . . .
> what [KSA] this is. (May 25, 2005)

The ways in which the three schools handled these alignment concerns contributed substantively to what the enacted curriculum looked like. Initially accepting the school district's claim that the instructional guides were aligned with state expectations, teachers' first strategy was to follow the pacing guidelines in the new curricula. When this proved to be a limited strategy in preparing students for the state test, teachers employed strategies that took them further away from the intent of the original curriculum framers.

The differences between the official reading curriculum and the assessed KSAs in reading were the result of the timing of the curriculum revisions and the implementation of the state's new NCLB-compliant tests. The reading curriculum, in development prior to NCLB, was written to be compatible with the former state assessment. In keeping with that assessment, the district's new reading curriculum valued attention to various genres, such as historical fiction, and practicing reading strategies within the reading of particular genres. In contrast, the new state assessment focused almost exclusively on specific reading skills.

Although teachers at all three schools used numerous strategies to align the taught curriculum to the state's assessed curriculum, strong themes predominated at each school. At Hawthorne, where circumstances produced a somewhat frenzied teaching environment, teachers actually suspended the official curriculum in order to prepare students for the test. Brookfield, with its stable, experienced staff and strong collegial relations, primarily supplemented the official curriculum. And at Cherry Ridge, the most at risk of the schools, teachers restricted the official curriculum to the assessed KSAs.

HAWTHORNE: SUSPENDING THE CURRICULUM

Hawthorne teachers initially attended strictly to Stevenson's instructional guides in mathematics and reading. In fact, no supplementary materials were even known to teachers until January. However, this was more a laissez-faire than a deliberative course of action. Teachers merely used the resources available to them in the school. As the March state test date drew near, teachers' curriculum orientation changed dramatically, largely because of the insistence of the principal, Ms. Everett. As reported in Chapter 2, she moved from her September stance of emphasizing adherence to the district's instructional guides and programs to a January position emphasizing the need to teach from commercially produced materials that were reportedly closely aligned to the content tested by the state. For example, the staff developer, Melodie Newkirk, told us that in late winter writing was no longer a priority at Hawthorne. The fifth-grade teachers went further, exclaiming: "Throw writing out the door," "Forget about writing," and "Science, social studies are basically . . . pushed aside" (May 31, 2005).

Mathematics Classes

Greta Shephard, Hawthorne's math content coach, was a strong proponent of the district's mathematics curriculum. She believed that the pace set by the curriculum was reasonable and good because "if the child isn't getting it, there's time built into the program where you can see in Unit 2 where you can reteach something, where you're not just reteaching it, but here's a good place for this to come in and be retaught" (December 13, 2004). She also distributed "alignment charts," prepared by the school district, to classroom teachers that laid out all the objectives in the district's instructional guides by grade level and unit. Those objectives that were assessed on the state test at each grade level were typed in bold. When asked about support for teachers, she commented on those charts, explaining that they showed teachers how the assessed KSAs designated on the chart matched the district curriculum.

With the help of these alignment charts, teachers began to resequence the district curriculum to cover concepts and procedures on the state test before the end of February. Although we did not observe classrooms on a daily basis, the daily logs that teachers completed asked them to indicate what topics in the curriculum they covered in the day's lesson. The daily log of a fifth-grade teacher at Hawthorne indicates that just prior to the state test, when the curriculum pacing guide suggested that statistics (Unit 4) would be the topic of instruction, the teacher was splitting time between rational numbers (Unit 3) and measurement (Unit 5). Over a 2-week period near the end of February, as much as 50% of class time was logged as spent on geometry.

A similar situation appears in the fourth-grade teachers daily math logs. The curriculum-pacing guide indicates that classes during January to the end of February be devoted to Unit 3 on fractions, decimals, and probability (an area in which there is application of fractions and decimals). However, a typical teacher log from Hawthorne shows that 30–50% of that time was spent on Unit 5 measurement topics. The argument supporting this deviation, voiced in planning sessions, was that area and volume, Unit 5 topics, were tested on the March state test. The problem was that Unit 5 was not scheduled to be taught until April and May.

In a group interview, fourth-grade teachers expressed the frustration involved in these efforts:

> KARLSEN: It was teach and go, teach and go, teach and go. Mastery did not matter, creativity did not matter, thinking did not matter.
>
> ZWILLER: Some things you had to teach in a day and then move on and say, "Sorry if you didn't get it. We'll try to come back to it later."
>
> SANCHEZ: Things were so out of order. . . . So we had to do a whole shift around and that was a real touch-and-go. I mean, that was no mastery at all. We were just, "Kids . . ." "This is what you do." Move on. I mean, literally, day to day, we were changing concepts on them, because of the [state test] pressure, and the way that the curriculum is not aligned. (June 8, 2005)

Part of the teachers' difficulty was that they were trying to prepare students for both the district's unit tests and the state's end-of-the-year (March) test. Teachers worried that the content of the two tests was not congruent. At their February 9 planning meeting, for example, the fourth-grade team was clearly annoyed that a unit test had to be graded and turned into the district office by March 8, right in the middle of the state testing period. Later, the teachers told us how they handled the situation: "That one unit test that came at the same time as [the state test]. You look and see the scores; they all dropped. Because the kids . . . half of the things on the unit test, they hadn't even seen. Because we were concerned with what was gonna be on the [state test], so that's what they were being taught"

(June 8, 2005). Teachers felt confident that they were putting the emphasis where the principal wanted it.

Fifth-grade teachers felt the same way. At a planning meeting in January, the teachers were reminded that when Ms. Everett visited their classes, she "expected to be able to see [state test] practice going on" (January 18, 2005). This indicated to them how seriously they were to approach test preparation. A couple of days later, when they were spending a full day preparing their test prep classes, Ms. Everett stopped by. This gave a fifth-grade teacher the opportunity to voice his concerns about mathematics. According to field notes:

> He said he'll have to take time away from regular teaching to do the test prep and the third unit assessment is coming up. Elaine said, "I don't care about that." She said the regular class work is important for assigning grades in the long run, but "as far as I'm concerned *you can throw away the unit test.*" (January 20, 2005)

Joy Karlsen, the fourth-grade team leader, explained the principal's reasoning in subordinating the official mathematics curriculum and unit tests to the state tests:

> The [state tests] are the top priority. I mean, they want . . . the kids to do well on the unit tests, but the state isn't gonna come over, come in and take you over because you don't do well on your unit tests. The [state tests] the whole state knows about; there's the takeover and situations like that. . . . Math units went by the wayside. It was all geared to [state test] prep. (June 8, 2005)

Reading Classes

For reading, teachers did not have to worry about juggling required unit tests while they were preparing their students for the state test. But, unlike Brookfield and Cherry Ridge, only a few of Hawthorne's fourth- and fifth-grade students were assigned to a reading intervention class. This meant that there was no designated period for reading test preparation. By default, the balanced reading period became "test prep" in the four weeks leading up to the state test. During that time, according to Heather Nichols, Hawthorne's reading specialist, only Guided Reading groups for low readers and test preparation were considered "sacred":

> We've always, the month before the assessment, done testing prep. We've bought from commercial companies what the district

has recommended in both math and reading, and we've had extensive test prep. The district, at least the Reading Department, is saying if you teach from the instructional guides, you will be prepared for [state test]. Elaine feels like we'd be doing a disservice to our children because we've done so well with this last minute, one month, like 4 straight weeks, of just—boom! Test, prep, practice. . . . The only thing that is sacred during that time is your Guided Reading groups and your math time. Everything else gets crunched. (December 22, 2004)

But teachers were not happy with this approach to test preparation. At their full-day planning meeting, it was clear that the fifth-grade teachers were frustrated that they had not been asked to do this test prep earlier and that materials were not readily available to them. Mr. Mitchell, for example, said he had been at the school for 6 years, the same amount of time as Ms. Everett, and "it's always been the same story every year. Nothing has changed" (January 20, 2005).

The following description of the fourth-grade team's planning for test preparation in reading helps explain that frustration. The team began by looking at the assessed KSAs on the state's recommended reading curriculum to determine what they had not covered. Without much difficulty, they produced a list of 30 items, including main idea, sequencing, author's purpose, summaries, compare/contrast, similes/metaphors, connotation/denotation, tone, mood, poetry, plays, and story elements. One teacher suggested covering an item a day until the test; another said that if they used Test Ready commercial materials each day, they would cover items on the list. With that, the team began creating a calendar, plotting out a daily schedule so each of the 30 assessed KSAs would be "covered."

But this planning gave rise to concerns about their regular reading instruction. When one of the teachers commented that they would need to stop teaching the curriculum for the next month, Sheila Wolfe, the newest teacher, conveyed the principal's message that they were to discontinue working on grammar because it was not tested and that they were to "suspend the curriculum" until after the state test. As recorded in field notes of the meeting:

The other teachers pressed her to be sure that that was the directive she'd been given to pass on to them. She was certain that was what Elaine told her to do and commented that *Elaine would be upset with her if she did not relay the message.* . . . The teachers do not like this. It became apparent to them that the test preparation will take over everything they are doing. They were not happy with any aspect of the task they've been given . . . [referring] to it as a "dined and dashed" [eat and run] . . . curriculum." (January 19, 2005)

A couple of weeks later, when the team was planning for a formal walk-through, they were reminded that the principal made it "loud and clear" that she did not expect them to be working on the curriculum in the weeks before the state test (February 9, 2005).

Reading test preparation affected not only coverage of the official reading curriculum, but coverage of science and social studies as well. Still having to assign grades in those subjects at report card time, teachers worried that they had no indicators of student achievement. Drawing on her years of experience, the fourth-grade team leader produced examples of reading worksheets with science and social studies content that could be used for dual-grading purposes (reading/social studies or reading/science).

Summary

The faculty and staff at Hawthorne began the year by following the district's curriculum. Test preparation was not a matter of concern. However, as the March testing date approached, there was frenzied attention given to test preparation and curriculum alignment. As a result the curriculum in mathematics was resequenced, fragmented, and rushed. The reading curriculum was essentially suspended so that the skills on the state assessment could be emphasized. Any attempt at curricular and instructional coherence was abandoned for the sake of alignment with the state test.

BROOKFIELD: SUPPLEMENTING THE CURRICULUM

Brookfield's faculty and leadership steered a fairly steady course in their attention to the official district curriculum. There were times when they taught content out of the recommended sequence so students would at least be exposed to key topics before the state test at the beginning of March. But they continued to cover the full scope of the curriculum, even while wishing there was more time to cover some things in more depth and in a more logical order. Their way of preparing students for the state test was with careful planning, additional time, and supplementary materials. Thus, while teachers followed the district curriculum, they supplemented instruction for key topics on the state test.

Mathematics Classes

Even Brookfield's veteran fifth-grade teachers complained about how "overly packed" the mathematics curriculum was, saying they needed more time for everything and wishing they could leave a unit out (June 2, 2005). The fourth-grade teachers talked about "smooshing" the curriculum (January 25, 2005). Aware of this problem, Laura Seibert, the math content coach, had previously mentioned that "the pacing is still difficult. So, that's something we still struggle with. . . . They fight me on that, but I say, 'We're tight,' and that's not the [school district's] fault either, because we have to teach them this curriculum by the time March comes around" (January 11, 2005).

As at Hawthorne, there were indications from teachers' daily logs that some rearrangement of the official curriculum order took place. The fourth-grade curriculum-pacing guide shows January and February devoted to Unit 3: fractions, decimals, and probability. Brookfield log data shows that attention to fractions predominated but that probability, a topic bypassed at Hawthorne, was also taught. In addition, and similar to Hawthorne, there was attention to measurement topics, part of a later unit, that were deemed important to teach prior to the state test.

Nonetheless, teachers did not dismiss parts of the district curriculum nor did they purchase commercial materials with mathematics problems aligned to state test content and format. Instead, they requested supplemental time from the principal. Consistent with her administrative style, Ms. Moore had teachers offer solutions:

> Fourth and fifth grades increased the number of minutes for math instruction for this year, and they did it by taking away time from their specials. That's pretty powerful. You know, they came to me as a grade level and said, "We need to increase our time with math. . . . Instead of taking the full maximum number of minutes for PE once a week, we're going to cut it down 10 minutes." Well, that's their planning time. That is their time. And they're taking away from their own planning time because they know instructionally they need more time with their math instruction. (September 28, 2004)

In addition to the formal after-school programs, individual and small-group mentoring occurred on a regular basis.

Teachers also supplemented mathematics instruction by expanding their own expertise. Considerably more than was the case for the other two schools, Brookfield teachers talked about pedagogy, how they taught according to the strengths and weaknesses of their students, and how they set up manipulative activities for their students. The math content coach shared resources and emphasized the importance of classroom discourse prior to students' tackling problems in writing. At one meeting we attended, she used Kilpatrick, Swafford, and Findell's (2001) *Adding It Up: Helping Children Learn Mathematics* from the National Research Council. She and the teachers reviewed its five strands of mathematical proficiency—understanding, computing, applying, reasoning, and engaging—that were the foundation of Stevenson's math curriculum. The teachers then used these to assess students' written responses.

At a before-school whole-staff meeting, teachers were engaged in strategic planning around mathematics instruction. Ms. Seibert asked them to list their additional training needs. The fourth-grade team wanted more strategies for helping students translate the understanding they had gained using manipulatives into words, symbols, and drawings, tasks they would be expected to perform on the state test. The fifth-grade team requested assistance in helping students understand what questions were asking. The support staff then worked with the Instructional Council to follow up on the expressed need for teaching strategies designed to help students write responses, unlock questions, engage in mathematical discourse, understand test rubrics, and express in writing understandings derived from use of math manipulatives.

Reading Classes

Although Brookfield teachers decided not to order supplemental, test-oriented materials for mathematics, they did order these materials for reading. There were several reasons for this. First, the principal had decided to adhere to the district's strong recommendation that the school offer a reading intervention program to supplement the regular reading program. These materials would be used during those class meetings. Second, the state's reading test was an even bigger challenge for their students than the mathematics test. And, third, the teachers found the new reading curriculum even more overwhelming than the mathematics curriculum. To eliminate some of the uncertainty about the alignment of instructional guides they had not yet seen, they agreed to use some commercially produced materials. It is noteworthy, however, that in contrast to Hawthorne and Cherry Ridge, these materials never replaced the official curriculum during the designated reading class. They were only used during supplementary "reading intervention" time. Even so, beginning in September, teachers resisted merely using a test-taking curriculum and struggled to "teach reading in accordance with the curriculum"

(September 29, 2004). This can be seen in their approaches to both read-ing and writing instruction.

In reading, both fourth- and fifth-grade teachers became increasingly dissatisfied with the supplemental reading intervention program as the year went on. They did not believe it was necessary, resented the time it took from social studies and science, and struggled to integrate it with their regular reading classes. For example, Emma Hinton, a fourth-grade teacher, openly questioned why the fifth graders had to have reading intervention when they had done quite well on the state test as fourth graders. Mid-way through the year, Leslie Gabriel, who had designed the fifth-grade reading intervention program, asked the same question. These teachers also worried that this test-oriented instruction was self-defeating. They noted that the state test assumed extensive knowledge of content that their students would normally have received in social studies and science. How-ever, the "test prep" reading intervention was encroaching on that time.

Until they were permitted to end reading intervention after the state test, the teachers tried to integrate this supplemental test preparation pe-riod more fully with their balanced reading instruction. Although for part of the year their reading students were reassigned to homogeneous groups for their reading intervention class, the fourth-grade teachers eventually succeeded in getting them back. As explained in Chapter 3, the teachers argued that their students were pulled out for so much supplemental in-struction that they did not know them well enough to teach and assess. The teachers' comments reflected their understanding not only of the way the learning of students was interrupted by these pullouts but also the way in which the teachers' learning about students' thinking and learning suffered.

While continuing to do the supplementary reading intervention, the teachers aligned it with the regular reading curriculum as much as pos-sible. They anticipated that the following year the alignment would be better because they would have been through all 4 quarters of the new instructional guides. On a day we observed her reading intervention class, for example, Ms. Hinton was reviewing the elements of a story, empha-sizing point of view, in particular, since that was a problem area for her students in their regular reading class. She decided to assign parts and have her students do dramatic read-alouds as a way to help them "hear" a first-person narrative point of view. She and her team mates called these class meetings the "Strategy Development Club" to characterize what they were attempting to do, in contrast to mere test preparation, which, to her, would be unethical: "We also wanted the parents to realize that it's not a test-taking class" (January 19, 2005).

In their approach to writing instruction, Brookfield's teachers again supplemented the state's assessed KSAs with recommendations from

Stevenson's new instructional guides. As Lottie Breman, the staff developer, explained, unlike the former state test, the current test did not assess writing per se. Instead, students' paragraph responses to questions were assessed strictly to determine students' understanding of the test questions. Test scorers were trained to ignore the quality (e.g., spelling, grammar, punctuation) of the writing. Nonetheless, Brookfield teachers continued to teach writing, using two strategies in particular: Six Writing Traits and AGOP (Ask, Gather, Organize, and Present), a program derived from William and Mary to help students write research papers. Thus Brookfield staff included specific attention to quality and organization of writing multiple paragraph texts. Karen McNeil, the reading specialist, thanked teachers at the end-of-year staff meeting for staying focused on writing "despite the attention to testing" (May 25, 2005).

Summary

The faculty and staff at Brookfield struggled to maintain the scope and sequence of the district's curriculum. In using supplementary instruction, they did little reordering or narrowing of the curriculum. Rather, their efforts to supplement might be viewed as distorting the emphases in that curriculum. Their discussions about how to meet the press of the state test were ongoing and included attention to the coherence of students' experiences as well as the alignment of the curriculum and the test.

CHERRY RIDGE: RESTRICTING THE CURRICULUM

Having once failed to make AYP, Cherry Ridge was even more pressed than Hawthorne to prepare students to be successful on the high-stakes state test. But the Cherry Ridge principal's systematic way of planning and allocating resources made the test preparation experience quite different from that at Hawthorne. First, as noted in Chapter 2, Julia Hancock used the school schedule to allocate as much instructional time to reading and mathematics as possible. She then made curriculum alignment issues a priority on meeting agendas and hired a consultant, Melany Batori, to help teachers with the "alignment challenge."

In her ongoing professional development work with teachers toward the end of the year, Ms. Batori expressed her alignment goals this way: "We're trying to teach what they [students] are expected to know. . . . We have only a limited amount of time, so we want to focus. . . . We want what you are supposed to be teaching to match with [the state test questions and answers]" (April 4, 2005). Teachers' systematic, targeted planning and instruction throughout the year meant that, unlike Hawthorne, Cherry Ridge never temporarily put Stevenson's official curriculum totally aside. Instead, they were carefully and purposefully restrictive in its use throughout the school year.

Mathematics Classes

The following description of a November fifth-grade team meeting is typical of the targeted planning that occurred at Cherry Ridge. Early in the school year, teachers began to plot out what content they had to cover by what dates in order to prepare their students for both the unit and state tests. Cecilia Kelley distributed a calendar on which she had laid out all the mathematics topics that needed to be covered from November through February, prior to the early March administration of the state test. Commenting that all the topics on the calendar were on the state curriculum, Ms. Kelley explained that upon completing Unit 2, they would do Unit 4, data and graphing. Only then would they come back to Unit 3, which covered fractions, decimals, and percents. But since there were no percent questions on the fifth-grade state test, they would skip that section of the unit. This schedule would give them time for "catch up and review" prior to the March test. Once the test was over, they would cover percents, objectives about circles, and the other Unit 4 untested objectives. Ms. Kelley also introduced the new teachers to commercially produced materials that would "coach" students for the test, warning them to review activities to be sure they were consistent with the state curriculum.

Fourth-grade planning occurred much the same way, with the math instructional guide, the textbook, and the state curriculum simultaneously used to map out each unit. This early, long-range planning was particularly important for the 4th-quarter units in the instructional guide that would not normally be taught until after the state tests in March. Teachers had to figure out what content in later units was on the March test and how best to at least "expose" students to that content so they had "a chance" on the state test (May 25, 2005).

As an example, teachers mentioned that "divisibility" was a fifth-grade objective in the district curriculum, but was on the fourth-grade state test. Amy Odett, the math content coach, was sympathetic to the demands this made on teachers: "The [school district] says that it's aligned . . . to the state curriculum, and it's not. And so the teams—third-, fourth-, and fifth-grade teams—had to spend pretty much time looking at the [state] curriculum in its detail, and then looking to see where objectives in the [state] curriculum appeared in the Stevenson curriculum" (June 7, 2005).

From a review of teachers' daily logs, the planning that was done appears to have been enacted. Recall that the curriculum-pacing guide suggests that January and February be devoted to Unit 3 on fractions, decimals, and probability. Fourth-grade teacher logs indicate that the majority of class time was spent covering these topics. However, on at least 8 days during this time period, teachers deviated significantly from the designated topics, devoting almost half these lessons to tested measurement topics, topics the official curriculum scheduled for April and May.

By the end of January, teachers had begun to approach their alignment work with more of a "test prep" orientation, reminiscent of Hawthorne. Despite their careful planning, there was a great deal of material they still needed to cover. At a meeting on January 26, Ms. Kelley handed her teammates a page of objectives that had not yet been covered and another page of objectives that unit test results indicated needed to be covered again. The teachers tried to figure out what topics could be "stuck" into warm-ups to lessons and what could be covered in science—for which they also were short on grades. Observing the way in which the official curriculum was resequenced, with assessed objectives emphasized and those not assessed moved or given little attention, the mathematics specialist on our research team dubbed the enacted curriculum "contorted," that is, grotesquely twisted out of shape.

Reading Classes

What most characterized reading instruction at Cherry Ridge was teachers' focus on "the 12 reading strategies." While struggling to learn and implement the new reading curriculum, teachers became aware of the mismatch with the state's curriculum and assessments, which paid less attention to literary genres and more to reading strategies independent of genre than did the district's curriculum. The teachers used their reading intervention period to explicitly teach reading strategies using commercial materials while continuing to use the district's instructional guides during their balanced reading block. However, as the year went on, teachers increasingly focused on reading strategies, such as main idea, sequencing, predicting, and inferencing in their balanced reading blocks as well.

In a fourth-grade class, for example, the whole-group objective, written on the chalkboard, was, "What are the characteristics of historical fiction?" (February 11, 2005). However, almost the entire lesson focused on making predictions and writing summaries using story elements. After introducing the text *The Race of the River Runner*, Ms. Winchester, the teacher, explained, "This is a historical fiction book. One of the things that makes it historical is that the setting and the clothing mean that it took place a long, long time ago." But instead of orienting the discussion and assignments around the characteristics of historical fiction, as would be expected from the board objective, Ms. Winchester quickly shifted to reading strategies: "The point in making a prediction is to help you think about what the book is about. At the bottom of your sheet, write one or two sentences indicating what you think the story will be about." Ms. Winchester then reviewed story elements with her students (e.g., problem, setting, characters, events) to prepare them to fill out independently a story map graphic organizer.

Similarly, Ms. Kelley, a fifth-grade teacher, used a text, "Air Travel," recommended in the official instructional guide, but for the purpose of practicing the kind of written response required on the state test (January 4, 2005). Her writing prompt was for the reading strategy of finding the main idea and supporting details: *Explain the contributions that Orville and Wilbur Wright made to air travel. Use information from the selection to support your answer. Write your answer on your answer document.* (A box with six lines was given for students to write their answer). In addition, considerable class time was also spent reviewing strategies to answer this type of test question (e.g., understand what the question is asking, be aware of important words, organize your thoughts, review your answer). The special educator, who was meeting with the small group of students with IEPs in the back of the room, had handed the students an even more explicit sheet of "test-taking tips."

These two classes reflect the strong emphasis on "reading strategies," an emphasis hard to predict from the new instructional guides but that reflect the school's independently purchased prep materials and the principal's directive. While the use and teaching of reading strategies is an important and research-supported activity, the extent to which teaching the strategies overwhelmed the exploration of the characteristics of genres and the messages of rich text seems not in keeping with the district's curriculum guide. An agenda for one Cherry Ridge staff meeting (November 17, 2004) left no doubt about the principal's perspective on reading instruction:

Grades 3, 4, 5 will focus on:

- aligning the assessed KSAs within the state test to the Stevenson Instructional Guides;
- reviewing the expectation for planning and teaching the 12 comprehension strategies rather than genre;
- demonstrating how teachers can incorporate the 12 strategies within the Guided Reading component of balanced literacy block.

Teachers clearly heeded the call. At a December meeting, one grade team listed topics they needed to cover from January 3 to February 18. The 21 dates for instruction were listed on the board and each of the 12 reading strategies was assigned to one or two dates. Dates to review three or four strategies were sprinkled throughout. The genres to be covered, tall tales and biography, were listed in parentheses, making clear that the purpose was to teach strategies, with genres the mere vehicles to be used.

A stark limitation of this approach was evident at a fifth-grade meeting where teachers were planning a unit on informational texts. Searching for a core lesson to anchor the unit, Ms. Franklin, the team leader, told the group she thought they should use a lesson titled "What's the Big Idea in a Feature Article." This lesson included a T-chart for students to differentiate facts from ideas, feelings, opinions, and questions and used the article "Tragedy of Sudan" from *Time for Kids*. Ms. Kelley had chosen this article before and recommended it, saying she was sure she could find a copy. However, the entire planning discussion revolved around problems students had in the past with the T-chart. Ms. Kelley said her students had a hard time writing something "solid" in that column, and Ms. Franklin thought it was because there were too many different kinds of things listed—that she might give them just one, such as questions, or feelings.

When we observed her class on March 21, Ms. Clemson, a new fifth-grade teacher, was using the article, not for separating fact from opinion, but to teach students how to sequence events, another one of the 12 reading strategies. One must wonder, and worry, about a curriculum approach that can make the tragedy of Sudan, which the United Nations has called the world's worst humanitarian crisis, a mere vehicle for teaching students how to sequence events or separate fact from opinion. As the observer saw the lesson unfold, the forced attention to reading strategies resulted in diminishing attention to the message and meaning of the text itself.

Cherry Ridge teachers also severely restricted writing instruction, a strong component of the district's instructional guides. Unlike Brookfield, where teachers taught the process of writing, the only writing instruction at Cherry Ridge was designed to demonstrate reading (or mathematical) comprehension. The state assessment included questions that required a short constructed response (SCR). The SCR questions in reading were assessed for content but not form and required students to fit their written statements into rectangles printed on the test materials. The focus on reading strategies that we saw in Ms. Clemson's class was repeated every week in every class at Cherry Ridge. The only variation was which reading strategy was targeted. As the fourth-grade team leader, Gayle Peterson, told us, "SCR after SCR, SCR after SCR. There was hardly any room for creativity.

... We had to stick to the plan, the state curriculum, you know, if we wanted to make—be prepared for the state test" (May 25, 2005). Teachers' professional development also centered heavily on writing clear prompts for the SCR practice and reaching consensus on how to judge the level of student answers (basic, proficient, or advanced).

As reported in Chapter 3, regretting that student writing was not part of the instructional day, the fifth-grade teachers requested that, after the state test, they replace the reading intervention period with writing for at least some of their students. Being strategic, they even called it "writing intervention" (March 1, 2005). This request was turned down by the principal, who considered the school year March–March and did not feel that the time would be well spent on anything that was not tested:

> Will I change the master schedule? No. Will I go back to putting a writing block in there? No. I am going to keep, until we show that this [making AYP] is not a fluke, I am going to keep that 90 minutes, and they're working on it right now, the master schedule's gonna keep the 90 minutes of balanced literacy. . . . Plus I have another sixty. . . . The writing that we do in this building has to be embedded. . . . Most schools in Stevenson School District that aren't Title I teach the six traits of writing, and they go through the writing process. I don't do that. (June 20, 2005)

Summary

The Cherry Ridge administrators and specialists strategically planned their approach to preparation for the state test. Teachers' attention was focused on the tested objectives, and specialists worked with teachers to plot out timelines and strategies. As a result the curriculum in mathematics was resequenced and the reading curriculum was essentially upended so that the skills emphasized on the state assessment took precedence over the balanced literacy program reflected in the district curriculum. At Cherry Ridge the pervasive strategy was that of narrowing, or restricting, the official curriculum to that which was tested.

CONCLUSION

Districts, such as Stevenson, develop or adopt curricula to define and focus on what knowledge is valued; to promote a reasonable, logical, and connected progression of concepts and skills; and, in our increasingly mobile society, to attempt to ensure equality of experiences, both in learning and assessment, from school to school. As noted above, Stevenson's beliefs about curriculum and the rationale for the new curricula were seen as efforts to provide such focus, quality, equity, and alignment.

Indeed, research has indicated that students are more apt to learn if their experiences connect with and build upon one another (e.g., Alexander & Murphy, 1998; Bransford et al., 1999). The argument for coherence is central in curriculum discussions in both reading and mathematics (e.g., Guthrie, Cox, Knowles, Buehl, Mazzoni, & Fasulo, 2000; NCTM, 2006). The likelihood of building understanding and sustaining skills is enhanced by experiences that provide time for such development. Student motivation to learn also increases in settings that provide connected and meaningful experiences (e.g., Alexander & Murphy, 1998).

A "coherent curriculum framework" identifies valued content, organizes it in a logical manner that also provides a smooth progression from grade to grade and from easy to more difficult subject matter, provides meaningful experiences, and aligns assessment and instruction (Newmann, et al., 2001). Stevenson's curriculum reflected many of the desirable characteristics of Newmann and colleagues' coherent framework. This was particularly true in mathematics, where unit and lesson topics were carefully sequenced within and across grades, asking students to reason about increasingly difficult subject matter. In reading, where the sequencing of knowledge and skills is less important, Stevenson attempted to support coherent instruction through curriculum frameworks and guides that would engage students in meaningful experiences with a variety of texts. But the press of state testing associated with NCLB frequently resulted in administrators and teachers taking actions that undermined the implementation of a coherent framework. Examples of such actions drawn from the preceding are revisited to illustrate this point.

Reading and writing are important forms of communication that are reciprocal, even for young readers and writers (IRA & NCTE, 1996). What students learn about language as they write not only improves their writing skills, but positively influences how well they can read. For this reason, Stevenson included writing in the curriculum as an important aspect of teaching children to be literate. However, writing quality was not directly assessed on the state test, not even on the SCRs, which measured how well children had comprehended the text rather than the quality of their writing. As a result, instruction that focused on writing quality was essentially eliminated at Cherry Ridge and was sharply curtailed at Hawthorne.

The limited attention given to writing in these schools not only would fail to help children develop more expertise in this important mode of communication, but also might well impede their progress in reading itself. The assessed KSAs drove the school-level decisions, and the adage of "what gets tested is what gets taught" applied.

In its preview to the instructional guides, Stevenson argued that curriculum should be organized in a "coherent and logical manner." So, for example, an important concept included in fifth-grade Unit 3 mathematics was that fractions, decimals, and percents all are used to express a relationship between two numbers. This lengthy unit includes attention to the meanings of these forms of rational numbers and how the four basic operations (addition, subtraction, multiplication, and division) are carried out with rational numbers. But, as noted above, the fifth-grade teachers at Cherry Ridge temporarily omitted the material on percents (because there were no assessed KSAs on percent in fifth grade) and planned to return to percent after the state test. On the surface, the separation of the teaching of percent from the teaching of decimals seems, to use a pun, irrational. But the staff's motivation for doing so, to provide coverage of assessed KSAs by the state test date, was highly reasonable. Nevertheless, the official curriculum's attempt to center instruction around the core idea that relates the different forms of rational numbers and to order curriculum in a logical manner was impeded if not destroyed by such reorderings.

Another goal of the official curriculum was to provide equity across schools. However, we have noted the differences in attention given to writing and the unevenness with which the full Stevenson mathematics curriculum was attended to across the three schools. While Stevenson provided the curriculum for all students, not all the curriculum was enacted at all schools. In the case of writing in particular, these differences in offerings were not nuanced differences prompted by teacher resistance or variance in teacher knowledge. Rather, it was a matter of school policy that advocated the need to align with the state test over the need to adhere to the district curriculum.

Finally, there is the issue of the alignment of curriculum goals and assessment. While the district's mathematics curriculum included unit tests that were aligned with the curriculum, teachers found that the alignment of these tests (and therefore the district curriculum) with the assessed KSAs was not ideal. In reading, the alignment of the official curriculum and the state recommended curriculum was even more problematic. Given the pressure to meet the ever rising goals in percentage of students at or above proficiency level, teachers and administrators generally opted to favor alignment with the state's assessed KSAs over alignment with the district's curriculum. This decision resulted in narrowing the focus and supplanting some of the values embedded in that curriculum.

In each of the three schools we studied, the Stevenson curriculum failed in some degree to have the impact for which it was designed. Good intentions of helping children be successful on the state assessments and avoiding punitive sanctions resulted in subordinating the official curriculum, thereby limiting its intended benefits. How the quest for alignment affected teachers' learning opportunities and the classroom instruction received by students is described in the following chapters.

Aligning Teacher Learning with Student Testing

Significantly elevating the quality of instruction by providing staff in participating schools with substantial opportunities for professional development . . .

—No Child Left Behind Act

We're trying to help teachers become more reflective and meet those [professional teaching] standards and at the same time we're introducing a thousand miles of new curriculum, of new everything. . . . Even with the support; all of us are supports for them, but we're not enough. How much change can you do at once?

—Staff developer

P ROFESSIONAL DEVELOPMENT was a high priority in the Stevenson School District. Realizing the learning demands being placed on teachers by the rollout of the new curricula and a new state test, as well as numerous other initiatives, Stevenson used a trainer-of-trainers model to assist schools in implementing these reform efforts. With its rapidly diversifying student population and interest in closing achievement gaps, the district also sponsored workshops on race, poverty, and second-language acquisition, encouraging principals to follow up at the school level. Aware of the consequences of inadequate yearly progress, the district promoted attention to the short constructed response (SCR) type of questions that were used on the state test.

In the way it delivered professional development, Stevenson modeled most recommendations found in the literature (see, for example, Desimone, Porter, Birman, Garet, & Yoon, 2002; Gamoran et al., 2000; Hawley & Valli, 1999, 2007). Professional development occurred in the school, with colleagues, and was closely related to the curriculum. Stevenson provided human and material resources to facilitate teacher learning opportunities, disseminated information about reform initiatives, and promoted a unified guiding vision of school improvement. With a comprehensive plan for professional development, the district aimed to "infuse an ethic of continuous improvement through professional learning communities of shared beliefs and accountability in which standards-based teaching results in consistently improving student learning."

To accomplish this goal, Stevenson relied on its district-level specialists to disseminate critical information and training to school-based leaders who were then responsible for professional development in their schools. This trainer-of-trainers model was supplemented with summer and school-year workshops conducted directly through the district's central office personnel or hired consultants. Stevenson also earmarked funds for a Substitute Teacher Project so that teachers could be released during school hours to participate in ongoing professional development. In addition to job-embedded professional development, the district's plan emphasized a common language and framework for teaching. Individual professional development plans, required of all teachers, were to be ongoing and linked to school goals. Collaborative activities were encouraged, and teachers had to use data to assess their growth. In all these respects, Stevenson was a model for employing a combination of pressure and support recommended in the reform literature (Firestone, Monfils, Schorr, et al., 2004). And despite the "trainer-of-trainer" language, the district promoted ongoing teacher learning that was more than technical know-how. Rather than merely training teachers in a narrow range of expected behaviors, its vision embraced a deeper and shared understanding of curriculum, subject matter, and student learning.

Supporting district efforts were the state Department of Education's professional development standards. Based on the standards of the National Staff Development Council (NSDC), the state standards called for professional development that was research based, was related to the learning needs of diverse students, occurred in learning communities, and was supported by adequate resources. Staff developers were urged to be data driven and learner centered, to evaluate the impact of their work, and to include teachers in the planning.

By the time No Child Left Behind was enacted at the federal level, consensus about this view of high-quality professional development was so widespread that it was incorporated in the legislation. Seen as an important policy lever in ensuring that all children receive a rigorous, standards-based education, professional development and technical assistance were to be ongoing, sustained, and intensive. Believing that school staff needed "substantial opportunities" for learning, NCLB gave states flexible funds for local professional development efforts. Title I schools received additional monetary support, and schools in improvement status (including Cherry Ridge) were required to use 10% of their funding for professional development in their area of need.

With a staff developer, reading specialist, and math content coach in each of the schools; time set aside for professional development; funds to hire teacher substitutes; and support from the state and federal government, Stevenson reasonably could have expected substantive teacher learning to occur in its schools. But what actually happened at the school level, and why? As indicated by the quote from the staff developer above, the district was ambitious in its reform efforts. While the school district is often the primary policy arena supporting school-based professional development, it can also be an obstacle (Newmann et al., 2000; Spillane, 2002). To support its numerous initiatives, Stevenson required teachers to receive implementation training. This included training in keeping running records on PalmPilots, new computer programs, the new grading and reporting system, the Baldrige system of school improvement, and multiple diagnostic tests. Following the trainer-of-trainers model, the school specialists were pulled out of the school two or three times a month for the training they were to conduct in their schools.

With each new initiative, teacher learning needs sometimes became overwhelming and professional development reduced to mere training. Instead of developing shared understandings within a comprehensive framework of teaching and learning, teachers simply acquired the knowledge and skill to accomplish prespecified, and seemingly unrelated, tasks (Spillane, 2002). Some information never made its way to the classroom. Consistent with variations in school capacity and curriculum enactment, approaches and commitment to teacher learning also varied. Each of the schools scheduled time for teacher learning, but what occurred during that time differed in focus, quality, and impact.

In this chapter, we look at the formal learning opportunities teachers had as well as their impact on classroom practice. We analyze separately two types of professional development that took place in these schools. The first type helped teachers learn about the district curriculum and classroom teaching. Its goal was the improvement of teaching and learning. The second type helped teachers prepare students for the state test. Its goal was meeting proficiency benchmarks on the state test. Even though the focus, quality, and impact of professional development differed in the three schools, each was pressed to concentrate on test-oriented rather than curriculum- and pedagogy-oriented teacher learning. In many of the instances we observed, professional development turned into narrow "training," with an emphasis on expected teacher and student behaviors rather than deepened understandings.

HAWTHORNE

Professional development at Hawthorne was hard to find. In the chaotic environment of Hawthorne, professional development became a dispensable part of school life—lost in daily demands and emergencies. Professional development sessions were delayed, interrupted, or canceled, leaving learning opportunities informal and haphazard. More often than not, professional development days were used for routine planning rather than teacher learning—especially as test time drew near and anxiety grew about finding curriculum materials that were aligned with test topics. Although inspiring plans for teacher learning opportunities were voiced at the year's first Task Team meeting, most failed to materialize. School leaders and teachers simply became too preoccupied with daily pressures to carry out ongoing, strategically targeted professional development.

The principal's dissatisfaction with directives and resources coming from the district also had an adverse impact on professional development. In response to a question about additional Title I support, she commented:

> It doesn't give you the resources that you need. You know, now I just have my little Helena Norton [Title I Specialist] driving me crazy all the time. It's like having this person around all the time, "Did you do this? Did you do this?" . . . Yeah, like, "Get out of my face." I mean, I'm not that friendly of a person anyway. You know, "Leave me alone. . . . You're asking me for stuff that I need to work on this stuff now. I don't need to meet with you. You're not my boss." (April 28, 2005)

In addition, teachers were generally excluded from schoolwide decisions, creating the impression that professional development was not for their benefit but rather forced upon them. Ms. Everett made decisions alone or in consultation with her small Task Team. As Ms. Newkirk, the staff developer explained, "We try to get input from teachers. However, I feel it's the administration that either overrides that decision or, you know, agrees with it but let's have another meeting and discuss it. And we do a lot of discussing but we don't do a lot of acting" (June 6, 2005). This imposed but chaotic implementation approach fostered a lack of direction and silent resistance. Although the grade-level teachers met weekly for an extended period, one fifth-grade teacher commented that the only time the team accomplished anything was when a visitor from the research project attended.

This confluence of factors played out as inconsistent investment in professional development. By neglecting professional development, the administration conveyed the message that teaching and improvements in teaching, rather than being institutionally valued, were individual matters. Simply getting through the school day with surface compliance was all that could be expected. While Brookfield and Cherry Ridge conducted formal professional development until the end of the year, we found no hint of such sessions at Hawthorne once the state test was given. The little professional development that did occur was primarily helping individual teachers with mathematics instruction. As described below, Hawthorne's pedagogy-oriented professional development was mostly individualized, diminishing opportunities to build the organizational and relational capacities of the school through collaborative effort. In the absence of a learning community, the primary influence on professional development was the state test. Attempts were made to help teachers learn about SCRs. But given teachers' responses, they appear to have been too little and too late.

Individualizing Teacher Learning

During its initial meeting in September, Task Team members had a lengthy discussion about how grade-level teams should operate. Their vision evoked images of high-functioning learning communities. The principal began by contrasting what often occurred at team meetings (e.g., deciding to cover lessons 1–8 and calling the meeting a success) with what she would like to see happen: looking at student work to determine what strategies were successful. The group then made a summary of the issues that should be addressed at team meetings: "What should a team meeting be? Planning instruction, examining data, reflection on lessons, examining curriculum, creating formative and summative assessments" (September 9, 2004). In our observations, however, "covering lessons 1–8" more aptly described the agendas of grade-level meetings.

Nor did we see strong efforts to transform the practices and agendas of grade-level meetings. This hands-off orientation seemed to be a result of the principal's effort to stop being perceived as a "micromanager" as well as the lack of collegiality at the school. Unfortunately, training efforts at Hawthorne often seemed to be viewed as criticism of their work. When the staff developer, Melodie Newkirk, used the third-grade team as an example of effective meeting practices, other grade-level teams interpreted the example as mandated practice and were resentful. They had similar reactions when instructional practices were recommended. Grade-level teams viewed these recommendations as directives even when that was not the intent.

The one area where professional development was welcomed was in new topics or strategies included in the new curriculum. Heather Nichols, the reading specialist, gave a training session on guided reading groups, which she videotaped for those who did not have a chance to participate. This training, as well as the guided reading training provided directly by the school district, was mentioned favorably by upper-grade teachers, who lacked experience guiding small reading groups. Guided Reading groups are teacher directed and led with a carefully prescribed approach (Fountas & Pinnell, 2001). Literature circles, also included in Stevenson's new instructional guides, are primarily peer led with the teacher playing a smaller and smaller role as the students gain in expertise (Brabham & Villaume, 2000; Noe & Johnson, 1999). In previous years, Stevenson allowed schools and teachers to choose one or the other or both. However, this school year, the district was requiring all schools to use Guided Reading. Because they had not used Guided Reading groups in the past, and because their role would be quite different, Hawthorne teachers appreciated the training. However, as the principal made clear, except for Ms. Nichols's one session on guided reading groups, there would be no group professional development in reading. Whatever occurred would be modeled in classrooms by an outside consultant because the reading specialist had too many other responsibilities with her test coordinator role.

Apart from this occasional modeling, the two vehicles left for professional development at Hawthorne were grade-level meetings and data meetings. Neither had the capacity to provide widespread learning opportunities. According to the assistant principal, Adam Fox, locating professional development at the grade level was the school's philosophical orientation, meant to avoid a "Band-Aid one size fits all" approach (May 24, 2005). Although organizing professional development at the grade level brought it close to the level of implementation, classroom instruction benefited little from that decision, as we will see in Chapter 6. Instead, with no expectations for the kind of feedback loop we will see at Brookfield, Hawthorne could easily ignore professional development—or pretend it went on when it did not. There were simply no mechanisms to make professional development visible and accountable to the larger school community. It remained hidden, unspoken, and undone. Although structured time for professional development was built into the school calendar, as it was at the other two schools, it seemed to spontaneously morph into planning and curriculum aligning, as the example below illustrates.

The fourth-grade team had its first whole-day professional development session in mid-October. Melodie Newkirk, the staff developer, had prepared an ambitious and purposeful agenda. Teachers were going to discuss key components of team planning, create long-range plans, complete a topic calendar for reading, become familiar with materials in the book room and math lab, and get an overview of the Junior Great Books

Program, a program more akin to literature circles than to Guided Reading. But half an hour into the meeting, Ms. Newkirk was called away to handle a disruptive kindergarten student. In her absence, teachers spent time in short-term lesson planning. They then went to the book room to see what reading materials might fit the new curriculum units. When Ms. Newkirk returned, she did not participate in the group, much less assume leadership, but let the group continue planning for the rest of the morning.

When teachers returned from a 95-minute lunch break, they went back to the book room, where Ms. Newkirk gave them an overview of the new leveled-reading materials. Even though these materials are better suited to Guided Reading, teachers decided to use them to introduce literature circles because of their brevity. They then spent most of the afternoon deciding what materials they wanted to use and what materials they should order from the core-reading book list. Starting at about 11:30, field notes are filled with comments about teacher fatigue, work coming to a standstill, and unsystematic planning. In summarizing the meeting, the observer wrote:

> There seems to be a great deal of attention to "effective meetings" in the rhetoric of the Task Team, Leadership Team, and at staff meetings. This meeting was to begin with an overview of key components of team planning, but that did not happen. Also, at the beginning of the meeting Melodie stressed the importance of long-term planning and stated that one of the purposes of this meeting was for the fourth-grade teachers to meet with specialists so they could think about the long term. Melodie was absent for about 90% of the meeting, and the meeting with Greta, the math specialist, lasted only for about 15 minutes. Overall, this team meeting accomplished only a small portion of the intended goals. (October 12, 2004)

Instead of this all-day session being an opportunity to help teachers create professional learning communities, it quickly deteriorated into short-term planning and material review. Although collaborative planning can be a source of learning, these teachers missed a valuable opportunity to learn about better team planning and materials selection. Left on their own, without guidance, they adopted a routine approach to their work: plugging in district-recommended lessons on their calendar and choosing books and other curriculum materials with which they were familiar.

Hawthorne's other vehicle with potential for professional development was data meetings. Although some teachers explicitly requested collaborative grade-level meetings, the data meetings maintained an individual teacher focus throughout the year. As described in previous chapters, at these meetings, the principal, reading and math specialists, an ESOL or resource teacher, and the staff developer met with a classroom teacher to discuss students who were receiving interventions or whose data indicated they were not achieving at grade level through regular classroom instruction. Teachers were of two minds about these sessions. Some found sharing information about students with learning problems helpful: "It's a great way for you to get together with all these other professionals that work with your children, and have advice, you know, different strategies that you can use to help them out" (June 8, 2005). For these teachers, the data meetings were genuine professional development experiences. However, as seen in Chapter 3, other teachers thought that preparing for the meetings was excessively time consuming and needlessly took instructional time by requiring them to administer DRAs—a source of data they were expected to bring to the meetings. Rather than enjoying collaborative support, these teachers experienced intrusion and pressure. They also viewed these meetings as a form of surveillance. Speaking with the confidence of her seniority at the school, the fourth-grade team leader told the data team, "I've taught here longer than a lot of you have been alive and I'm . . . my palms are sweating. . . . The perception of this [data meeting] is that it's a witch hunt" (January 31, 2005). Had teachers been permitted the collaborative data meetings they requested, the "witch hunt" experience might have been avoided. Instead, Hawthorne's individualistic culture and low relational capacity undermined its attempts to promote teacher learning.

Cramming Test-Oriented Training

Hawthorne also used an individual approach to test-oriented professional development. This was done by modeling in teachers' classrooms, mostly by the math content coach, Greta Shepard. Because of the reading specialist's test coordinator assignments, Ms. Everett would not allow her time to be used this way. Ms. Shepard, however, took what she learned from the district's trainer-of-trainer sessions directly into teachers' classrooms: "This year we did get more information on the SCR and how the children can answer a mathematics SCR. I was trained on that, and then I went in and modeled . . . for the teachers as well as showing the children how to do this. I did that in every room including special ed, Grades 3, 4, and 5" (June 6, 2005). The only other opportunities for learning how to prepare students for the state test occurred at grade-level meetings that were crammed into the few weeks prior to the state test.

Prior to this training, Hawthorne teachers lacked even the most fundamental knowledge about SCRs. One Hawthorne teacher described overall understanding as merely "aware" of SCRs (December 13, 2004). In late January, only a few weeks before the state test, Hawthorne teachers did not even realize that a standard rubric existed for the scoring of SCRs. The observer noted, "[The teachers] were concerned that there didn't seem to be any set criteria or rubric for SCRs. One of the teachers believed that the rubric was a three-point scale, but no one seemed to have an interpretation of the three points" (January 18, 2005). One teacher commented that she had been using a rubric from the district curriculum, but later discovered that this rubric was intended for writing rather than reading. At one team meeting, teachers developed a plan for teaching SCRs in reading. But visibly absent from that plan was any reference to using the state rubric for scoring SCRs or sample responses for modeling what a proficient response looks like. These tools could have proved highly useful for both students and teachers and were used extensively at the other schools.

Helena Norton, the Title I specialist whom Ms. Everett wanted to "get out of her face," led a few grade-level SCR training sessions. She essentially carried out the same professional development for fourth- and fifth-grade teachers, who seemed willing to participate but reluctant to expend much time or energy this close to the state test. During one fourth-grade meeting, Ms. Norton asked the teachers questions about the SCRs to make sure they were all assessing the same things. As indicated by field notes, teachers appeared to be learning the most basic SCR vocabulary and foundational concepts:

> Helena asked, "What is the indicator we're assessing?" Answer from teachers, "The main idea."
> Helena, "What is proficiency?" The teachers questioned whether students needed to reference the text in order to receive a good answer on the SCR. (January 26, 2005)

When asked to identify features of high, medium, and low-level work, the teachers offered answers such as, High kids knew the main idea and used "strong and vivid" language. Absent from teacher responses was any mention of the state rubric for evaluating SCRs. Instead, teachers offered characteristics of good writing (strong and vivid language) as criteria for a proficient answer (Rinke & Valli, in press).

The same series of events occurred at the fifth-grade meeting a month later. When Ms. Norton asked the fifth-grade team what types of strategies students could use to respond to a SCR, teachers responded with suggestions such as "Organize," "Be specific about details," "Use descriptive language," and "Vary sentence structure." Ms. Norton pointed out that these were writing qualities and the SCR was to assess reading. Although the problem was identified, it persisted throughout the meeting. When Ms. Norton prompted teachers to identify what middle-level students should do on a SCR, the observer noted, "The teachers continued to describe the written structure of the students' answers, 'give some description, order the paper.'" Once again, the teachers were "confusing writing assessment for reading assessment" (February 22, 2005). At this point, the state test was just a week away.

Because Hawthorne teachers' opportunities to learn about SCRs were crammed into a few high-pressured weeks immediately before the state test, it became an isolated test preparation strategy rather than a comprehensive instructional approach. While teachers felt compelled to use SCRs with their students, they had little time to implement them thoughtfully. One fourth-grade teacher commented that SCRs were good "because they get the kids to learn how to explain their thinking and how to back up their answers." However, she wished they had been used more systematically throughout the year, rather than just "all at once, to just push them into the kids" (June 8, 2005). A colleague echoed that sentiment: "I don't feel comfortable . . . teaching this concept, this concept, this concept, this concept, now you're gonna write a SCR. This is all in the same 90 minutes of reading. . . . I would rather have seen it done once a week and say . . . 'Here's your SCR. Here are all the anchors. How can you improve it? Please rewrite it and improve it.' I had no time for redos" (June 8, 2005).

Apart from Ms. Shepard's modeling SCR use in mathematics classes and Ms. Norton's work on using SCRs to assess reading comprehension, not writing skill, Hawthorne teachers had little assistance in learning how to prepare students for the state test. As discussed in Chapter 4, the all-day professional development sessions scheduled for that purpose in January were rushed and haphazard. Instead of teacher learning being their goal, it was simply preparing for the state test. Few advance preparations were made and little attention given to a teacher learning component except to make sure teachers understood that their purpose was "to teach kids the format of the test" and give them test-taking strategies (Greta Shepard, January 19, 2005).

The day before these meetings were to occur, materials were still not ordered. Interrupting a fifth-grade meeting to announce that she was on her way to another school to pick up sample materials, the principal talked about the urgency of getting copies before the fourth-grade team met the next day. Ms. Everett had not reviewed any of these materials herself, but other principals told her that they were closely aligned with the state test. Field notes ended with the following reflection:

Poorly prepared professional development. Elaine was clearly flustered about getting the teachers ready to begin [state test] prep with their students. The professional development for fourth grade would start the next day, followed by the fifth grade a day later, but she had only begun to examine materials to present to them on this day. This was an example of crisis management, and it was evident to the teachers. (January 18, 2005)

Summary

Investment in teacher learning at Hawthorne was erratic. While professional development did attend to SCRs, and even used some modeling techniques, the implementation strategy fostered a sense of test preparation training rather than in-depth understanding. Hawthorne's attempts at aligning teacher learning with student testing were at the 11th hour, too late to affect the cognitive change necessary to understand the purpose of SCRs and develop effective pedagogical strategies. In the absence of a collaborative culture, professional development reverted to individualized assistance, mentoring, and informal networking. Specialists did what they had time for with individual teachers behind closed classroom doors. These efforts were sometimes at the request of the administration or the teacher, or because the specialist saw a need. Although the reading specialist's time was filled with test coordinator tasks, the math content coach tried to do instructional modeling in individual teacher classrooms. But these opportunities were isolated, were prescribed by an outside source, were limited to particular skills, and lacked comprehensive school-wide investment.

BROOKFIELD

Institutional investment in professional development was strong and systematic at Brookfield. Liz Moore, the principal, favorably contrasted it with the undesirable "drive-bys" that once characterized teacher learning opportunities. In contrast to Hawthorne, Brookfield exemplified how professional development is enacted in a high-capacity school with leadership that fosters teacher commitment. In Brookfield's familial environment, learning opportunities were embedded in the daily fabric of the school. They occurred throughout the year in both whole-school and grade-level meetings. Unlike the case at Hawthorne, where professional development efforts were often viewed as criticism, Brookfield administrators and teachers shared roles as learners and experts. The leadership team made use of

Baldrige school improvement procedures to focus teacher learning on SCR instruction, assessment data, grading and reporting, curriculum implementation, and writing instruction.

Professional development sessions were structured around what teachers said they needed to learn. The staff developer explained that she and the specialist teachers, "try to get the input from staff, what it is that they need in order to be able to do their job . . . and try to base the year's staff development" on their input (May 17, 2005). Ms. Moore, the principal, encouraged teachers to tell them, "What do I need to learn more? Do I need more help with problem solving? Do I need more help with number relationships? Because that was something that my kids last year didn't get when I did the assessments?" (Sepetember 28, 2004). The staff developer, reading specialist, and math content coach organized and led professional development, often assisted by teacher volunteers. Teachers willingly and ably stepped into the staff developer's role if she was unexpectedly called away.

But the district's penchant for simultaneous, multiple agendas made a sustained focus for teacher learning difficult. As Ms. Breman, the staff developer, said,

> Each year more and more mandates come down from above. So, if we could stick with our school priority it would be nice but . . . here's grading and reporting you got to do. That's not one of our real priorities here in the school. It's improving instruction. But that's a mandate from above. These Palms coming in. This is another one—OK, we got to put our priority aside because we've got to spend time training on these Palms. Yeah, they pay for substitutes coming in but then again the teachers are being pulled out of the classroom. So, you lose instruction time. (June 7, 2005)

While school-level staff were trying to enhance knowledge for teaching, the district was diverting their attention through organizational requirements. This work was so demanding that the reading specialist often stepped out of her role designation to help out with initiatives such as the new grading and reporting system and the organizational improvement system, things that "didn't really have a lot to do with my job" (January 15, 2005). As fifth-grade teacher, Eddie Wilson, complained, too much was being "thrown" at teachers at once: "And when everything is important, nothing's important" (June 2, 2005).

In the following section, we illustrate the nature of professional development at Brookfield with examples of curriculum rollout and writing instruction. We then look at the professional development that teachers received to prepare students to write short-constructed response (SCR) answers on the state test. In each of these areas, the focus was on developing understandings for improved teaching and learning, consistent with the district curriculum. Teachers were encouraged to be reflective learners who monitored their own understandings in all their learning opportunities. This, in turn, was the type of learning they envisioned and promoted for their students. Because of the stability of the staff and strong, shared norms about metacognitive, learner-centered instruction, the process of professional development consistently modeled high-quality teaching that could be transferred to classrooms. Even the SCR sessions transcended mere training on state test requirements.

Maintaining Collaborative Teacher Learning

Brookfield teachers had numerous opportunities for professional development as the new reading curriculum and instructional guides were rolled out. Half-day meetings were set aside each quarter for this purpose. The reading specialist's goal was to help teachers practice different types of instruction in the guides and share their understandings with each other. Because this was the first year that Stevenson had instructional guides for reading, following them was a big change for teachers. In the past, teachers had considerable autonomy during the reading/language arts period. Now, along with the guides, they had to think about covering the content that would be on the state test. Ms. Breman told us that "looking at the end first was a big change for teachers because now you've got this goal that you have got to really focus on. Going down the road you've got to be sure you can see that end there and not, you know, just flounder and take all these little forks in the road. . . . Now it's like, OK, it may be a very good lesson but why are you doing it?" (May 17, 2005).

At the rollout of the 3rd-quarter curriculum to the fourth- and fifth-grade teams, Ms. Breman and Ms. McNeil gave an overview of the voluminous instructional guides. They had prepared a number of key handouts: "Guiding Questions/Expectations," "Characteristics of Guided Reading/ Small Group," "Levels of Implementation," "Strategies for Teaching Questioning," "Before, During, and After Reading Strategies." With a small group of five teachers, the meeting was conducted as an informal sharing of ideas, concerns, and information. It was a time when teachers saw the types of literature covered during the quarter and could note the need for additional chapter books, such as realistic fiction and science fiction, which always seemed to be in short supply. It was also a time when the staff developer could point out connections that the instructional guide made to science and social studies.

As indicated by the handouts, the topics for this meeting were differentiating reading instruction and questioning strategies. Because Brookfield teachers had long been using Guided Reading groups and were comfortable with the approach, this material seemed like a review for them. As they were guided through the materials, they discussed what kinds of questions caused their students difficulty, the types of questions they liked, and the before, during, and after reading strategies they used. They specifically discussed strategies for special needs students. Each teacher spent some time examining an unfamiliar reading strategy to present to the group, such as "Save the Last Word for Me," an activity in which children identify and discuss the most important ideas in a passage.

Throughout the meeting, teachers expressed how overwhelmed they were with the scope of the new curriculum. In response, Ms. Breman reminded them that they did not need to teach everything in the guides—that the selection decisions were theirs: "Don't worry about the specific lessons. Be sure the indicators are covered. Teachers can decide how. . . . You can't do it all. . . . Just remember, you're not teaching 'this,' you're teaching children" (February 5, 2005). This exchange highlights the student orientation at Brookfield as well as the professional respect that school leaders displayed toward classroom teachers, something we saw throughout the year.

Toward the end of the year, teachers continued to be engaged in professional development. Even though writing instruction was part of the new reading/language arts curriculum, Brookfield was the only one of the three schools to foster teacher learning in this area. Brookfield's commitment to writing instruction went back several years, when the school district started promoting the use of the Six Traits of Writing, now incorporated in the new instructional guides. As Lottie Breman recalled:

> It's probably one of the best years we've had for staff development because it was a true focused year. And what we did was nothing but Six-Trait Writing: What is it? How do you get kids to write? What is good writing? And so we spent the whole year. . . . We talked about bringing in student work and looking at just that one trait of writing and monitoring that piece. And then we'd move on the next month and try to combine the two that we were working with, and then the three and then the four. (June 7, 2005)

Ms. Breman believed that writing instruction and student writing had improved considerably because of the training teachers had. Before that, she said, some teachers thought that writing instruction just meant having students practice.

In contrast to this sustained focus, during the year of our study, professional development and training touched on numerous topics, with SCRs receiving the most attention. Thus, professional development for writing, which teachers were often reminded was not tested, was low priority. Sessions originally intended for Six Traits were used for more pressing matters. At a final staff meeting in May, Ms. McNeil apologized that the meeting on looking at student writing had been postponed so many times and was sorry that it was so late in the year to revisit the topic.

Nonetheless, in addition to this meeting, we witnessed two other whole-staff meetings, in September and January, where Six Traits were the main part of the agenda. As with other staff development sessions at Brookfield, teachers were actively and purposefully involved in a series of well-planned activities. For the September meeting, they came prepared with samples of student writing and their writing rubric so they could discuss overall class strengths and weaknesses, priority areas for instruction, and students who needed extra help (September 28, 2004). Before the end of the meeting, grade-level representatives turned in a written plan so the reading specialist could assist them in achieving their goals.

With clear expectations that they were regularly using these September plans for writing instruction, teachers were asked to share their successes and concerns at follow-up meetings in January and May. Again arriving with samples of student work, teachers discussed their experiences in both grade-level and cross-grade groupings. They were asked to discuss, and to submit answers to, in writing, "In what areas did your class show growth? Have any particular students that you targeted shown improvement? How? What areas are you now planning to target? How can you relate your target areas into our SCR writing goal?" According to field notes of the January meeting, "This meeting demonstrated the continuity of professional development activities at Brookfield and how that continuity seemed to facilitate a high level of collaboration in a short meeting time. . . . The teachers had clearly been acting on the directives they were introduced to at professional development meetings" (January 11, 2005).

A primary goal of the May session was "vertical articulation," the process of building instructional coherence across grade levels. About this meeting, the observer made a similar observation:

> There is an ongoing effort at Brookfield for teachers to understand what learning looks like at the different grade levels. This was one of several meetings in which teachers were asked to work with teachers at grade levels other than their own. The teachers take this kind of information sharing very seriously. . . . It was a very collegial environment and very serious for so late in the school

year. These teachers were still very much at work with their students. (May 24, 2005)

Transforming Test-Oriented Training

Brookfield's systemic investment in teacher learning also permeated professional development efforts around SCRs. Meetings on SCRs were carefully designed, with Instructional Leadership team teachers involved in planning and presentations. The principal, Ms. Moore, requested teacher volunteers, saying, "It is always more powerful if teachers participated in presenting" (October 7, 2004). At that same meeting, a substantial part of the discussion was led by teachers: "Leslie Gabriel suggested that they have examples of SCRs from prior years. Examples of what is a '1' response, '2' response, and '3' response. . . . Teachers identified other sources of examples of SCRs" (October 7, 2004). In these exchanges, the principal's was but one of the valued voices.

Furthermore, teacher learning about SCRs at Brookfield was a school-wide endeavor, with professional development taking place at whole school meetings as well as grade-level sessions. School leaders emphasized the importance of students at all grade levels developing SCR skills: "Karen and Lottie discussed the district's goal to reinforce students' ability to write SCRs. They argued that teachers needed to look at what is expected of students by the fifth grade and then lay out and model expectations at each grade. Considerable emphasis on vertically aligning what teachers were doing at all grades to prepare students for SCRs" (October 7, 2004). Even teachers of the youngest students participated.

At a whole-school meeting later that year, teachers across all grade levels brainstormed age-appropriate approaches to preparing students for math SCRs. Some of the areas in which they wanted more assistance were helping students understand the question, teaching students how to transfer their thinking while using manipulatives into a written explanation, and modeling a pre-writing response (January 25, 2005). Teachers worked in grade-level teams to develop action plans for teaching SCRs. The fourth-grade team, for example, had the following strategies in their action plan: asking students if they understood the question, explaining the scoring rubric, giving students guidelines for writing good answers, and having students check their work as a group.

During these meetings, professional developers used a variety of instructional strategies. At a meeting aimed at developing a common understanding of SCRs, teachers were taught using an information packet, a treasure hunt, a summarizer, and other strategies that could be translated into classroom instruction for students. The meeting began with teachers being asked to monitor their own understanding of SCRs. With the help of the light-hearted type of graphics they might use with their students, teachers did not hesitate to signal that they needed support. The reading specialist instructed teachers to "cut out a go, slow, or stop sign from the sheet of paper at their table indicating where they were with their knowledge of SCRs and post it on the bulletin board by the appropriate signal light on the graphic" (November 30, 2004).

At the end of the meeting, teachers were asked to answer the following question: "Using what you know about SCRs, explain how your knowledge of SCRs has changed or stayed the same. Use information from our staff meeting to support your answer." They were then told that this summarizer was itself an SCR, further incorporating teacher use of SCRs into professional development. Just as metacognitive strategies such as these enhance student learning, they also support teacher learning. Modeling good teaching, the staff development team regularly incorporated self-reflection into these sessions (Rinke & Valli, in press).

Teachers were also asked to consider what SCRs looked like at different grade levels in different subjects. A specific goal for the Leadership Team that year was to help teachers see the relationship between SCRs in both mathematics and reading assessment, that they would use "the same instructional strategies" for both (January 11, 2005). At one professional development session, teachers completed a Venn diagram comparing and contrasting SCRs in reading with SCRs in mathematics. The teachers distinguished between content-specific aspects, such as using information from the text in reading and using equations in mathematics, and general features of SCRs such as critical analysis and specific vocabulary. In addition, teachers shared strategies they had found to be successful in teaching SCRs, such as using different colors to underline relevant parts of the text, examining the question with students, and having students check each other's work. "The strategies the teachers devised to teach students how to answer SCRs were specific, enabling other teachers to interject comments about each others' ideas" (November 30, 2004).

At the end of the year, the staff developer commented about the various ways in which Brookfield teachers had engaged with SCRs: "We spent a lot of time developing and working with the teachers on the use of the SCRs. . . . They have gone over the kinds of questions that need to be asked and answered and how they should be answered and the expectations for the kids, as well as how to score" (June 7, 2005). Nonetheless, learning how to help students write SCRs did not captivate teachers. Even though the math content coach named learning how SCRs on the state test were scored as the best professional development she had had that year, she had a hard time getting teachers equally excited about this focus for learning: "A lot of my stuff that we go over might have to focus on testing and things of that sort, and so it's not really like, 'Woo hoo!' . . . It's hard because sometimes you feel that, 'Oh I'm one of those people putting more on them,' which, you know, it's not your intention" (January 11, 2005).

Summary

Both types of teacher learning opportunities illustrate many of the defining features of Brookfield's orientation to professional development—features we witnessed throughout the year: teacher involvement, emphasis on knowledge for teaching, modeling good classroom instruction, metacognitive awareness, collaboration within and across grade-levels, and sustained whole-group investment over time. Teachers were asked to engage in a variety of ways over time with the concept and techniques of SCRs, offering them the opportunity to develop in-depth understanding in this area. Because of this, even Brookfield's SCR sessions transcended the narrow training orientation of the other two schools. Brookfield teachers were learning how to help students critically evaluate their own writing and, through it, their comprehension of subject matter.

None of the teachers' current involvement in learning, however, seemed to compare to their personal investment in the Six Traits of Writing instruction. Summarizing her recollections from a previous year, Ms. Breman said:

> Some of our trainings that year . . . it was very emotional, especially when we got to voice. I mean, we'd have teachers in tears looking at—because we bring student writing back, OK, so we're covering this, let's bring it back and share. So then each team then came back and shared some of their writings that they had gotten students to be able to work through and some of it was just incredible what they were doing. It was like tears of joy. It was like—we would often have staff meetings where they would applaud. (June 7, 2005)

The district's numerous initiatives and the high stakes attached to students being able to successfully write SCRs made that type of professional development impossible to re-create.

CHERRY RIDGE

Cherry Ridge had some professional development constraints not found in the other two schools. As a high-poverty Title I school that had missed

AYP, Cherry Ridge had to abide by guidelines that did not affect the other schools, such as using 10% of federal funds it received for professional development in the area in need of improvement. And because of the school's "watch list" status, the principal did not use the district's substitute policy to release teachers from classes for curriculum rollout training. She was concerned that valuable instructional time would be lost, jeopardizing the school's chances of making AYP once again. Ms. Kladowski, the reading specialist, called this a "double whammy" for teachers because so many of them were new: "And I feel like our teachers are kind of getting short-handed a little bit because I know that's what they're doing in other schools. And so we have the double whammy of they're not getting it plus they're brand new teachers. And so that's difficult" (December 1, 2004).

Nonetheless, reflecting the school's strong organizational capacity, professional development was deliberately planned from the start of the year. But unlike Brookfield, Cherry Ridge used whole-staff meetings infrequently. The preferred venues were School Improvement Team (SIT), Instructional Leadership Team (ILT), and grade-level meetings. Therefore, most of the direct learning opportunities that classroom teachers received were with their grade-level teams. In these meetings, informal mentoring occurred, with experienced teachers sharing ideas and resources with newer teachers. This tiered structure meant that the professional development that occurred at SIT and ILT meetings relied on team leaders to disseminate the information and training they received. Following an implicit trickle-down theory, with training flowing from district leaders to school leaders to grade-level leaders to classroom teachers, this approach added one more layer to, and frequently diluted, the "trainer of trainers" model.

Because Cherry Ridge lacked a strong professional community but had extra Title I funds, the principal hired an outside expert, Melany Batori, to guide teacher training in the most critical topic, SCR instruction. Ms. Batori was also actively engaged in frequent, ongoing follow-up with teachers. School leaders, on the other hand, were given responsibility for sharing information and teaching strategies that were perceived as less crucial to AYP success. In contrast to the priority given to learning about SCR instruction, there was often little time, especially for new teachers, to deepen and expand their professional learning and teaching repertoire in areas other than SCR instruction. As we shall see in this and the following chapter, the direct assistance that teachers received through Ms. Batori had more impact on how they spent classroom time. But even though the classroom focus became more aligned with the state test, there was little indication that teaching improved.

Minimizing Teacher Learning Opportunities

As one of the highest-poverty schools in the district with a large population of ELL and African American students, Cherry Ridge administrators devoted considerable staff development time to issues of poverty, race, and language acquisition. They also carved out time throughout the year for ongoing rollout training for the mathematics and reading curriculum. As at Brookfield, these sessions were all led by school staff using the Baldrige system. But, unlike Brookfield, Cherry Ridge did not incorporate action plans as a core component of these sessions. Because few of these sessions were for the whole school staff, action was dependent on grade-level follow-through. Given other priorities, this rarely happened, as seen in the poverty, race, language acquisition, and curriculum training sessions.

Tapping into the trainer-of-trainers model, some staff members had attended district-sponsored diversity training that incorporated Ruby Payne's (1996) popular book *A Framework for Understanding Poverty*. Cherry Ridge, like many district schools, followed up with in-service training for its entire staff. During this school year, participants read and discussed a series of articles by Ruby Payne on No Child Left Behind. Beginning with the premise that NCLB benefits children of poverty, discussion focused on the importance of schools promoting excellence and equity, ways to involve parents, and learning modalities.[1] Some practical ideas were shared, such as using Title I money to transport parents to the school, and we did see one grade-level team use a concrete strategy recommended in *A Framework for Understanding Poverty* (i.e., using folders and envelopes to help students organize information they were gathering on a research topic). Some ESOL and special education teachers also praised the framework training for helping teachers develop more concrete representations of subject matter for students: "The fourth-grade teachers are using a lot of the visuals. . . . In reading they're using the graphic organizers. . . . In math they're using . . . visuals. . . . That's been very helpful to the teachers to be able to use that, to copy the Ruby Payne information and to use that with the kids for math" (June 2, 2005).

But with no systematic plan for action accompanying readings and discussions at these training sessions, the observer's overall impression was that "too much was crammed in too little time with, in the end, little applicable use for school staff" (December 6, 2004). One of the grade-level team leaders confirmed this. After an Instructional Leadership Team meeting on conversations about race, we asked her what would happen next. Ideally, she said, the grade-level teams would discuss the article. But because they spent so much of their time planning and analyzing student work, there was little time for these kinds of discussions. Later in the year, reflective field notes from an ILT meeting on English Language Learners raised the same kinds of questions about implementation:

> I thought the ESOL articles were pretty sound theoretically and offered a lot of good strategies. However, I wondered how much impact they would have on instruction. There was no ESOL teacher present and there was no clear strategy for implementation. Clearly time was a factor, but leaving team leaders on their own to make grade-level improvements is a big leap of faith. . . . One easy thing would have been to have team leaders decide on the one or two strategies they thought would be most helpful at their grade level and give two or three ways they would ensure more attention to that in classroom instruction. (March 21, 2005)

Observers also noted a similar approach to training in reading and mathematics instruction during SIT and ILT meetings. On the one hand, excellent information was disseminated. On the other hand, little time was allotted for internalizing and using the information. At a fall SIT meeting, the school's speech pathologist and a special education teacher shared information about the problems that all students, but especially special needs students, had with the state's reading standards. Using analyses of diagnostic reading assessment provided by the school's data team, they shared important vocabulary associated with reading processes as well as instructional strategies. However, rather than having the SIT work with their handouts identifying specific grade-level needs, the reading specialist had participants identify lessons from their instructional guides that matched the state's reading process content standards. Preparing students for the end-of-year assessment was such an overriding concern at Cherry Ridge that neither presenters nor participants seemed to notice that the professional development focus had shifted from vocabulary instruction to aligning instruction to the state test.

There were similar in-depth presentations on language acquisition and instructional strategies, especially for ELL students, at a December SIT meeting. But again, at the end of the meeting, the observer wrote that there was

> relatively small likelihood that teachers will incorporate suggested practices into existing repertoires. Cecilia Kelley and Vicky Winchester shared that there is no time left to use the "Vocabulary Triangle" and other suggested strategies. This is a case where the information presented might be enlightening and relevant, but where the logistics of daily instruction, formatted to teach to

testing, leave no room for something else that might be "new." . . . [Teachers] are truly on an overload, incessantly being told how to adjust their instruction to ensure meeting AYP. (December 6, 2004)

As found in another high-stakes accountability context, the test became the "reference point" for teaching, learning, and the implementation of professional development (Boardman & Woodruff, 2004).

At a January SIT meeting, the same kind of comments were written about learning opportunities for mathematics instruction. On the one hand, the observer was impressed with the quality of professional development the math content coach provided, particularly her modeling and discussing "how the various [instructional] strategies could be adapted to different levels and explaining the rationale for the strategies." On the other hand, the observer "wondered how much teachers use and pass out what they get at these SIT meetings" (January 31, 2005). Implementation depended on SIT members following through at grade-level meetings, which Ms. Odett tried to attend. But her half-time appointment as math content coach and competing obligations often made this difficult. When she did attend, conversations were often about math family night, homework, planning a 60/30 lesson format, and assessments. Commenting on a grade-level meeting of the fifth-grade team, for example, the observer wrote, "The agenda again is largely strategic and related to testing and timing. There is relatively little mathematics or mathematics pedagogy professional development here. I was disappointed that no Cherry Ridge student work was reviewed; I thought this was to be the hallmark of team math meetings" (January 7, 2005). As discussed below, when student work was reviewed as a basis of teacher development, understanding the state's SCR expectations for mathematics was the primary goal.

Maximizing Test-Oriented Training

Unlike the professional development sessions that focused on student diversity, curriculum rollout, and instructional strategies, the SCR sessions took place at the grade level; were frequently guided by the outside consultant, Ms. Batori; and required highly specified action plans. At these meetings, teachers generated examples of SCR questions, discussed key elements of a proficient response, and examined the state's scoring rubric. Unlike Hawthorne, where there was little mention of SCRs until January, Cherry Ridge teachers began to work with them from the start of the school year. The consultation sessions with Ms. Batori were seen as so critical that they were among the few times teachers were pulled from classrooms: four times for each grade level team between mid-December and the end of January.

At her first set of hourlong meetings, Ms. Batori introduced each grade-level team to the state's diagnostic protocol for examining student work. At that meeting, and the ones to follow, Ms. Batori followed the procedure set out in that protocol. First, teachers were to come to meetings with the text and objective they were using; the SCR question they had constructed; and enough copies of a high, medium, and low response for the group. Second, there was discussion about the nature of the text (e.g., fiction or not) and the targeted objective to ensure common understanding. Third, each teacher presented the three samples giving reasons for the high, medium, and low rankings. Fourth, the rest of the participants were asked for their feedback.

Ms. Batori believed that the hardest part of this work was reaching consensus on what they were looking for in answers. She saw the state protocol as an invaluable tool and was explicit in emphasizing state test preparation: "This process is meant to help you focus your attention and time on preparing kids for [the state test]" (December 13, 2005). She stated that as long as the teachers strategically picked from top, middle, and bottom papers, and continued to diagnose, their students would improve on the state test while acquiring long-lasting academic skills. Throughout these sessions, Ms. Batori stressed the importance of teachers clearly identifying the objectives they were assessing in order to compose relevant SCR questions, achieve consensus around expected answers, and track the objectives they were assessing in order to avoid useless redundancy. During all these sessions, much time was spent on analyzing student work in order to obtain increasing numbers of proficient responses. As one teacher described the process:

> We pick an SCR that the kids do, and we pick whatever our
> objective is, and we match it up to the recommended curriculum,
> and then we decide what we're looking for from the kids to write
> in their SCR, and then the following week . . . we all discuss it. . . .
> We usually pick a high, medium, and low student; we bring the
> same student each week; and then we'll have a dialogue going
> between the whole team about strategies that we might use. So
> that has really influenced our teaching . . . to really make sure that
> we are reteaching and revisiting those SCRs, and not when they
> finish it, that we're moving on right away. (May 26, 2005)

A weekly plan that one grade-level recommended to others was to teach a reading comprehension strategy on Monday, Tuesday, and Wednesday; start a practice SCR on Wednesday; continue on Thursday; and test on Friday.

But despite all the attention to SCR questions and answers, there was surprisingly little emphasis on suggesting strategies for improvement. So while teachers devoted extensive time in their team meetings to generating reteaching strategies for SCRs, as required by the protocol, their repertoire of instructional strategies remained fairly limited. In one instance, a teacher attempted an instructional strategy with a struggling student, faced the same difficulty the following week, and again decided upon the same failed instructional strategy. The observer explained:

> Lisa began the SCR discussion by saying that she had pulled out the same kids whose SCR had been discussed last week, to see if there was any progress in their performance on this new SCR, as a follow-up. She shared that for this one student, last week's identified problem was that he did not "pull out evidence," and that the diagnosis had been to "highlight text." She said that in this week's SCR he again did not use evidence from text. . . . She said that for next time she would ask him to highlight where there are examples in the story. (January 11, 2005)

This teacher, Lisa Franklin, was the fifth-grade team leader, with years of teaching experience. She taught only reading, including gifted and talented classes, and was regarded as a highly skilled teacher entrusted with mentoring others on her team, all first- through third-year teachers. But even for her, analyzing student work for teaching implications remained a formidable task. It did not become the type of helpful formative assessment described in Chapters 2 and 3.

Cherry Ridge teachers put in the time necessary to develop students' SCR skills, but used the same strategies over and over with seemingly little progress. The impact on teaching seemed minimal. This may have been because of the way the school linked professional development and accountability (Rinke & Valli, in press). As described previously, each time grade-level teams did work around SCRs, teachers were required to fill out "capture sheets" that were submitted to the principal. On these sheets, teachers had to summarize from the SCR discussions what individual students knew and needed to know to be proficient on that question. From this analysis, they needed to indicate what they would do next with individual students as well as what they needed to reteach the entire class. This exercise seemed to foster a sense among teachers that professional development sessions were hoops to jump through for accountability purposes rather than authentic learning opportunities for them. One fourth-grade teacher commented, "I don't like rushing so we can show on paper that we're doing this" (January 27, 2005).

Summary

As a long-standing Title I school that was in school improvement status, Cherry Ridge was awash in professional development resources and requirements. Its long-term principal, who excelled at management, strategically targeted those resources to its greatest need area. While teachers were willing participants in professional development, it was often experienced as a tool to make AYP rather than to enhance their learning. The principal's approach toward documentation and accountability, such as requiring "capture sheets," created an atmosphere in which teachers simply went through the motions to accomplish all of their tasks. The investment in an outside consultant and released time only for SCR training, conveyed a message about what was valued. Having to rely on much of their professional development to trickle down from leadership meetings marginalized many, potentially rich, learning opportunities. Although teachers participated in professional development, apart from learning how to use SCRs to identify problem areas, its impact often seemed negligible.

CONCLUSION

Despite similar policy environments and resources, the organizational and relational capacities of Hawthorne, Brookfield, and Cherry Ridge produced different versions of professional development. With its limited capacity, Hawthorne individualized opportunities for teacher learning and crammed training to prepare students for the high-stakes state test. With its strong capacity, Brookfield was not only able to maintain quality professional development for the improvement of teaching, but also transformed SCR training into rich learning opportunities for teachers and their students. Strong organizationally, Cherry Ridge systematically provided teachers with SCR learning opportunities. But in doing so, it minimized pedagogy-oriented teacher learning. Even the SCR training lacked a pedagogical emphasis. Teachers did not learn how to make teaching decisions from their analysis of student work, but simply relied on the limited strategies they already had.

The message that teachers at Hawthorne received was that the need for professional development was a sign of inadequacy. With the school's lack of relational capacity and classroom modeling targeting weak teachers, professional development seemed more threat than opportunity. Because of the chaotic school climate, professional development was ignored for much of the year. Even the regularly scheduled data meetings had limited payoff in relation to the extensive investment of resources they required. Teachers felt as though they had to spend inordinate amounts of time to prepare and experienced the sessions as judgment rather than assistance. Coming late in the school year and without strong administrative support, SCR training also lacked the power to effect teacher change.

Brookfield seemed to have maintained high-level professional development despite rather than because of external messages; it "weathered" policy pressure. This suggests that a better strategy for school improvement is developing leadership, school culture, and capacity rather than imposing regulations for outcomes (Gamoran et al., 2000; Mintrop, 2004).The message that Brookfield teachers received was that ongoing learning was integral to being a professional, part of the professional culture of the school, and vital to their teacher identity and to meeting the challenges of helping students learn. Attention was given not just to professional development itself, but also to classroom implementation. The strong tradition of being a professional learning community carried over into learning about new initiatives, including new test-taking requirements. These new requirements, however, detracted from the strong pedagogical orientation that the professional staff previously had on student writing. Although high-quality professional development continued, the focus of teacher learning changed. It became simultaneously fractured across multiple initiatives and primarily pulled toward SCR teaching.

At Cherry Ridge, where the most professional development occurred, little attention was paid to classroom implementation except SCRs. The message that teachers received was that professional development was expedient to get off the state watch list, not for professional growth. The school's reading curriculum rollout and other types of professional development were displaced by the SCR-training focus, narrowing opportunities for teachers to learn. Unlike Brookfield, SCR-training emphasized test-taking skills rather than teaching and learning skills. Although professional development was ongoing, job embedded, collaborative, and closely linked to student learning expectations, the test-taking orientation transformed genuine professional development into narrow training. Test-taking behaviors and test outcomes mattered more than developing teacher and student understanding.

Ironically, urgency to make AYP did not result in professional development focusing on the improvement of instruction. Instead, professional development time was spent on aligning curriculum and instruction with the state test content and format. Teachers' collaborative work and opportunities to learn centered on test-taking skills rather than on subject matter and pedagogy. Even at a strong school like Brookfield, professional development time was devoted to learning how to help students write the kinds of SCRs required on the state test. Thus, opportunities to "scale up" good teaching practices, such as those taught in the curriculum rollout training were minimized. Although teachers learned how to assess student needs, they did not necessarily learn how to make appropriate instructional adjustments. The dominant message that teachers received was that professional development related to test taking was of utmost value to district, state, and federal officials. Those learning opportunities, however, were often for narrow skill training, not the rich cognitive growth found in the literature.

Eroding Quality Teaching

Ensuring the access of children to effective, scientifically based instructional strategies and challenging academic content . . .
— No Child Left Behind Act

We glaze over things. Kids aren't given the opportunity . . . to get in-depth . . . because, we prep the heck out of them. . . . But if you ask those kids half that stuff now, they wouldn't know it . . . because it was quick and dirty.
— Special Ed teacher

I N THIS CHAPTER, we examine what occurs as teachers attempt to fulfill the charge of NCLB: providing every child access to effective instructional strategies, challenging content, and high expectations. Stevenson was well positioned to fulfill this vision. The district's curriculum and instructional guides in mathematics and reading reflected national standards and effective instructional practices. Stevenson had provided resources to schools to support professional development that would enable teachers to implement the curriculum and instructional guides and to evaluate how well each child was meeting high expectations. However, a mismatch existed between Stevenson's curriculum and the state test, and the three schools differed in organizational and relational capacities available for navigating the resulting pressures and conflicts.

In this chapter we show how assessment and accountability policies affected teachers' thinking about the meaning of teaching, especially high-quality teaching, classroom experiences for teachers and students, and teachers' personal images of what it means to be a good teacher. We also show how assessment and accountability policies heightened educators' sense of responsibility for individual student learning, but also the challenges of differentiating instruction. Certainly, the intent of NCLB is to improve instruction and learning for all students. However, the increased expectations for schools and teachers often seemed to make improving teaching and the conditions for improving teaching more difficult. They also reinforced deficit views of students.

CONCEPTUALIZATION OF HIGH-QUALITY TEACHING

The three schools felt pressures to construct teaching in ways that were quite different from ideas about high-quality teaching that we, as researchers, brought to this study. Based on our understandings of the literature in cognitive psychology and reading and mathematics education, we regard high-quality teaching as that which promotes the principled learning of content; encourages the development of cognitive and metacognitive skills; motivates students to engage deeply in subject matter; addresses student differences; and creates inclusive, affirming, and successful learning environments. In keeping with these principles, reading instruction would promote dialogue about interesting and challenging texts of a variety of genres, make connections across the curriculum, and embed skills instruction in meaningful interaction with text (IRA & NCTE, 1996). Similarly, mathematics instruction would engage students in high-level tasks, promote conceptual as well as procedural understanding, require students to explain their thinking, give them opportunities to use alternative problem-solving methods, help them make connections between and among mathematical ideas, and show the usefulness of mathematics outside the classroom (NCTM, 2000).

Our conception of high-quality teaching is similar to what Fenstermacher and Richardson (2005) have described as *good* teaching. Good teaching reflects disciplinary standards and is motivating, age appropriate, moral, and aimed at enhancing the learner's competence with the disciplinary content. Good teaching is *learner sensitive*. The teacher ensures that content is explained, defined, demonstrated, and interpreted. The teacher provides for correction and informative feedback. The teacher's goal is to motivate, encourage, evaluate, reward, or punish students in a manner that is honest, tolerant, compassionate, respectful, and fair. For their part, students are engaged substantively with the lesson, motivated, excited, connected, and demonstrating that they understand the content. Observers seeing these teacher and student behaviors would characterize instruction as good teaching without waiting for the results from student assessment per se.

This last point evokes a vivid scene from *The Practice of Teaching*. In that book, Jackson (1986) points to the absurdity of evaluating teaching based solely on what a teacher is doing and how the students are responding. He postulates a scenario in which an observer believes herself to be watching a teacher who is "well and properly engaged in his or her craft" and students who are responding enthusiastically and appropriately. However, the teacher and students actually are actors rehearsing a scene from the play *The Prime of Miss Jean Brodie*. Referring to their own analogous scenario, in which the teacher is real but the students are actually robots, Fenstermacher and Richardson (2005) argue that *quality* teaching, as opposed to *good* teaching, must also be *successful* teaching. That is, students must learn what the teacher intends for them to learn. In contrast to *good* teaching, which we have already described as learner sensitive, *successful* teaching is *learning dependent*. And the learning must be measured somehow.

Successful teaching receives far less explication from Fenstermacher and Richardson than does good teaching. The authors review research results that suggest that direct instruction, time on task, and providing lots of academic-learning time lead to the student learning what is tested on standardized tests. The teacher presents material to the students, students receive and practice the new knowledge and skills, and at some point they are asked to reproduce what they have been taught in the same or similar form. Instruction does not encourage teachers or students to engage in thinking logically about important curricular ideas. Successful teaching as described here would appear to be almost antithetical to good teaching. And yet Fenstermacher and Richardson argue convincingly for the necessity of both in quality teaching.

Because these two types of teaching are so strikingly opposite in educational research, it is unlikely that they exist in equal proportions in quality teaching. Indeed, our conceptualization of high-quality teaching puts more weight on what Fenstermacher and Richardson describe as good teaching. We did, however, take learning-dependent successful teaching into account when we originally chose to study moderate- to high-poverty schools that demonstrated higher-than-expected scores on standardized tests. As we will demonstrate below, teachers at the three schools differed in how they conceived the balance between these two types of teaching. Nonetheless, as March testing time approached, teaching that matched the features of learning-dependent successful teaching became progressively more prominent at all three schools.

Fenstermacher and Richardson (2005) admit that research studies focusing on learner-sensitive good teaching have failed to demonstrate successful teaching clearly. The problem is how to measure easily the new understanding that students have constructed as a result of good teaching with readily interpretable and reliable standardized results. For

Stevenson schools, the state test was a given, and it had not been designed to measure knowledge construction and understanding. Instead, it measured skills in reading and mathematics that lent themselves to fill-in-the-bubble responses and short constructed responses (SCRs), as we have already described. Successful teaching had to prepare students to do well on this test.

With the press of high-stakes assessments, teachers in Stevenson schools seemed to be adopting learning-dependent successful teaching that showed fewer and fewer signs of learner-sensitive good teaching (Fenstermacher & Richardson, 2005). This change is evident from the nearly 400 pre–classroom observation interview forms collected from the three schools that year. In preparation for collecting time-sampling data, observers recorded the lesson focus, lesson objective, and materials used. The year of the case study was the first time observers reported that test preparation was a substantial proportion of lessons: 16% of the observed lessons at Brookfield, 18% of the lessons at Hawthorne, and 22% of the lessons at Cherry Ridge. By comparison, these test preparation lessons occurred, on average, only 8% of the time in the three schools the previous year. Although proponents of NCLB might argue that this test preparation is exactly the intent of the legislation, these actions raise questions about the quality of education afforded all children. This emphasis on test practice was also heard in teacher discourse. In conversations with us and with their school colleagues, teachers focused on curriculum coverage, aligning content to assessments, pacing the curriculum, monitoring student performance, modeling assessment formats in their classroom assignments, practicing for the test, and providing better accommodations for students during the test.

In addition to teaching practices being characterized by test preparation, time-sampling data across all study schools indicate that, with the increased press of test accountability, lessons became less cognitively demanding. Table 6.1 shows a three-year comparison of indicators of cognitive demand in mathematics and reading, from our total sample of teachers, 64–76 depending on the subject and year. There was a decline in every category that signified cognitively complex instruction and either a rise or constancy in instruction that placed little cognitive demand on students.

More specifically, teachers in both subject areas were most likely to be managing an activity and posing lower-order questions and tasks, as reported in Table 6.2. Students were most likely being managed, listening, or giving simple answers. Instruction in both subjects was most likely to occur in whole-class settings with the teacher in charge, and during reading, in a mixed organization in which children took turns working independently at their seats and meeting with their teacher in small groups

Table 6.1. Level of cognitive demand by year across 25 schools (percent of lessons).

	Mathematics			Reading		
	2002–03 (N = 266)	2003–04 (N = 606)	2004–05 (N = 539)	2002–03 (N = 266)	2003–04 (N = 552)	2004–05 (N = 536)
Teacher high cognitive demand	11	11	7	14	10	10
Teacher low cognitive demand	21	20	20	13	17	17
Student response/work high cognitive demand	18	17	10	20	18	16
Student response/work low cognitive demand	33	32	39	24	24	26
Lesson content high cognitive demand	19	11	7	33	29	28

Notes: Mathematics teacher and student high cognitive demand 2002–03 and 2003–04 are significantly higher than 2004–05 at the .01 confidence level; student low cognitive demand 2004–05 is significantly higher than 2002–03 and 2003–04 at the .01 level. For content, all years are significantly different from one another at the .01 level. Reading teacher high cognitive demand 2002–03 is significantly higher than 2003–04 and 2004–05 at the .01 level; student high cognitive demand 2002–03 is significantly higher than 2004–05 at the .01 level; teacher low cognitive demand 2003–04 and 2004–05 are significantly higher than 2002–03 at the .01 level; student low cognitive demand 2004–05 is significantly higher than 2003–04 at the .05 level. For content, year 2 is significantly higher than year 4 at the .05 level.

for Guided Reading. For both subjects, most students were on task three fourths of the time. Although there were a few minor differences, instruction was remarkably similar in the two subject areas in its learning-dependent teaching orientation.

Stevenson teachers did show some evidence of learner-sensitive teaching as well. As Fenstermacher and Richardson (2005) and others have noted, the research on successful teaching has tended to ignore curriculum, which has been the province of studies on good teaching. Stevenson's curriculum demonstrates many of the features of good teaching, reflecting the NCTM and IRA/NCTE standards. NCTM standards promote conceptual understanding in addition to procedural proficiency. According to

Table 6.2. The three most frequently observed teacher activities, student activities, content foci, and types of classroom organization across 16 schools, 2004–05 (percent of observed lesson time).

Rank	Mathematics	Reading
	Teacher activity	Teacher activity
1	Manage activity (17%)	Manage activity (16%)
2	Pose low order (16%)	Pose low order (14%)
3	Read aloud (10%)	Listen (11%)
	Student activity	Student activity
1	Simple answer (23%)	Simple answer (19%)
2	Listen/watch (19%)	Management (18%)
3	Management (18%)	Listen (18%)
	Content focus	Content focus
1	Procedural (44%)	Text elements (20%)
2	Conceptual (24%)	Resource management (17%)
3	Resource management (18%)	Reading (9%)
	Classroom organization	Classroom organization
1	Whole group (56%)	Whole group (51%)
2	Individual (22%)	Mixed small group and individual (22%)
3	Small group (7%)	Individual (13%)

Table 6.2, mathematics lessons focused on both procedural proficiency and conceptual understanding, although procedural proficiency was the instructional focus almost twice as often as conceptual understanding. IRA/NCTE standards promote student understanding of text patterns, such as the elements in narratives (settings, characters, plots, and themes) and expositions (main ideas and supporting details). Reading lessons were more likely to focus on these elements than any other type of content (e.g., personal responses, vocabulary, decoding). In both mathematics and reading, we saw some evidence of curriculum-based good teaching.

Within these general outcomes, however, were important differences among the three schools. From these differences we have gained valuable insights about the effects that organizational and relational capacities can have on instruction and the limits of even robust capacities to protect a school from the negative impact of assessment and accountability policies.

HAWTHORNE: TEACHING AS CRAMMING
FOR THE TEST AND REGROUPING

Hawthorne struggled under the impact of assessment and accountability policies more than did the other two schools. Teachers abruptly shifted from the Stevenson curriculum to a test-taking curriculum in the 2 months leading up to the state test. Opportunities for staff development occurred infrequently and, when they did, focused far more on logistics than substance. Not surprisingly, Hawthorne's struggles also affected classroom instruction, efforts to meet the instructional needs of all students, and teachers' professional identities.

Classroom Instruction

Classroom instruction at the beginning of the year at Hawthorne looked very much like the instruction in other Stevenson schools in our study, which we have described in Table 6.2. However, teachers were even more likely to pose low-order questions and activities during both mathematics and reading than teachers in the larger sample, and students were more likely to be completing routine exercises in mathematics. Similar to the larger sample, instruction in mathematics and reading looked remarkably alike: teaching in both subjects matched the characteristics of learning-dependent far more than learner-sensitive instruction.

Instruction in Hawthorne classrooms changed abruptly in January, although the change looks subtler in the time-sampling data than in other types of observations and interviews. The changes in reading instruction are more evident than the changes in mathematics. During January and February, teachers were even more likely to pose low-order questions in reading, and "reading aloud" replaced "listening" to students in frequency. Lessons focused on literal comprehension (details that can be easily identified in the text) rather than text elements, and students were more likely to be completing seat work than working with the teacher in Guided Reading groups. In mathematics instruction, the major change was a drop in the focus on conceptual understanding.

Hawthorne teachers were engaged in what has been called decontextualized test preparation during much of January and February. This is the form of test prep that "consists of special 'cramming' shortly before the test is given and intensification of conventional, didactic practice" (Firestone, Schorr, & Monfils, 2004, p. viii). And lest there be any doubt, teachers let their students know what they were doing. In comparison to the rest of the year, where Hawthorne teachers mentioned the relationship between class content and tested material less than 1% of the time, during January and February they made statements about class content being on the test approximately 10% of class time. This percentage far exceeded "will be on the test" motivational statements at either Brookfield or Cherry Ridge. Indeed, cramming for the test was such a widely accepted practice in Hawthorne that when the Title I specialist asked the teachers what they were doing in classes, they responded that they were doing test preparation. Laura Zwiller, a fourth-grade teacher, did not hesitate to add that she tells her students "they're in boot camp" (January 26, 2005).

There were numerous indications of this test prep orientation. The fifth-grade team formally decided to use half their mathematics class to teach the curriculum and the other half for test preparation. Greta Shephard, the math content coach, made the rounds of third- through fifth-grade classrooms to tell students about the test, and teachers regularly used worksheets from commercial materials that were aligned with the state test in both content and format. So, for example, a fourth-grade teacher gave her students a brief overview of perimeter before the test, but then did not return to the topic until May 11. As one observer wrote about a fifth-grade teacher: "This lesson on perimeter and area was taught because it will be on the [state test] and the teacher had not yet covered it. Topics are being taught in isolation and out of sequence until the [state test]. The curriculum has been 'abandoned' according to this teacher" (January 22, 2005).

Teachers voiced similar concerns about reading instruction. Commenting during a February planning meeting that students were still having trouble with topics such as finding the main ideas and using context cues from texts, one of the new teachers lamented, "I hope they're getting it. I don't know if they're getting anything." But instead of strategizing how to avoid this "cramming" approach to teaching and engaging in pedagogical discourse, the team leader suggested doing something "nice" for students after the test like taking them outside or getting them ice cream (February 7, 2005).

On a number of occasions when members of the research team were formally scheduled to conduct observations of reading classes, teachers were even using that time to give their students test preparation in mathematics. For example, an observer annotated for three consecutive episodes (3-minute intervals): "The class has incorporated math test prep into reading time and is doing no reading at the moment . . . still doing math . . . still doing math in test prep booklets" (January 28, 2005).

During their joint end-of-year interview, the staff developer, math content coach, and reading specialist commented on this extensive test preparation practice, which had now become part of the school's established routine:

Ms. Newkirk: After a couple of days of testing and they [students] get to the writing piece and it's seven SCRs right in a row. They were just dying.

Ms. Shephard: I think the tests are too long. You can find out what the children know in a lot less.

Ms. Nichols: And unfortunately it's causing the teachers to change their teaching to practice things like that. They know, based on last year, if there's seven SCRs in a row we've got to get our kids able to do seven SCRs and not fall asleep so that we know that they were practicing that extensive writing. (June 6, 2005)

Indeed, toward the end of February, one of the fourth-grade teachers decided that the students had to practice for the length of the state test. The observer wrote, "Teacher is preparing students to have to sit for 3 hours during the state test. She has assigned a lot of work all at once, and they will have to sit to finish them [*sic*]. Students are not happy about it" (February 23, 2005).

The resulting teacher and student stress clearly showed in observers' annotations immediately before and after the test, particularly for the four newest teachers. As examples, observers wrote:

Behavior and classroom management are both horrible, classroom is out of control, and teacher cannot seem to regain order. (February 16, 2005)

Class is talking over the teacher and teacher is not handling it very well. She's yelling, and when that doesn't work she just stops talking, and they continue to talk. (March 14, 2005)

Meeting the Instructional Needs of All Students

One way in which Stevenson school district sought to leave no child behind was by differentiating instruction. The new mathematics and reading instructional guides offered numerous strategies that regular classroom teachers could use to differentiate for students above and below grade level. The district also supported the use of supplemental or remedial programs beyond regular classes. Nonetheless, the teaching that occurred in Hawthorne's regular classrooms showed little evidence of differentiation. More than half the time, students were meeting with the teacher as a whole class. By January and February, students were either meeting as a whole class or working at their desks on the same tasks more than 80% of the time.

According to Stevenson guidelines, during reading instruction students were to spend most of their time (70–85%) either meeting with the teacher in a small, homogeneous, Guided Reading group or working at their desks on individualized tasks. As indicated earlier, by January and February, children were much less likely to be meeting in Guided Reading groups, even though the reading specialist had given a workshop on small-group, Guided Reading instruction. In mathematics classes, observers recorded differentiated instruction occurring less than 2% of class time. Instead of in-class instructional differentiation, Hawthorne teachers relied on other strategies to differentiate: pullouts, regrouping, and reteaching.

Students who were low achievers in mathematics and reading were pulled out for additional instruction. Hawthorne was the only one of the three schools to give low achievers a "double-dip" of mathematics instruction. These students met with the math content coach for an extra 35 minutes a day, when they either previewed or reviewed the content from their assigned class. When Stevenson School District instituted the reading intervention program, Hawthorne employed a similar model, pulling low readers for specialized instruction. However, in this case, as with ESOL, the pullouts were not always a double-dip, but replaced part of the reading block.

Often these pullout programs had little relationship to classroom instruction. One of the academic support teachers, Ms. Boyer, mentioned that, unfortunately, she did not need to talk to classroom teachers about class content and student learning needs, that with the prescribed reading intervention curriculum she had to follow, "it doesn't matter what they do in the classroom. I know what I'm doing with them" (June 6, 2005).

Pullout programs themselves typically were not differentiated according to student needs. Ms. Turner, a special education teacher who was also required to teach reading intervention from highly structured programs, complained that even when the lessons were too basic and boring for the students, she could not skip them because the materials required that she follow the prescribed sequence and not omit any topics. She also believed that the demands made on students were unrealistic:

We glaze over things. Kids aren't given the opportunity for repeated practice and to get in depth, and to apply the skills, which is what they need to really retain the information and learn it, because, we prep the heck out of them for [the state test]. But if you ask those kids half that stuff now, they wouldn't know it . . . because it was [snapping fingers] quick and dirty. (June 6, 2005)

Some children were being pulled out of class so often that their classroom teachers complained of having them in class too infrequently. Although the classroom teachers were the teachers of record, many of their students went to specialists for reading intervention, ESOL, and other types of support. One of the fifth-grade teachers, for example, had nine ESOL students in her class who were pulled out of her reading class. Although she only saw these students for 40 minutes of her 2-hour reading period, she was still the one held responsible for their learning and test scores. She worried about having to move ahead too quickly for students to attain mastery of the content.

A special education teacher had similar frustrations over pullouts from her regularly assigned class:

> Almost every single child in my room does get pulled out for speech support. And she can't take them all at once. Literally every day, I have three or four kids that go off to speech. So for me it's difficult to remember, OK, who's going to be gone this day, and what can I do with these kids that are left that the kids who are out aren't going to have missed, so that when they come back tomorrow, they don't know what's going on. (Nicky Turner, June 6, 2005)

Even though considerable investment was made in these special programs, classroom teachers and specialists were dissatisfied with this approach to differentiation. And we see no evidence that these pullout programs addressed student needs. The one exception would be the math double-dip that was highly integrated with regular classroom instruction and did not disrupt the lesson or student learning by pulling students out of those classes.

A second strategy that Hawthorne teachers used, and about which we heard no complaints, was reassigning students to different teachers to achieve as much homogeneity in group composition as possible. This reassignment occurred only in mathematics classes in which district-developed unit tests monitored student progress. Used as differentiation tools, unit tests assisted in the regular regrouping of students across classrooms. Because students varied in their achievement rankings on unit tests, maintaining homogeneity meant that teachers made reassignments after every unit. When asked how often teachers regrouped, the math content coach, Greta Shephard, answered, "At the end of unit tests for sure, because . . . the assistant in my room has their lists and has to put in their data and they [*sic*] go, 'Oh, they switched again!' And that's the whole point" (December 13, 2004).

This constant switching may, however, have made it difficult for teachers to get to know their students. In mid-February, teachers still did not know which of the students they would be monitoring during the state test should receive accommodations such as the use of a calculator. As the observer noted about the meeting, "I found it odd that the teachers didn't know which of the students from their homerooms needed accommodations in math. There are not that many students in the fourth grade, and with all the talk about accommodations and the preparation for the [state test], it would seem that they might have discussed this already" (February 16, 2005).

The one, within-class differentiation strategy that we heard about was reviewing and reteaching mathematics content that students within a homogeneously grouped classroom found difficult—especially if that content was assessed on the state test. When they met for unit planning, grade-level teams tried to leave a few days free so they could plug in review time: "We always leave gaps so that your class might need to do some extra review on a certain topic whereas my class might be able to jump ahead to another topic" (Charles Swindell, January 26, 2005). To achieve instructional coherence, Ms. Shepard tried to help teachers reinforce prior learning by seeing the natural connections within the curriculum:

> For instance, if you taught multiplication, and they didn't get the multiplication, when you teach area—area is multiplying length times width—therefore you're reteaching the multiplication again. So there are places that you can do some reteaching. It's not always that easy to see, but there are places where the reteaching can happen. (June 6, 2005)

Based on our time-sampling data, however, we would have to judge Ms. Shephard's efforts as ineffective. Of the three schools, Hawthorne teachers made the fewest connections to prior instruction in both reading and mathematics—less than 1% in each subject area. So, while Hawthorne teachers might have "retaught" content by leaving gaps in unit planning, they failed to take advantage of the inherent connections within subject matter.

Through differentiation, Hawthorne teachers could have been switching their focus from learning dependent to learner sensitive. But students were identified for differentiation because they probably would not perform well on the state test, and the response, at least whenever students were given extra time spent on test practice, was to prepare them better for success on the test. The differentiation seems much more learning dependent than learner sensitive. We are reminded of Black and Wiliam's

(1998b) caution about formative assessment: that it requires a whole new set of instructional strategies to be successful. To our knowledge, Hawthorne's teachers received little professional development in instructional strategies that are particularly effective with children who are failing to flourish in mathematics and reading. Lacking this institutional support, they relied heavily on their past experience and the highly structured published materials that they were given.

Constructing Self as Teacher: Missing Autonomy

The new teachers at Hawthorne said they never envisioned that they would be doing test preparation as they studied to become teachers. They thought they would enjoy the work of teaching much more than they did. Nicky Turner, a more experienced special education teacher, similarly described what a prescribed curriculum and testing accountability did to her sense of professional identity:

> On one hand it's great to have the curriculum . . . but on the other hand, I think it takes so much away from teaching. I spent 6 years between undergrad and grad school getting my degree in education, and it frustrates me to be given eight binders at the beginning of the year, and this is what you're gonna teach and this is exact, the lesson is planned out for you and everything. . . . I spent years, particularly in grad school, studying all . . . the research about what's best practice and how do kids learn. . . . And then you get in the schools, and it's like . . . throw that out the window because you've gotta do test prep, and we have this lesson already given to you. . . . Anybody could come in here and read through that curriculum guide and be a teacher. (June 6, 2005)

Brandon Mitchell, then in his 6th year of teaching, said he found it scary to be a teacher in the present policy climate. Giving the example of an ESOL student who, after 181 days in the United States, had to be treated the same as everyone else relative to test taking, he asked rhetorically, "What have you done? Taught a kid to take a test" (May 31, 2005).

In contrast to their present teaching reality, experienced teachers such as Joy Karlsen and Anita Lopez recalled the days of teaching centers and independent contracts, when students had some choice in what they wanted to learn, might not even realize they were learning, and were not just doing "crunch time SCRs" (June 8, 2005). Ms. Lopez, for example, used to teach a unit on change from the William and Mary reading program, designed for a gifted and talents population, but used by Ms. Lopez with her heterogeneous class, which included a large number of ESOL students. In teaching students the concept of change, Ms. Lopez began by having them bring in a number of photographs of themselves and put them in chronological order. Students, many of whom were from impoverished and war-torn regions of Central America, eagerly shared their family histories through their photos, often speaking with Ms. Lopez in their native Spanish. This opening activity prepared them for writing autobiographies and an interdisciplinary unit on understanding positive and negative aspects of change as it occurs in nature and society. The contrast between this unit and the current reading instruction was striking.

Ms. Karlsen explained, "I don't like the teacher I've become." She said she felt compelled to explain to her students that the teachers had a lot of pressure on them to improve test scores and that is why they were doing all of these test prep activities, even though they were not necessarily interesting or enjoyable. Each of the teachers described showing students the test score graphs from last year and explaining how they had to improve on them this year. Laura Zwiller said she was so frustrated that she told her students that she could be fired if they did not do well on the state test. She said she now felt bad about having said that and asked, tongue in cheek, "Does this make me a terrible teacher?" (February 9, 2005). Another teacher stated that some of the students were worried that they could not go to the fifth grade if they did poorly on the test, and the others said they had heard similar fears. However, teachers said they were so pressured about the test that they did not discourage that false notion. They believed they had to keep the pressure on their students because they were afraid that students would shut down on test prep work if they did not.

BROOKFIELD: TEACHING AS SCAFFOLDING LEARNING

Not surprisingly, based on the portrait that we have painted of Brookfield so far, teachers at Brookfield exhibited *good* teaching more obviously than did those at either of the other schools. As a staff, they had a shared sense of what they meant by good teaching. This stable staff had spent time over the years developing that collective sense. Indeed, at times teachers seemed to be balancing good and successful teaching in a manner that we believe Fenstermacher and Richardson (2005) would have readily identified as *quality* teaching. During January and February as the state test approached, the balance shifted more and more from learner-sensitive toward learning-dependent instruction. Even this school with strong organizational and relational capacities struggled to retain good teaching under the impact of assessment and accountability policies.

Classroom Instruction

At the beginning of the year, classroom instruction at Brookfield demonstrated learner-sensitive good teaching more frequently than what occurred in the other Stevenson schools in our larger study. In addition to posing lower-order questions and managing resources, teachers in mathematics elaborated on their questions and tasks rather than reading aloud to practice test accommodations, and teachers in reading were more likely to pose higher-order questions than listen. Similar to the larger sample, the content focus tended to reflect standards in mathematics and reading. In addition, reading included a focus on vocabulary, important in a school with a substantial ELL population. In mathematics, students were less likely to be completing independent seat work than in the larger sample, and in reading they met in Guided Reading groups almost as often as they participated in whole group instruction. Most students were on task 85% of the time, a higher rate than in other schools in our larger sample, suggesting that students were engaged substantively with the lesson. These outcomes from the observation protocol hint at classroom instruction at Brookfield. Interviews, field notes, and other data collected during the observations complete the picture.

Brookfield teachers' regular instructional practice reflected disciplinary standards. According to the *Standards for the English Language Arts* (IRA & NCTE, 1996), students must be able to draw on their background knowledge and their knowledge of text patterns to create, critique, and discuss a wide variety of texts. Based on lesson handouts and interviews, we could see that teachers frequently had students fill out chapter organizers, character maps, and literature webs in preparation for small-group reading discussions about substantial texts. They also distributed organizers for previewing both narrative and expository text. The narrative organizer for previewing had students predict what might happen next (before reading), determine whether their prediction was right or not (during reading), and explain why their prediction was right or wrong (after reading). For expository text, the organizer for previewing had students ask themselves before reading, "What do I know or think about when I look at this text?" and to generate questions about the text. While they read, students were to write answers to their questions, followed by additional questions they had about the text when they finished reading. These organizers provided students with a format for using K-W-L, an instructional approach developed to support expository text comprehension in which children ask, "What do I know?" "What do I want to know?" "What did I learn?" (Ogle, 1986).

The language that Brookfield teachers used in describing teaching success underscored their desire to enhance their students' love for and

competence with disciplinary content. In an interview, two special education teachers distinguished teaching success by students' love of the
subject instead of by test scores. For example, Evelyn Keller explained:

> I feel the most successful when students in my particular math
> class come in the beginning of the year saying they all hate math,
> and at the end of the year they say they love math. And to me,
> having someone really turned off turn into a love of reading or a
> love of math, maybe love's a little strong, but who really are
> excited about it and look forward to it, and feel successful at it. And
> I think, for most teachers, even though you can take great pride in
> your schoolwide successes, that reaching children on an individual
> basis is where we get our satisfaction. (June 16, 2005)

These themes were echoed by Eddie Wilson, a fifth-grade teacher, who
described his delight in watching students "play with" different ways of
representing probability answers on a unit test: "When they understand
that math is not this fixed, cement thing, that it's actually malleable and
that they can change it to suit their understanding . . . that's when they
begin to appreciate it" (June 2, 2005).

Students will be far more likely to gain a love for a discipline if instruction draws connections to prior knowledge in the content area, to
other content areas, to real-world contexts, and to students' personal lives.
Fenstermacher and Richardson (2005) describe good teaching as motivating and aimed at connecting the learner with the disciplinary content. By
helping students make these connections, teachers both scaffold learning
and demonstrate concern about more than the immediate lesson. They
show an interest in who their students are, what students know, the experiences students bring with them to the classroom, and what students
might do with their new knowledge and skills. These connections have
both a cognitive and a motivational component. As one teacher said, "I'd
much rather connect it [a reading strategy] to the books we're reading than
just follow a cookbook. I'd rather connect it to something that really means
something to them" (Emma Hinton, January 19, 2005). In addition to
facilitating deeper, more long-lasting learning (Bransford et al., 1999), these
connections create personal ties between teachers and students beyond
their institutional roles (Valli & Chambliss, 2007).

While these kinds of connections were relatively rare phenomena at
all schools in the larger study, teachers at Brookfield used them two to six
times as frequently as did teachers at Hawthorne and Cherry Ridge. In
reading, for example, our time-sampling data show Brookfield teachers
connecting their instruction to prior learning, other content, personal

experience, or the real world more than 13% of the time, whereas at Hawthorne these practices occurred only about 2% of the time. Our data also show that students at Brookfield completed instructional activities in which they related their personal lives to what they were reading 9% of the time in contrast to the other two schools in which students engaged in similar activities about 3% of the time. This means that, in literature discussions, for example, Brookfield students had substantially more opportunities to discuss similarities between themselves and characters in a story, to share their feelings about a character's actions, or to hear questions such as "Have you ever faced a dilemma like that?"

Helping students recognize and use text patterns, connecting to what they know, and teaching them strategies to construct meaning from what they read would all enhance student metacognitive understanding. This kind of instruction is regarded by cognitive psychologists as essential for sound academic growth. Students learn how to monitor their progress, reflect on their strengths and weaknesses, evaluate their performance, and correct errors (Alexander & Murphy, 1998; Kilpatrick et al., 2001).

Midway through the year of data collection, one of the team members assigned to Brookfield tentatively summarized the various priorities that teachers sought to accommodate in their teaching:

> Both fourth- and fifth-grade teachers feel three pulls: what they perceive as the needs of their students, the school district curriculum, and [state] test preparation. I've put this list in order of my understanding of the teachers' priorities. Teachers have rescheduled their days to give students more experience with the curriculum. The reading specialist has shifted the curriculum for the pullout program away from Corrective Reading (the district-recommended program) to another program that she believes fits the needs of their students better. This school is trying very hard to put the needs of the students first. (February 17, 2005)

Without awareness of the researcher's perception, Leslie Gabriel, a long-time fifth-grade teacher at Brookfield, echoed this summation almost verbatim in her end-of-year interview. Explaining that although curriculum and assessments had always guided teaching, she said that teachers' most important guide is always their students.

Teachers at Brookfield managed these tensions in part with what Firestone and colleagues have called "embedding" test preparation during regular instruction (Firestone, Schorr, & Monfils, 2004). In this approach to test prep, there is little that distinguishes a test preparation lesson from a regular lesson: sound instructional strategies were used in both types. Although we found instances of decontextualized test preparation at Brookfield (Valli & Chambliss, 2007), it was not as frequent or as pronounced as at the other two schools even as the state test approached.

In the ways in which they prepared students for test taking, Brookfield teachers continued to keep features of good teaching in mind. We saw this orientation, in particular, in the ways in which they had students practice writing SCRs. Like teachers at the other two schools, Brookfield teachers spent considerable time teaching students how to write SCRs. But unlike teachers at the other two schools, Brookfield teachers taught students how to analyze their responses, to judge the quality of these responses, and to justify their answers.

Early in the school year, students were given a general guide for answering questions about written text, called "5 Steps to a Better Answer." Students were walked through the process of reading the question; finding information in the text; using the text, background knowledge, and clear language to answer the question; rereading the question; and reading and revising the answer to make sure they answered all parts of the question, thought about important ideas, and made necessary connections (Pat Kim, October 18, 2005). Instead of learning to follow a set of algorithms, students were learning to think, revise, and express their ideas clearly.

Rather than keeping the state test rubric a secret, teachers gave copies to their students, discussed it, and had them be the assessors of SCR samples. In this way, students were developing metacognitive skill, learning how to independently evaluate the quality of their own writing. So, as an example, Ms. Kim, a fourth-grade teacher, used a reading intervention class period to have students assess SCRs on author's purpose and audience. She gave them three examples for two different SCR questions ("What are some things that the author does to achieve this purpose?" and "How does the tone of the two selections show you that they are meant for different audiences?"). Students worked in small groups to come to an agreement on rubric scores and were directed to "discuss the reasons for each score" (January 5, 2005). Small groups then explained their scores and reasoning to the whole class for further assessment.

The fourth-grade teachers explained that they initially settled on this approach to SCR test practice because of time constraints. There simply was not time for students always to do the writing themselves. But more than that, the teachers wanted their students to become "analysts":

> We twisted it [SCR practice] a little bit this year. . . . Instead of just taking a test, going over the test, taking a test, going over—they had to analyze themselves. . . . We would put them in groups and give them three choices for the SCR that would match that reading,

and they had to score them. We had gone over the rubric. What would you give this? A 3. Why? And so they had to, in the class they had to justify it so they turned into analysts. (May 17, 2005)

Nonetheless, we saw revealing differences in the time-sampling data during January and February. Teachers were more likely to make statements than ask higher-order questions in reading. The focus on procedural proficiency in mathematics increased, while the focus on conceptual understanding decreased substantially. In reading, the focus on vocabulary decreased while the focus on literal comprehension (details that can be easily identified in the text) increased. Otherwise, class organization and the proportion of students who were on task remained about the same. These outcomes hint at a shift in balance away from learner-sensitive good instruction toward learning-dependent instruction as the state test approached.

And as we watched the regular classroom teachers plan instruction during the months preceding the state test, we witnessed their frustrations as they tried to juggle their priorities with the realities of external expectations. During a January planning meeting, the teachers expressed concern about the time the school was devoting to upcoming practice sessions for state assessments. In addition to giving three practice sessions in 2 weeks, they wanted to have accommodators for all designated students at each of the sessions, so had to make those arrangements. When a special education teacher expressed frustration that the use of calculators would impede her students' developing understanding of long division, she was told that this accommodation was mandatory.

Later that month, one fourth-grade teacher, Ms. Hinton, came to the planning meeting with a printout from the state's Web site that showed the curriculum indicators that would be tested at that grade level. She had printed out sample test items as well. As they reviewed these materials, the teachers realized that they would need to get through all the "time stuff" (e.g., elapsed time) the following week and had to add problems concerning money before the state test. Ms. Hinton's teammate, Ms. Kim, complained that this kind of planning was unfair to the students, that the teachers were trying to cover too much before the state test and could not work on topics in depth (February 16, 2005). Brookfield teachers voiced concern about doing too much direct teaching and reteaching rather than engaging students in inquiry and reasoning.

Meeting the Instructional Needs of All Students

As we have already noted, differentiating instruction to meet student needs was a strong theme in the new Stevenson school district curriculum.

Brookfield's emphasis on learner-sensitive good instruction could lead to effective differentiation. Indeed, throughout the year students met in whole-class instruction in reading less than half the time. The district had directed third- through fifth-grade teachers to use small, guided group instruction to differentiate reading instruction. As principal Liz Moore told us at the start of the year, using Guided Reading would not be a problem for her staff, who had been using this mode of differentiation for a number of years. This claim was borne out by our time-sampling data, which indicated that in reading classes, Brookfield teachers differentiated 56% of the time, mostly through the use of small-group instruction. This contrasted with 44% at Cherry Ridge and a strikingly lower 25% at Hawthorne.

Brookfield, like Hawthorne, also used a pullout strategy for ELL and special needs students, which caused its own set of problems. Students were pulled from their regular classes for speech therapy, basic reading intervention, and so forth. This differentiation strategy conflicted with teachers' desires for close instructional bonds with their students. Pullouts during reading classes, in particular, were so noteworthy at Brookfield that observers assigned to collect time-sampling data often felt compelled to write comments such as "three students left for music 10 minutes ago. . . . Six students just arrived from an ESOL specialist" (Emma Hinton, May 16, 2005); "Three students have been pulled out of the classroom for supplemental ESOL instruction" (Pat Kim, February 16, 2005); "Seven students have left the classroom—to work with specialist?" (Eddie Wilson, January 26, 2005); "Six students have left to work with other teachers" (Leslie Gabriel, April 6, 2005).

In one of our last interviews, Lottie Breman, the staff developer, reflected on the status of differentiation as it was practiced at Brookfield:

> The hardest thing in both reading and mathematics is the differentiation piece, is the grouping, and the pullout that goes on in the classroom. The teachers are really, really good at taking the instruction, looking at indicators and objectives that need to be taught, and teaching that, but when you have children being pulled out for ESOL, children being pulled out for resource, children being pulled out for reading intervention and it's constant all day, trying to find the time to teach, it gets kind of hard. And I would say that would be their biggest concern this year (June 7, 2005).

At one point, Ms. Gabriel became so upset with the disruption to her lesson and concerned for students' well-being that she refused to allow a specialist to take her students until the lesson was over. This same motivation had led the fourth-grade teachers to request a change in the homogeneous-grouping policy for reading intervention so they could keep their homeroom students for both the regular reading and the reading intervention class.

Sympathetic to classroom teachers' concerns, their ESOL colleague tried to accommodate. In an interview after the close of the school year, Malinda Marek told us:

> The teachers really don't like the kids to get pulled out, and it's always a constant struggle for the ESOL teacher because we have our own curriculum that's been proven to be effective to help them acquire the language but the teachers also—a lot of these kids who are in ESOL are also the struggling readers so they're getting pulled out for the special reading program, and they're the ones that are being pulled out for . . . special ed. . . . [The teachers are] like, "We never see them. So please come plug in." So I did a lot of plug-in. (July 13, 2005)

Brookfield teachers did not find a perfect solution to the tension between knowing their students well and realizing their needs for specialized assistance. Throughout the year, they made adjustments, which were invariably supported by the principal. They also extended themselves beyond their regular assignments for differential needs. The ESOL teacher, for example, who was fluent in Spanish, was frequently called on to assist in communications with Spanish-speaking parents, about a third of Brookfield's population. She took phone numbers home with her over weekends and the summer so parents would be sure to hear about vaccination requirements, field trips, meetings, and so forth. The teachers had also created an after-school mentoring program for about 40 students. Unlike many after-school programs, which specifically targeted areas of academic deficiency, this one had a strong relational component. Teachers selected students whom the teachers believed needed an adult role model to help them become more connected to school.

The irony in Brookfield's response to differentiation by pulling children out of the regular classroom and setting time aside for reading intervention is that many of the instructional strategies used in the regular classrooms during reading/language arts are strategies that have been found particularly effective with students who fail to flourish (Graham & Harris, 2000). Drawing connections, teaching vocabulary, teaching students to recognize text patterns and to use effective strategies for constructing meaning, enhancing students' metacognitive understanding, and embedding test preparation in regular instruction would be effective instructional approaches for all children that could indeed bring good and successful teaching into balance. Pulling children out of regular classroom instruction or spending time on interventions instead of social studies or science might very well have been doing more harm than good.

Constructing Self as Teacher: Caring About Students

Consistent with findings from numerous other studies (e.g., Darling-Hammond, 1997; Huberman, 1993; James, 2006), Brookfield teachers considered themselves caring professionals. Getting to know their students personally was important to them, so they were torn between accepting the district's stance that knowing the students' needs meant knowing their assessment data and their belief that the information they garnered through interacting with them was equally valuable. The time taken away from instruction because of testing was not, from the perspective of most of the teachers, worth the price of diminished relational roles with their students (Valli & Buese, 2007). This orientation to the test bothered the fourth-grade teachers so much that they said they no longer felt as though they were good teachers (May 17, 2005).

Brookfield teachers attributed this feeling to the number of pullouts from their classes, their lack of familiarity with the new reading curriculum, and the pressures of AYP. Mr. Wilson, the fifth-grade teacher who initiated the after-school mentoring program, was so upset with the demands and unrealistic expectations of NCLB that, after spending his entire teaching career at Brookfield, starting when he was a teaching intern, he resigned in favor of a position in a private school. Nonetheless, as a group, Brookfield teachers did not express the same level of frustration as teachers at the other two schools. Teachers, the support staff, and the principal and her intern all worked together to try to solve problems created by the pressures from the high-stakes state test. We suspect that the strong organizational and relational capacities at the school provided a level of support at Brookfield that teachers at the other two schools did not experience.

CHERRY RIDGE: TEACHING AS TARGETING STUDENT DEFICIENCIES

As the only one of the schools to have missed AYP, Cherry Ridge exhibited learning-dependent teaching more obviously than either of the other two schools. In contrast to Brookfield, Cherry Ridge embraced the recommended state curriculum that was closely aligned to the state test and restricted Stevenson's curriculum, which reflected disciplinary standards. Professional development maximized test-oriented training while minimizing pedagogy-oriented teacher learning. Because the category of inadequate progress was reading for special education students, these students were monitored the most closely, followed by ELL reading, which was on the borderline of inadequacy. But instruction of all students was affected by this emphasis on successful test-oriented teaching.

Classroom Instruction

Classroom instruction at the beginning of the year at Cherry Ridge showed little evidence of the learner-sensitive good teaching that was evident at Brookfield. In comparison to other Stevenson schools in our study, teachers were far more likely to pose low-order questions and activities during both mathematics and reading, and students were more likely to be completing routine exercises in mathematics. Teachers did not ask higher-order questions during reading or elaborate on the tasks they had posed in mathematics, as had Brookfield teachers. In both subject areas, teachers were more likely than either the larger sample or the other two case study schools to be engaged in management. Instruction in mathematics did focus on conceptual understanding more than the larger sample. Otherwise, the content focus in mathematics and reading was similar to that of the larger sample. During reading, teachers at Cherry Ridge used whole-class instruction more and Guided Reading less than did teachers at Hawthorne and Brookfield and in the larger sample. Except for the focus on conceptual understanding in mathematics, instruction at Cherry Ridge matched the characteristics of learning-dependent far more than learner-sensitive instruction.

Monitoring students frequently to guide instructional decisions is crucial in learning-dependent successful teaching. Accordingly, the school tested students regularly and targeted deficiency areas. The head of the data team, Carmen Ledwich, worked with teachers on interpreting test results and was pleased with the progress they were making in becoming data-based decision makers. A shortcoming to that approach, however, is that discrete skills and small, isolated bits of knowledge are the easiest to quickly assess. These became the targeted areas for instruction, as the description with which we opened this section would imply.

Interviews, field notes, and other materials gathered at the observations further characterize the learning-dependent goals that guided instruction at Cherry Ridge. Teachers prepared students for the state test by having them practice SCRs, including test accommodations for special education and ELL students. As test time approached, students were writing two or three times a week, so students would "know what is expected," even though they were turned off by the mere mention of writing SCRs (January 14, 2005). This instructional practice was pervasive in both reading classes and reading intervention classes, where pre-observation interviews with teachers and handouts from observed classes provided numerous examples of SCR prompts: "Write a summary using the story frame." "The little girl in the poem said, '. . . .' What do you think she meant by that?" "Explain whether or not *One Little Can* is a good title for this story." "What is this article mainly about?" "Identify the reason the author may have written this text." "Did the author make the sequence of steps easy to understand?" These questions were invariably followed with, "Support your answer with details from the text." And the texts were short, the length that they would be on the test.

At first glance, these prompts would appear to elicit the same types of metacognitive thinking that occurred at Brookfield. However, strictly following the format of the state test, the teachers did not embed SCR practice in instruction. Without the type of instructional scaffolding that Brookfield teachers provided, students at Cherry Ridge could be expected to struggle with these prompts. SCRs were written for narrative text, expository text, and poetry—but always on the 12 decontextualized reading strategies prescribed in the recommended state curriculum: for example, finding the main idea, predicting, and summarizing.

Ms. Hancock, the principal, regularly visited team planning meetings to remind teachers that students had problems with particular types of SCRs such as inferencing and identifying the narrator's point of view (February 23, 2005). Those were to be practiced most frequently, but unlike with SCR work at Brookfield, we saw no indication that teachers were helping students develop self-monitoring skills. This approach to writing about text was patterned and formulaic. Perhaps because teachers were themselves still unsure about how to word SCR questions and how to assess them for reading comprehension and not writing ability, they seemed reluctant to deviate from the strictly applied formula.

In mathematics instruction, teachers used SCRs to fulfill two purposes: test preparation and evidence of student writing. Teachers were required to assign students a writing grade in mathematics. They used SCRs to assign this grade. But, as seen in the previous chapter, teachers were not always clear about SCR expectations. Using SCRs to obtain writing grades might have added to the confusion since, on the state test, SCRs were used to determine comprehension in reading and mathematics, not writing ability. Indeed, it was perfectly acceptable on SCRs in mathematics for students to present equations or graphics rather than written explanations.

At Cherry Ridge, ELL students were particularly encouraged to use equations or graphics instead of words.

In addition to preparing students to answer SCR questions, Cherry Ridge teachers prepared them for multiple choice questions. They distributed a district handout titled "Strategies for Answering Multiple Choice Questions" and TerraNova's "Test-Taking Tips and Reminders for Reading/Language Arts." Unlike the metacognitive "5 Steps to a Better Answer" distributed at Brookfield, these "tips" did not aim to help students develop skills to monitor and improve their writing in response to text. Rather, their goal was simply "to get the right answer," offering such tips as look for clues, look at the picture, read the title, try each answer to see which makes the most sense.

As at the other two schools, classroom instruction at Cherry Ridge changed during January and February as the state test approached. The differences were most marked in mathematics instruction where teachers were more likely to be managing an activity than posing low-order questions and tasks, and students were more likely to be working on routine exercises than giving simple answers. Teachers and students were talking with one another about the content less than had occurred at other times of the year. Instruction focused substantially more on procedural proficiency and less on conceptual understanding, and the amount of time in which students were engaged in seat work was higher than for the rest of the year. In reading, the most marked difference was the decline in Guided Reading groups and the increase in whole-class instruction. These changes aside, Cherry Ridge was preparing students for the test all year long. The dramatic changes that occurred at Hawthorne were not evident at Cherry Ridge. Nonetheless, as test time approached, teachers expressed the tremendous pressure that they felt to cover content on the test, resulting in content incoherence.

During the intense (and tense) period leading up to the test, teachers were reminded to target students for whom they had hopes of moving from the basic to the proficiency category. As Chavaun Baker, a special education teacher, told the fifth-grade team as they listed mathematics topics that needed review: be sure to focus on students who are on the "bubble" (January 26, 2005). But teachers struggled to agree on how to focus on special education and ELL students in particular, as seen in this exchange between a regular and special education teacher:

> Vicky and Audrey went over the lesson plan for the next 2 weeks. Vicky was the leader in this exchange, telling Audrey what lessons she needed to concentrate on and giving her some instructional

strategies for carrying out the lessons. . . . The special ed teacher was advocating a slower approach; the classroom teacher was advocating a sort of brutal reality check. Pressures of performing on tests is certainly palpable. (November 12, 2004)

This tension between preparing students for the test by covering all the relevant KSAs and attending to background knowledge and development needs persisted throughout the year. In her exit interview, one of the experienced special education teachers shared her frustration:

When we're doing our math curriculum, you're teaching this [topic] this day. You're teaching this [another topic] the next day. You're teaching—and it goes so fast. Well, if they missed Monday, forget Friday, you know, they haven't gotten there. And it's just something that even with the support it may take 3 days to get that concept across but we don't have 3 days to teach it. (June 2, 2005)

This teacher was still feeling pressure to cover topics at the end of the school year even though the test had occurred in March. As the principal reminded teachers, the school year at Cherry Ridge now ran from March to March, that in June teachers must be preparing students for the test the following March.

Meeting the Instructional Needs of All Students

Unlike Brookfield and Hawthorne, which frequently used pullout strategies to differentiate, Cherry Ridge was using full inclusion in mathematics, regular reading, and reading intervention. Dissatisfied with the test scores and behavior of the past year's special education classes, the principal voluntarily implemented the state's inclusion initiative early as a way of dispersing those students in regular classrooms.

But differentiating through inclusion did not provide a simple solution to meeting students' learning needs in a coherent instructional environment. Simply figuring out how to use specialists as resources consumed huge amounts of joint planning time. According to the district, reading classes were to be divided into whole-class instruction and blocks of time during which children would rotate between Guided Reading in a small homogeneous group meeting with their teacher and individualized seat work. At one meeting we observed, the fourth-grade team leader had prepared a worksheet with all fourth-grade student names, their teacher of record, and columns that broke their reading block into four segments, with specialists' availability listed for each segment. Specialists would be moving from classroom to classroom to provide their own instruction to students who needed their help. The team then spent the next 50 minutes trying to determine how to group and schedule students so they could meet with the appropriate specialist. The final schedule relegated whole-classroom reading instruction where all students were working with their classroom teacher from 3:00 to 3:20, the very last segment of the day (October 20, 2005). As one observer noted during a fourth-grade class, "When the two teachers [ESOL/special ed] enter, the noise level rises considerably—very distracting. I don't know how the teacher can teach! Way too much noise for any one group to concentrate!" (October 12, 2004).

In mathematics classes, teachers generally did not have specialist assistance, so they used a different mode of differentiation: a 60/30 lesson format. Amy Odett, the math content coach, had persuaded the principal to extend the mathematics block to 90 minutes. Teachers could follow the normal 60-minute whole-group lesson with 30 minutes of differentiated instruction similar to the Guided Reading approach for students who needed review, were on level, or could be accelerated. Ms. Odett met regularly with classroom teachers to help them plan for this differentiation, and the principal monitored classes so that whole-group instruction would not encroach on differentiation time. Ms. Hancock believed strongly that students' mathematics scores would improve "if we do a better job with the 60/30, and if we help them [teachers] more with how you differentiate, and who does what in that 30 minutes" (June 20, 2005). The formal template for the mathematics period that teachers were expected to use was essential question, math warm-up (5 minutes), focus problem/lesson (25 minutes), individual practice/evaluation (25 minutes), closure (5 minutes), guided/independent practice (25 minutes) (October 6, 2004).

In a discussion with the fourth-grade team about the purpose of the "guided/independent" segment of the class, the principal asked one of the teachers to summarize his understanding from a prior meeting. His answer was, "Work with the students close to proficiency, focus on their strengths and weaknesses, and give them TLC [tender loving care]," making explicit the expectation to target those students who could move out of the basic level on the state test (January 14, 2005). Elaborating on "TLC," the principal said that the idea was to help students develop confidence that they could do the work. She indicated that teachers should still see all students, but that they could adjust times to give more to those who were close to proficiency. The certified teachers were to give attention to the close-to-proficient students; paraeducators could work with others.

New teachers found the 60/30 format hard to organize and manage, having to plan not only their central 60-minute mathematics lesson, but also a differentiated 30-minute follow-up. They often felt as though they had not adequately covered the lesson in the 60-minute period, when they had to stop and shift content focus—going back to "old" content that students had not mastered. This difficulty shows up in time-sampling data, where, as we have already indicated, Cherry Ridge teachers spent considerably more time during their mathematics lessons managing activities and materials than their Brookfield and Hawthorne counterparts (28% versus 18% and 19%) and where Cherry Ridge students used up a lot of learning time in management tasks (25% versus 7% and 12%). Teachers' difficulties with the 60/30 format might also account for the fact that our time-sampling data show less differentiation than would be expected, only 7%. Teachers apparently did not always adhere to the 60/30 directive even though the principal frequently monitored their classes.

Wasted instructional time also occurred for the majority of students during lessons when classroom teachers practiced accommodations with individuals or small groups. For students to qualify for a particular accommodation, they had to receive it at least 80% of class time. This requirement created a dilemma for classroom teachers. On the one hand, they did not always have the resources to provide these accommodations, which often had to be given individually. In schools with pullout programs, the ESOL or special education teacher would have provided the practice. On the other hand, if students had not practiced accommodations during class time, they could not be accommodated on the test. This increased the possibility that the student would not pass the test and the danger that the school would fail to meet its proficiency targets for the special education and ESOL cells. For example, if a student had a "read aloud" accommodation, the teacher would read the passage or the word problem to the student. Sometimes teachers could read a passage to a small group. But a writing accommodation required the teacher (or classroom assistant) to sit with the student and act as scribe. In efforts to simulate the testing environment, teachers would not engage in any coaching or instruction while working with students during test-practice time.

These examples of brief notations, written by an observer of Barry Mott's fourth-grade regular reading class, describe the interactions between two students and Mr. Mott as he provided writing accommodations:

- The student is an IEP student who is dictating his answer directly to the teacher—this is an accommodation that he is allowed to have for [the state test]. I do not have an item that corresponds to this particular interaction between teacher and student.
- An IEP student with allowances for accommodations has been now thinking about giving his answer to the teacher for a while—

because the teacher is taking down the dictation, he cannot help him formulate his answers (under testing stipulations).

- Again, an IEP student is dictating to teacher her answer, and teacher is writing it down.
- Still same IEP since last 3-minute episode—she is thinking about her response and the teacher is waiting for her response so he can write it down. (January 13, 2005)

While the teacher worked with these students one by one, the rest of the class worked independently in preparation for the state test, assisted only by a paraeducator.

Cherry Ridge was the only school where we saw classroom teachers doing accommodations during regular reading instruction. Indeed, the observer could find no item in the time-sampling protocol, which included such items as posing problems, listening, and responding to students, that matched Mr. Mott's actions. Even though the research team had spent a year developing the protocol with the assistance of district teachers, no one foresaw this type of "test accommodation" practice occurring during class time. The closest item on the protocol to capture this teacher activity, and, we would argue, an appropriate one, is "no obvious instruction or management." As one special educator said to us, it's fine to accommodate, but it would be nice to spend the time teaching students how to read on their own.

Constructing Self as Teacher: Feeling Stress

Teaching was clearly a stressful occupation for teachers at Cherry Ridge, with one teacher referring to it as "the dark place." Reflective field notes and interviews were filled with comments about teachers' stress levels, such as, "As union rep, [Carmen] gets a lot of teachers coming to her about how stressed out they are. She's had four or five teachers come to her crying, saying that they don't even like teaching any more" (October 21, 2004). This stress was directly associated with AYP and administrative actions related to AYP. As Barry Mott said, in addition to new curriculum, inclusion, and other initiatives, "You have the AYP floating in the back of your head, you have to make AYP, otherwise we have another intervention, and what's that going to make life like? . . . It's stressful" (May 25, 2005).

The stress was so palpable that one of us felt compelled to step out of her researcher role to reassure a first-year teacher who, leaving a planning meeting in tears, said she did not know if she could keep doing this for another year. Linked as they are to accountability policies, these increased levels of stress and anxiety are clearly, as others have argued, the result of workplace cultures, not psychological characteristics of teachers (Cohen & Kottkamp, 1993; Hargreaves, 1994). Not surprisingly, the teacher turnover rate at Cherry Ridge was 60–70% a year, one of the highest in the district. Julia Hancock had not hired a tenured teacher in years and said that once teachers received tenure they tended to move to less stressful school environments.

CONCLUSION

Few would argue with the goal of NCLB to ensure "the access of children to effective, scientifically based instructional strategies and challenging academic content." There is much to be commended in the emerging, data-based, decision-making orientation to teaching. As numerous studies have shown, students cannot learn what they are not taught. The simple opportunity to learn subject matter has become, in and of itself, a key component of research on teaching (Cohen & Hill, 2000; Porter, 1989; Spillane & Jennings, 1997). Furthermore, there is widespread agreement that schools have not served well those children who are most disadvantaged by reason of socioeconomic, linguistic, or racial status. So disaggregating student achievement data on these criteria in order to target students' needs seems to be compensating for years of educational neglect.

Responding to student needs by differentiating instruction is recommended throughout virtually all the research on student diversity (Dilworth & Brown, 2001; Gersten, Baker, & Pugach, 2001; Mercado, 2001). Participating teachers in this study talked about and valued opportunities to develop a common understanding of curriculum expectations, ways to assess student understandings, and differentiated instruction. In this chapter, we examined what actually occurred as teachers attempted to fulfill the charge of NCLB: providing every child access to effective instructional strategies, challenging content, and high expectations.

But operationally defining teaching as aligning curriculum and assessments, targeting student needs, and differentiating has its limitations as well. As critics have noted, alignment is only as good as the assessment (Firestone, Mayrowetz, & Fairman, 1998). The assessment that so strongly influenced Hawthorne, Brookfield, and Cherry Ridge was the state test, a response to the accountability provisions of NCLB. And the state test assessed skills in reading and mathematics that could be measured easily by fill-in-the-bubble items and short constructed responses. The nature of the test affected teachers' thinking about the characteristics of effective teaching, classroom experiences for teachers and students, and teachers' personal images of what it means to be a good teacher. Ironically, the characteristics of this test and the pressures that the three schools felt to prepare their students to perform well seemed to work against ensuring children's access to "scientifically based instructional strategies and challenging academic content" as defined by professional organizations in mathematics and reading.

Within these general observations were important differences among the three schools. Lacking in both institutional and relational support, the teachers at Hawthorne seem to have been most negatively affected by assessment and accountability policies. Unable to find a balance between good and successful teaching, they shifted abruptly from instruction that followed the Stevenson curriculum and therefore showed some characteristics of *good* teaching, to instruction that followed the recommended state curriculum, which was more closely aligned to the state test, and therefore showed some characteristics of *successful* teaching. Indeed the pervasive test preparation caused stress and distress among teachers and students alike.

Brookfield teachers worked in a very different context, one that provided both institutional and relational support. Of the three school staffs, Brookfield teachers were able to react to assessment and accountability policies in ways that achieved a reasonable balance between good and successful teaching. Working together, they found approaches to test preparation that also exemplified good teaching. While Brookfield teachers acknowledged the importance of the state test, they also valued outcomes that demonstrated students' reactions to academic content, such as a love of mathematics or reading. We were more likely to see good teaching at this school that resisted using the state test as the only measure of success.

Teachers at Cherry Ridge neither abruptly changed their instruction as the test approached nor found a balance between good and successful teaching. Instead, their teaching was pointed toward the state test from the beginning of the year and is best characterized as learning-dependent teaching. Using the format of the state test as a guide, teaching tended to become formulaic, rather than ensuring access of children to a wide range of "effective, scientifically based instructional strategies" or "challenging academic content." The policy environment of assessment and accountability seemed to make improving teaching at Cherry Ridge and the conditions for improving teaching even more difficult. Because AYP was determined by the percentage of students in the proficiency category, NCLB promoted teaching practices that would leave some children even further behind. "Bubble" students were to receive special attention, not those who were functioning toward the bottom of the basic category.

Perhaps the most serious problem for all three schools was finding an effective approach for differentiating instruction so that all children would be ensured access to quality instruction. Pullout programs at Hawthorne and Brookfield decreased curricular and instructional coherence, disrupted classroom instruction, and interfered with teachers' ability to know their students well enough to design effective instruction for them or even to assign grades. Even more troubling, the pullout programs tended to be rigidly structured and unresponsive to the individual needs of particular children. Cherry Ridge used full inclusion, bringing specialists into classrooms to address the needs of individual children rather than having the children pulled out. But this approach also disrupted classroom instruction, often did not lead to differentiated instruction to meet student needs, and created time-consuming scheduling problems. Even with the expending of substantial resources and the sincere desire of teachers and specialists at all three schools to meet the needs of students who were failing to flourish, we frequently saw little evidence that the attempts to differentiate were indeed meeting the needs of individual children. The lofty goal of leaving no child behind may well be eroded by the very policies enacted to reach this goal.

CHAPTER 7

Weathering High-Stakes Accountability

Holding schools, local educational agencies, and States accountable for
improving the academic achievement of all students . . .
                                          —No Child Left Behind Act

AS THE PRECEDING chapters indicate, there are good reasons to question
the wisdom of high-stakes accountability policies. In the three schools
that we studied, policies associated with No Child Left Behind (NCLB)
distorted the official curriculum, undermined instruction, and created a
test-driven culture that transformed school life in troubling ways. Although each of the schools responded differently to the challenges posed
by high-stakes accountability, life at each school became increasingly
centered on testing and test results, especially as the school year approached the month for the annual state assessments. If this greater
focus brought with it greater capacity to increase student learning, these
intensified efforts to raise test scores would be laudable. However, during the year that we studied the three schools, we saw little evidence
that increased testing prompted students and teachers to deeply engage
subject matter. On the contrary, and as we described in the preceding
chapters, instruction became increasingly focused on narrow, sometimes
disjointed tasks aligned with the fill-in-the-bubble and short-constructed-
response items that characterized the assessments.

A question that immediately arises is whether this is a local phenomenon or a phenomenon of broader national interest. We think the latter
is the case, particularly in schools that serve similar student populations—
racially diverse schools with half or more of their students qualifying for
free and reduced-price meals service (FARMS) and roughly one quarter
of their students being English Language Learners (ELL). Moreover, the
schools that we observed resided in what can only be called a relatively
resource-rich school district with a history of standards-based reform. Staff-
to-student ratios were relatively low (8:1) and class sizes ranged between

15 and 20 students in classrooms where students were taught reading and mathematics. In other words, the schools that we observed could be thought of as "critical case studies" (Patton, 1990) of high-stakes account-ability. They provide a portrait of the potentially harmful effects of high-stakes testing in schools with relatively high levels of resources and a tradition of standards-based reform. Based on this logic, schools with fewer resources and weaker traditions would be even more vulnerable to the potentially corrosive power of high-stakes testing. What we saw may be only the tip of the iceberg.

Other studies have also documented the transformation of school life associated with high-stakes accountability, providing further proof that what we observed in Hawthorne, Brookfield, and Cherry Ridge is not unique. Studies of individual schools, particularly schools that serve his-torically disadvantaged student populations, describe how testing has be-come the central focus of school life (Perlstein, 2007; Sunderman et al., 2004), and, at times, has weakened the integrity of teaching as a profes-sion (Nichols & Berliner, 2007; Sunderman et al., 2005). National and state studies of how schools are responding to the challenges of the high-stakes testing provisions in NCLB report how schools have narrowed the curriculum (Au, 2007; Bailey et al., 2006; Center on Education Policy, 2007b) and increased practices typically referred to as "teaching to the test" (Firestone, Schorr, & Monfils, 2004; Sunderman et al., 2005), all in an effort to boost test scores and meet annual yearly progress (AYP) goals. The re-sults of these studies and our own suggest that the challenges of high-stakes testing pose similar constraints and temptations for elementary schools, even elementary schools with substantial access to resources and tradi-tions of standards-based reform.

Proponents of high-stakes testing may still object to our bleak inter-pretation of findings. Even if life in schools is being transformed by high-stakes testing and policies such as those of NCLB, isn't that a positive outcome if it leads to higher levels of achievement, particularly for his-torically disadvantaged students? Anecdotal evidence suggests that some low-income elementary schools have made substantial gains in school performance during the past 5 years, and these success stories have been used as evidence by those who support an expansion of NCLB (Spellings, 2007). There is also evidence, albeit modest, that the implementation of NCLB has resulted in increases in achievement scores for students and decreases in the achievement gap in at least nine states for which the Center on Education Policy (2007a) was able to compare test scores before and after the implementation of NCLB. Our argument, however, is that even if some schools have taken actions that increased test scores, there is still the question of how those actions affect other desirable outcomes in schools, including classroom climate, curriculum coherence, teacher professionalism, and opportunities to engage students deeply in subject matter. It is quite possible that specific actions that raise test scores in elementary schools have detrimental effects for the quality of teaching and learning in those same schools.

Opponents of high-stakes accountability may embrace our interpretation of findings as proof that the assumptions of high-stakes accountability are deeply flawed and policies such as those of NCLB should be abandoned (Nichols & Berliner, 2007; Noddings, 2007). Although we share the concerns and sentiments of many of these critics, it is doubtful that Congress will revert to earlier policies that focused on targeting resources to schools that serve low-income families, at least not without including provisions aimed at ensuring accountability through mandatory testing. As we write this book, Congress debates the next reauthorization of the Elementary and Secondary Education Act of 1965 (ESEA). The administration's plan would extend aspects of NCLB to high schools, increase choice options for parents, and give local authorities additional power to take control of troubled schools (Spellings, 2007). Other recommendations call for more assistance for schools to develop comprehensive improvement plans, statewide data systems capable of tracking cohorts of students over time, better professional development opportunities, increased expectations for student performance, greater flexibility in forms of assessment, and greater support for research (Center on Education Policy, 2007c; Fulton, 2007, September). There is little serious discussion of ending NCLB or deviating from forms of accountability that require testing and some demonstration of equitable outcomes for students.

Moreover, there are aspects of high-stakes accountability policies that resonate with educators, even when they have reservations about how the policies are being implemented and the manner in which high-stakes testing has become a central focus of school life. As Greta Shephard, the Hawthorne math coach, remarked, "Not that I love NCLB, but I . . . definitely think that . . . it makes people aware of all students." Policymakers and educators have attempted to enhance the educational opportunities afforded historically disadvantaged children since the middle of the 1900s, but our success in doing so has been limited. Even though schools should not be made the scapegoat for failures in broader social and economic policies (Rothstein, 2004), acknowledging this fact does not make schools unaccountable for the educational failures of students. Rather, schools, along with other social and democratic institutions, share responsibility for the inequalities that exist in our society and the creation of more equitable educational outcomes for children (Elmore, 2005). As challenging as high-stakes accountability policies can be, they do address a fundamental policy issue and a moral responsibility acknowledged by many teachers.

In our opinion, the immediate issue is how to integrate legitimate concerns about accountability with the desire for classroom instruction that promotes deep understanding and excellence in education, not just for privileged populations of students but also for students who have been poorly served by the nation's public schools. As we argued in the prior chapters, even under the best of circumstances, in schools with faculty demonstrating a strong commitment to learner-centered pedagogy (Alexander & Murphy, 1998; Fenstermacher & Richardson, 2005), the pressure to teach to the test is almost overwhelming. Where these commitments are not deeply rooted in the collective life of students, teachers, and administrators, there is reason to believe that merely raising test scores will become the mantra for schools, regardless of the consequences for teaching and learning. Addressing this issue requires two considerations. First, how is it possible to safeguard the positive pedagogical reforms that have been made in some schools while implementing accountability measures required by districts, states, and the federal government, and, second, how can accountability measures be structured in such a way that they promote desirable forms of teaching and learning in schools rather than the minimal focus on test scores?

To prevent the erosion of high-quality teaching and learning, standards-based curriculum reforms, especially those advocated by professional associations, need to be well rooted at the school and district levels. By most accounts, these reforms are only tentatively rooted, making them especially vulnerable to the eroding effects of test-driven mandates. The more rooted these reforms are, the more likely it is that they will be able to survive the pressures of high-stakes accountability and perhaps even transform these pressures into positive environments for students. As we saw, teachers at Brookfield were better able to weather the assessment storm than those at Cherry Ridge and Hawthorne. With Brookfield's greater relational and organizational capacity, teachers were able to maintain a sense of professional community while addressing the demands of district, state, and federal mandates. They were better able to preserve high-quality teaching in the current climate of high-stakes accountability without becoming barren landscapes of teaching and learning.[1]

The second part of the question urges a consideration of the forms of accountability that encourage deep engagement in subject matter and equitable outcomes for students. Responding to this part of the question requires considerably more speculation because it was not directly investigated as part of the study. Nonetheless, we believe that there are some modest recommendations that might be drawn from the study and the existing literature. These recommendations urge policymakers to consider not only performance-based forms of accountability but professional-based forms of accountability; to create more flexibility in the range and types of formative assessments used to monitor student performance; and to support more research into how students, teachers, and educational leaders respond to high-stakes accountability policies. We summarize first what we consider to be key findings gleaned from the study and then outline a series of recommendations for school leaders, district administrators, and state and national policymakers.

KEY FINDINGS

Our case studies of Hawthorne, Brookfield, and Cherry Ridge provide insights into how schools are responding to the challenges of high-stakes accountability. In examining those responses across the different dimensions of school life presented in the previous chapters, five themes emerge: high-stakes testing has a corrosive power, motivation is not enough, more data are not always helpful, leadership matters, and there is an important role for capacity in determining how schools respond to high-stakes testing. We also speculate about what factors might explain differences between the three schools in their profiles of capacity.

Corrosive Power of High-Stakes Testing

Principals and teachers are faced with an enormous challenge to raise student achievement in a short period of time. In states that set relatively high proficiency levels, the goal of achieving proficiency for all students by 2014 can be daunting. One possibility is that schools simply need more time to work out the bugs and implement reforms more effectively. The year that we observed Hawthorne, Brookfield, and Cherry Ridge was only the 3rd year after NCLB had been signed into law. Although all the schools had experience with high-stake testing—the state's former accountability program required annual testing and sanctions for schools that failed to meet performance standards—teachers and principals had to adjust to a new state curriculum, new district curricula in reading and mathematics, and new state assessments. With time and effective professional development, we might anticipate that teachers and administrators would do a better job of identifying effective instructional practices, aligning the local curriculum with the state's assessed curriculum, and developing organizational routines to minimize the demands of testing.

Although we think that some of the story told in the preceding chapters has to do with implementation and time, we do not believe that this is all or even the major explanation for what we observed. Schools are being asked to accomplish unprecedented gains in achievement, and they are being asked to do so within a limited time frame. To address these pressures, schools do what is expedient—narrow the curriculum, group students by ability, teach to the test, and reorganize school activities around the requirements of testing. While these activities may result in higher test scores, they do not necessarily result in more meaningful or desirable forms of learning. When the drumbeat for higher test scores is combined with serious consequences for teachers and administrators, there is tremendous pressure on schools to streamline instruction and curriculum to focus more school resources on raising student test scores. In the three schools that we observed, the pressure to raise test scores and meet AYP became corrosive, especially as the date for the state assessments approached.

Even at Brookfield, the school with the greatest capacity to address the challenges of high-stakes accountability, there was substantial pressure to distort the curriculum and restructure school life to meet the demands of testing. Testing issues competed with pedagogical issues on meeting agendas, professional development topics leaned toward content thought to be included on the state assessments, and the media center was unavailable during part of the year to accommodate the demands of the district's diagnostic testing regime. Students were reshuffled, at least temporarily, into homogeneous groups for the purpose of participating in reading interventions, and students most at risk of failing to meet proficiency were pulled out of classes for testing and additional instruction. Teachers at Brookfield resisted these pressures by sustaining pedagogically oriented professional development activities, incorporating pedagogical content into test-taking instruction, limiting pullouts, and redesigning reading interventions so that students could remain with their homeroom teachers, but they felt these pressures nonetheless. Teachers at Hawthorne and Cherry Ridge were less successful in preventing the requirements of high-stakes testing from supplanting the goal of improving pedagogy.

Motivation Is Not Enough

A fundamental assumption of high-stakes accountability is that a primary problem with America's public schools is a lack of will. Teachers supposedly have low expectations for their students, particularly historically disadvantaged students. Teachers fail to present rigorous materials and tasks to their students, fail to press students to develop a deeper understanding of materials or to achieve at higher levels, and generally spend too little classroom time devoted to "scientifically based" instruction. From this perspective, low achievement is primarily a problem of commitment. High-stakes accountability practices are meant to expose schools where a low commitment to learning, on the part of both adults and children, undermines education. Any doubts about the ability of schools to meet the achievement standards set forth by NCLB are seen as evidence of weak commitment or, worse, as evidence of what proponents of NCLB characterize as the "subtle bigotry of low expectations" (see Noddings, 2007, for a discussion of the language used to curtail critiques of NCLB). Our observations suggest that this is a simplistic and potentially destructive perspective on how to improve teaching and learning in America's public schools.

Although we do not deny that low teacher commitment and discriminatory practices exist in American schools, these phenomena did not characterize the schools that we studied. For the most part, teachers took seriously the challenges of high-stakes accountability and sought to implement policy enactments successfully and positively for their students—often working beyond "normal" working hours, tutoring students, developing training materials, and organizing data. We discovered little evidence of "sloth" or "an absence of will" that seems to characterize contemporary indictments of public education. Teachers often appeared overwhelmed by the demands of teaching coupled with the demands of implementing new testing regimes, newly aligned curricula, and additional policies designed to promote effective school improvement. Nonetheless, even when teachers expressed their frustration with the multiple demands made on the school day, most continued to demonstrate a commitment to their school, colleagues, and students.

What makes this perspective potentially dangerous is that it can undermine a teacher's traditional commitment to the well-being of the *whole* student—that is, it can distort what it means to be a highly motivated professional committed to educating children. Rather than helping teachers feel responsible for all aspects of a student's development, high-stakes testing encourages teachers only to focus on whether students meet the currently established proficiency standards on the state assessments and, even then, only in reading and mathematics. The emphasis on reaching accountability goals—and the sanctions associated with even doubting those goals—can stifle teachers concerns for how specific practices might harm students. Forcing students to do practice tests over and over again, even if the practice stifles their desire to be in school, is "OK" if it helps the school achieve AYP. From the perspective of NCLB, Cherry Ridge's principal's reaction to language-minority parents who take their students out of school or keep them home when they have a headache is evidence of a highly motivated and committed administrator, because she recognizes that these actions could threaten the school's ability to meet AYP. The danger of focusing exclusively on raising test results is captured well by a comment made by Heather Nichols, the reading specialist at Hawthorne, "I don't always know them [the students] by face; I know them by data."

More Data Do Not Always Help

Another assumption underlying high-stakes accountability and NCLB is that more data will help teachers design more effective instructional practices that pinpoint students' misconceptions and instructional needs. As we saw in Chapter 4, the district sought to use state assessments and a new regimen of diagnostic tests to develop a more extensive data set on student knowledge, skills, and instructional needs. In all but 4 months of the school year, half or more of the students at Hawthorne, Brookfield, and Cherry Ridge were taking either district- or state-mandated tests. But these activities were relatively unsuccessful as judged by the extent to which teachers were able to use test results to inform instruction. Even though Stevenson School District invested in professional development designed to help teachers understand testing results, teachers were uncertain about how to use these data to improve teaching and learning. As a special education teacher at Hawthorne noted, "They did the testing, but then it was difficult to really use any of the data or information. . . . They're [the students] taking so many tests but what do we actually see from any of that? Not enough."

Developing a coherent set of assessment practices is far more difficult than often is portrayed by proponents of NCLB, even in schools with substantial resources. Data from diagnostic tests are only loosely linked to the state assessments—that is, it is not easy to determine how weaknesses or strengths on one test correspond to weaknesses or strengths on another test. Even if data identify a weakness in a comparable tested area, these test results do not identify what teachers should do to improve the skill set associated with an area of weakness. Under the best of conditions, assessment data help to identify what students know and can and cannot do; assessment data are rarely prescriptive. Although formative assessment are a fundamental component of what has been described as effective, quality teaching (Black & Wiliam, 1998a, 1998b; Shepard, 2001), they are effective only to the extent that they are used wisely. Teachers still need to make professional judgments about how to build on students' prior knowledge to facilitate a deeper understanding of content and the development of more complex cognitive skills.

Under some circumstances, more data may also be detrimental. In all three schools, the demand for testing, including the district's mandatory diagnostic testing, distracted resources from classroom teaching and professional development focused on improving pedagogy. Teachers were appreciative of being able to review test results for individual students, but they often did not know how to interpret the data or use it to develop more effective instructional practices. Some of this inability might be explained as a failure in professional development or a failure in selecting tests that are clearly aligned with the state assessments, but an equally legitimate observation is that NCLB places too much trust in "informative" test results and too little in the professional expertise required to interpret test results. When these aspects of data-based decision making are not clearly understood, schools and district are tempted simply to provide teachers with more and more data about student performance. Nonetheless, as we saw in the three schools that we studied, data about student performance is neither obviously prescriptive nor easily used by teachers to design new instructional programs. Formative assessments can be a powerful pedagogical tool, but only if teachers know how to use data to identify students' misconceptions, link those misconceptions to the curriculum, and design instruction that promotes desirable forms of learning.

Leadership Matters

A fourth finding from our observations and interviews is that leadership matters. Leadership was severely impaired or even absent at times at Hawthorne. Although Elaine Everett, the principal at Hawthorne, created leadership structures similar to those at the other two schools, these structures failed to function either efficiently or effectively. As the school calendar approached March, the month for the mandated state assessments, the consequences of weak leadership were increasingly apparent. Ms. Everett, who sought to adopt a strategy used by another school in the district to raise test scores, required teachers to suspend the district's official curriculum and cover content supposedly on the state assessment. The result was a frenzied instructional pace with disjointed lessons focused primarily on guaranteeing coverage. As one teacher described the effort, "It was teach and go, teach and go, teach and go. Mastery did not matter, creativity did not matter, thinking did not matter." Although Hawthorne made AYP in 2005, it failed to do so in 2006 for its special education population.

At Brookfield and Cherry Ridge, leadership was strong, albeit in different ways. At Brookfield, Liz Moore led by fostering leadership in others. She respected and trusted her teachers and she distributed leadership responsibilities widely throughout the school. Although the ultimate responsibility for the school's success rested with her, she saw her teachers as resources and collaborators in addressing the challenges of high-stakes

accountability and other policy mandates. During the year that we observed the school, Ms. Moore was assigned a principal intern, Luke Comer,
who took over the principal role during most of the spring. As part of the
internship, Ms. Moore was given assignments in the central office, leaving her teachers and Mr. Comer to deal with the pressures associated with
preparing for the state assessments. Although teachers at Brookfield
struggled to sustain their focus on improving pedagogy and maintaining
the richness of the district's curriculum, they were more successful at
doing so than teachers at any of the other schools. Despite the absence
of Ms. Moore, her leadership style was so deeply ingrained in the school's
culture that her absence did not seriously threaten the school's success.
In the spring of 2005, Brookfield made AYP in all areas, as it had done in
the past.

At Cherry Ridge, Julia Hancock relied heavily on a bureaucratic model
of leadership. She delegated but retained control over the school's agenda,
priorities, and decision making. She clearly stated that getting off the state
school improvement list was the school's primary goal, and she dedicated
most of the school's resources toward doing so. She relied little on the
professional judgment of her teachers and did little to create the type of
collaborative structures that we observed in Brookfield. From the beginning to the end of the school year, Ms. Hancock directed her teachers to
focus on preparing for the state assessments. Specialists worked with teachers to plot timelines and strategies for addressing test content in lessons.
As a result, there was no indication of chaotic or frenzied activity as the
date for the state assessments approached, only a relentless emphasis on
reading and mathematics instruction designed to raise test scores. Cherry
Ridge made AYP that spring and achieved its goal of being removed from
the state improvement list in June of 2005, but not without severely restricting the curriculum, embracing drill-and-practice instructional routines, and creating a stressful environment for teachers and students.

The Important Role of Capacity

One of the most fundamental observations that we made about the three
schools is that school capacity determines how schools respond to the
challenges of high-stakes testing. Brookfield clearly weathered the storm
of high-stakes testing better than Hawthorne or Cherry Ridge, though even
here there were signs that even pragmatic responses sometimes created
conflicts between teachers' desires to sustain a professional community
and teachers' desires to make AYP. Nonetheless, with its greater organizational and relational capacity, Brookfield was better able to sustain rigorous pedagogical practices, implement the district's curriculum, and

respond to the challenges of test-driven mandates than the other two schools. A primary difference was that Brookfield had a strong collective sense of what constituted quality teaching. Teachers felt professionally accountable for not only the quality of instruction in their own classrooms but also the quality of instruction in classrooms throughout the school. This provided Brookfield with additional resources that could be used to sustain a pedagogical focus, at the same time that teachers sought ways to prepare students for the state assessment. Although there were disagreements at Brookfield, including about priorities and practices, teachers worked together to solve problems and sustain their image of a professional community.

Cherry Ridge had greater capacity than Hawthorne, but its capacity was strongly centered in the school's bureaucratic structures. The bureaucratic structure of the school allowed the principal to deploy resources to enhance the effectiveness of organizational practices; increase efficiencies in preparing students for the assessment; and generally focus the entire school's efforts, from the beginning of the school year to the end, on attaining AYP. While Cherry Ridge was high on organizational capacity, higher than Brookfield, it developed this capacity at the expense of the school's relational capacity. Whereas in Brookfield accountability was derived from the relational ties that defined the school as a professional community, in Cherry Ridge accountability was derived from the hierarchical structures that specified and monitored teacher behaviors. There were very few opportunities for teachers to collaborate on mutually identified problems or to gain confidence in the professional judgment of their colleagues. Although these bureaucratic structures proved useful in raising test scores, they restricted the capacity of teachers to work jointly on more complex tasks, such as how to extend student test-taking competencies to a deeper understanding of content.

Hawthorne lacked both organizational and relational capacity. Unless faced with a crisis, responses to external policy mandates were sporadic and largely ineffective. Although teachers worked in teams, served on committees, and participated together in professional development activities, there was modest collaboration. Teachers exercised their professional judgment, but typically in the privacy of their own classroom. We observed few efforts to develop systematically either the organizational or the relational capacities of the school. Even though the school made AYP the spring of 2005, it did so at great cost to teachers and students. As pressures mounted to prepare students for the state assessments, the school had neither the organizational nor the relational capacity required to develop a systematic, coherent plan that contained some pedagogical value. Rather, from January to March, life at Hawthorne was a chaotic "cramming for the test." Students were forced to practice assessment-like items under assessment-like conditions, sometimes for as long as 3 hours without a break. Teacher morale declined significantly and student behavior became more problematic. Despite the relatively rich school district in which Hawthorne was located, the school could not make efficient use of these resources because it lacked the capacity to do so.

Differences in Capacity Profiles

Although there are many anecdotal stories about elementary schools that have made substantial increases in achievement scores, there are very few in-depth studies of how schools develop relational and organizational capacity within the context of high-stakes testing. Elaine Everett had been the principal at Hawthorne for 6 years, whereas Liz Moore had been principal at Brookfield for 15 years and Julia Hancock had been principal at Cherry Ridge for 20 years. Greater tenure of the principals at Brookfield and Cherry Ridge may have provided them with more of an opportunity to develop capacity at their respective schools. Additional time, though, may not guarantee that schools will be able to develop either the organizational or relational capacities needed to weather the demands of high-stakes testing. For schools like Hawthorne that lack these resources, even beginning the process of building school capacity can be difficult, especially when teachers feel the high-stakes pressure associated with preparing students for the state assessments. Without external expertise to help schools organize more effectively and break the cycle of crisis management, schools like Hawthorne will continue to "cram for the test" to meet AYP.

Although Ms. Moore and Ms. Hancock had longer tenures at their school than Ms. Everett, their schools had two very different profiles. Brookfield was high on both organizational and relational capacities, while Cherry Ridge was high on organizational capacity and low on relational capacity. These profiles mirror the leadership styles of the two principals. Ms. Moore relied heavily on the professional judgment of her teachers, distributed leadership responsibilities broadly, and encouraged collaboration and mutual problem solving. These activities built both relational and organizational capacities at the school. Ms. Hancock, on the other hand, made clear that developing interpersonal relations with her faculty was neither a strength nor a priority for her. She felt more comfortable leading through bureaucratic structures that delegated responsibilities and dictated instructional priorities. Principals like Ms. Hancock may find developing relational capacities difficult without external expertise and guidance.

Besides leadership style, context may also play an important role in the types of capacity developed at schools. Brookfield was the smallest of the three schools that we studied. It also had a lower student mobility rate and less teacher turnover. All three of these factors may have made Ms. Moore's work in building and sustaining relational capacity easier. Communitarian forms of organization, such as the professional community that we observed at Brookfield, are more likely to occur in smaller schools than larger schools and in schools with stable memberships than unstable memberships (Bryk & Schneider, 2002; Rosenholtz, 1991). The small school structure, along with a stable membership, provides greater opportunities for teachers and families to develop social bonds and norms of interaction conducive to cooperation, collaboration, and mutual trust. Where these opportunities do not exist, school leadership may have more difficulty building and sustaining relational capacity.

RECOMMENDATIONS

These findings provide some insights about how elementary schools are responding to the challenges of high-stakes accountability policies. The major challenge that we observed was for schools to sustain or develop sound pedagogical practices while addressing the demands of high-stakes testing. In Hawthorne and Cherry Ridge, the demands of testing overwhelmed school life. Only in Brookfield were teachers able to prevent the demands of testing from subverting their interest in providing students with a rich and rigorous learning environment. Safeguarding pedagogy from the pressures of high-stakes testing requires recognition that even when schools successfully meet AYP, doing so may have detrimental effects on school life and other desirable outcomes for students.

To that end we present a series of recommendations, focusing first on the school and district and then on state and federal policymakers. These recommendations urge policymakers to consider not only performance-based forms of accountability but professional-based forms of accountability, to create more flexibility in the range and types of formative assessments used to monitor student performance, and to support more research about how students, teachers, and educational leaders respond to the challenges of high-stakes accountability policies.

School and District

A central challenge facing schools is how to sustain and develop pedagogical reforms at the same time that schools prepare students for high-stakes tests.

In the three schools that we observed, school capacity determined how well schools addressed this challenge. Districts can assist schools in building capacity by supporting school leadership, creating a favorable organizational context for capacity building, promoting comprehensive professional development, facilitating effective assessment practices, and ensuring a coherent policy environment.

Strong leadership. Leadership played a pivotal role in how each school responded to the challenges of high-stakes testing. Although bureaucratic styles of leadership can focus available resources on preparing students for the assessments, as well as promote sound and effective organizational practices, a more collaborative style of leadership is often required to create professional communities focused on pedagogical improvement (Rosenholtz, 1991). Districts can assist schools in maintaining a pedagogical focus despite the corrosive power of high-stakes testing by selecting principals who have strong pedagogical skills themselves, value collaboration, and understand organizational principles. Where principals with strong leadership skills feel uncomfortable with either the organizational or relational dimensions of their role, districts should consider assigning other administrators capable of complementing the principal's skill set. The overall goal for the district should be to provide every school with a leadership team that understands the importance of building *both* organizational and relational capacities and is capable of doing so. Because there is always a limited pool of potential leaders skilled at capacity building, districts should give priority to those schools that serve the most challenging student populations and are at the greatest risk of failing to meet AYP.

Favorable context. The Stevenson School District sought to provide a favorable context for schools that served large numbers of low-income students by hiring additional staff, reducing class size, and providing substantial opportunities for professional development. Although these actions did not guarantee success, as seen in the case of Hawthorne, they did provide a favorable context for capacity building, one that Brookfield and Cherry Ridge took advantage of, albeit in different ways. Other factors that could create a favorable context for capacity building are exploring ways of creating smaller elementary schools, where necessary; ensuring greater stability in teacher assignments; and providing a school's leadership team with sufficient time to invest in and develop school capacity. Districts also could provide incentives for teachers with strong pedagogical skills to work at schools most at risk of not making AYP. Strong teachers, when combined with a strong leadership team, offer the strongest defense against the pressures of testing overwhelming good pedagogy.

Comprehensive professional development. Professional development activities are a primary mechanism for building capacity in schools, but, as explained in Chapter 5, the provision of professional development does not guarantee that schools will use these learning opportunities to enhance pedagogy as opposed to test preparation. Although schools should have the flexibility to identify professional development needs, they should be encouraged to participate in professional development opportunities that not only promote learning for individual teachers but also expand school capacity. Professional development activities that promote professional community, strong leadership, program coherence, and information about new forms of technology or material resources have been found to increase a school's capacity and promote desirable pedagogical and organizational outcomes (Newmann et al., 2000). While we saw these forms of professional development at Brookfield, where Ms. Moore and teachers worked collectively to align professional development with the school's instructional program, we saw less evidence of these forms at Cherry Ridge and especially at Hawthorne. Because schools with low levels of capacity are more likely to implement professional development programs that focus on individual learning or isolated aspects of capacity (Newmann et al., 2000), districts need to help schools in developing comprehensive professional development programs that will increase their organizational and relational capacities.

Effective assessment practices. A significant body of research points to the importance of instructional guidance systems that are skillfully implemented to support classroom teaching. This requires a sustained focus on supporting and nurturing good teaching with professional development, curriculum frameworks, accessible materials, and effective assessment practices. As we saw in Chapter 3, however, effective assessment practices are not easily developed. More information is not always helpful, especially if teachers do not know how to use the data to promote learning or if the data are not aligned with the school's instructional program. Districts can help schools develop effective assessment practices through professional development activities that help teachers interpret data and model collaboration in developing instructional responses. Technologies and other technical tools that reduce the burden on teachers of collecting and organizing data can also be useful. Although Stevenson School District provided professional development and technologies to Hawthorne, Brookfield, and Cherry Ridge, there was little modeling of how to actually use assessment data to improve instruction. Studies of assessment practices suggest that the monitoring of student learning can be a powerful component of an instructional guidance system, provided teachers know how to interpret data and work collaboratively to use data to direct instructional resources (Cohen & Spillane, 1992; Sharkey & Murnane, 2006; Shephard, 2001).

Coherent policy environment. Although school districts face pressures based on state and federal policy mandates, they are in a unique position to help shape the policy environments that surround schools. All too often schools face a bewildering array of policy initiatives that divert resources and energy from the central mission of schools—teaching and learning. Stevenson School District was in the midst of a broad range of initiatives the year that we observed the three schools, including new grading and reporting protocols, curriculum frameworks, diagnostic testing regimes, performance management systems, and reading intervention programs. Addressing the uncertainties associated with these new initiatives, along with addressing the pressures of high-stakes testing, proved overwhelming for the teachers at Hawthorne, stressful for the teachers at Cherry Ridge, and frustrating for the teachers at Brookfield. Districts can help schools more successfully address the challenges of high-stakes testing by creating a coherent policy environment that emphasizes capacity building, pedagogical reforms, and accountability for more than just test scores. Initiatives that distract from these fundamental tasks should be reconsidered, rescheduled, and even eliminated. Doing so would help schools weather the pressures of high-stakes testing and pursue the more pedagogically satisfying challenges of standards-based reforms.

State and Federal Policymakers

Accountability is a legitimate concern for the public and policymakers, and performance-based forms of accountability are an important response to that concern. The challenge for state and federal policymakers is to develop accountability systems that promote desirable forms of teaching and learning while safeguarding against the corrosive powers of high-stakes testing. State and federal policymakers can do so by providing support for schools to go beyond raising test scores, permit districts and states to experiment with a broader range of assessment formats, and support research that examines the ways in which high-stakes accountability influences not only achievement but other aspects of school life.

Going beyond test scores. State and federal policymakers can help to promote more rigorous pedagogical reforms by highlighting the importance of going beyond raising test scores. Although schools that raise test scores should be celebrated for their accomplishments, they should also be held accountable for the manner in which they do so. If current accountability measures are not to become a drive to teach to the test, restrict the curriculum, and reduce instruction to fill-in-the-bubble and short-answer practice, state and federal policymakers must make clear that this is not the intent of policies meant to promote greater accountability for school performance. State and federal policymakers can help to identify schools that serve challenging populations that meet AYP *and* provide rich landscapes for learning; they can caution districts and schools against practices that may raise test scores but undermine education; and they can promote policies supportive of the practices that we recommended for schools and districts. By setting aside funding for comprehensive professional development programs designed to build school capacity and promote desirable forms of teaching and learning, state and federal policymakers can help to sustain a focus on the pedagogical reforms at the heart of the standards-based-reform movement. State and federal funding should also support research on schools in different social and organizational contexts that have sustained or implemented successfully pedagogical reforms while meeting AYP. Such schools may serve as illustrative examples of how to address the challenges of high-stakes testing while promoting learner-centered instruction and more desirable forms of learning.

Alternative forms of assessment. States have substantial flexibility in determining assessment formats and thresholds for proficiency. However, many states have opted for standardized assessments and relatively low levels of proficiency (Fuller et al., 2007). Under these circumstances, "teaching to the test" not only sets low standards for teachers and students but also creates an ethical issue about whether schools are being held accountable for relatively high standards for all students (Darling-Hammond, 2004). The current federal requirements for accountability focus on grade-by-grade results without considering the possibility for substantial gains in individual achievement. Alternative assessment models that examine individual learning over time, as opposed to the current grade-cohort models required by NCLB, provide more accurate and pedagogically useful information about individual student learning and the distribution of learning among students at different proficiency levels (Choi, Seltzer, Herman, & Yamashiro, 2007). State and federal policymakers can facilitate the exploration of accountability measures supportive of pedagogical reforms by permitting states to consider alternative forms of assessment and procedures for establishing AYP. By encouraging an examination of alternative forms of assessment, as well as alternative strategies for establishing AYP, state and federal policymakers can reinforce the message that higher test scores are not a substitute for more meaningful forms of learning.

Research on the effects of high-stakes testing. We have argued that high-stakes testing has the potential for being a powerfully corrosive influence on pedagogical practice. Nonetheless, little research has been focused on the possible negative effects of high-stake accountability, particularly current forms of accountability that emphasize increasing test scores. State and federal policymakers can promote more meaningful forms of teaching and learning by supporting research that examines the consequences of high-stakes testing for the quality of school life, including school climate, teacher satisfaction, pedagogical practices, and students' orientation to learning. Although current policies support research on what might be termed "best practices," less support is available for researchers who desire to investigate the "unintended consequences" of high-stakes accountability. If state and federal policymakers are unwilling to consider the possibility that current actions encourage undesirable forms of teaching and learning, administrators and teachers are also unlikely to do so. Ultimately, the goal of standards-based reforms is to enhance the educational opportunities afforded all children. If we do not consider the quality of those opportunities, we fail to address the ultimate challenge—creating more meaningful and equitable opportunities for teaching and learning.

Key School Personnel

	Hawthorne	Brookfield	Cherry Ridge
Principal	Elaine Everett	Liz Moore	Julia Hancock
Assistant principal *or* principal intern	Adam Fox	Luke Comer	Bonnie Strauss
Staff developer	Melodie Newkirk	Lottie Breman	Carrie Bristol *(fall)* Jodie Foster *(spring)*
Reading specialist	Heather Nichols	Karen Mcneil	Opal Kladowski
Math content coach	Greta Shephard	Laura Seibert	Amy Odett
Fourth-grade teachers	Joy Karlsen Anita Sanchez Sheila Wolfe Laura Zwiller	Emma Hinton Pat Kim	Gayle Peterson Barry Mott Vicky Winchester
Fifth-grade teachers	Amber Keats Brandon Mitchell Mona Olson Charles Swindell	Leslie Gabriel Eddie Wilson	Nora Clemson Lisa Franklin *(reading)* Cecilia Kelley Patty Simpson
Special education and academic support teachers	Nicky Turner Vicki Romero Melissa Boyer	Clarice Grant Evelyn Keller	Chavaun Baker Maria Escabar
ESOL teachers	Ruthann West Donna Nestie	Mia Butler Malinda Marek	Allison Koors Lena Varner
Data team chair			Carmen Ledwich

Notes

Chapter 1

1. Performance standards and the actual application of sanctions vary, sometimes dramatically, between states. Nonetheless, NCLB requires a level of accountability for schools that far exceeds the requirements of previous federal legislation (McGuinn, 2006).

2. See Croninger & Valli (forthcoming) for more detailed information about the larger study.

3. Throughout the book, we use the school district's official language and categories to describe student populations. We provide more detailed information about each school later in this chapter.

4. Numbers and percentages reported in Table 1.1 have been rounded to protect the identity of the school district and schools.

5. Under NCLB, states may create exceptions—safe harbors—for schools that generally meet AYP but barely fail in one or more categories. In the case of Hawthorne, although it failed to meet AYP for two subpopulations, the percentage of students who failed to reach proficiency declined by at least 10%. Consequently, as determined by the state's safe harbor provision, Hawthorne was deemed to have met AYP for its ESOL and special education populations.

Chapter 2

1. NCLB requires each state to establish statewide annual measurable objectives (AMOs). Set separately for each tested area (i.e., reading and mathematics), AMOs identify the minimum percentage of students required to meet or exceed the proficient level on the state assessment. To move toward the requirement that all students be proficient by the 2013–14 school year, AMOs increase, sometimes substantially, from one year to the next. For example, in 2003–04, AMOs for Hawthorne, Brookfield, and Cherry Ridge were only 2–3% higher than they were the previous year. But in 2004–05, the year of our study, AMOs increased 9.5% in reading and 11.5% in mathematics.

2. "Double-dipping" was a term used for supplemental instruction. Students were taken out of classes in other subjects to receive additional instructional time in reading or mathematics.

3. Test accommodations, or adjustments, are made for students with disabilities and English Language Learners in order to provide equity and help ensure test validity by eliminating irrelevant obstacles to test performance. Because NCLB requires that students be included in statewide assessment programs "to the fullest extent possible," states develop policies for the selection, administration, and evaluation of these accommodations. Accommodations might include allowing extra time, offering bilingual dictionaries, providing a reader or scribe, or changing the test location. Before they are approved for testing purposes, accommodations must be based on each student's individual needs, documented, and used during classroom instruction.

Chapter 5

1. This framework for understanding poverty has been criticized by some for perpetuating negative and simplistic notions of a culture of poverty (see, for example, Gorski, 2006). One of the sessions we observed seemed to reinforce social-class stereotypes by informing teachers that children of poverty were "reactive, nonverbal, and concrete thinkers." The school's goal, and way to promote excellence and equity, was to help them become more like middle-class students: "proactive, verbal, and abstract thinkers" (November 15, 2004).

Chapter 7

1. We acknowledge Maxine Greene's (1978) initial use of this and related metaphors used in this chapter.

References

Alexander, P., & Murphy, P. K. (1998). The research base for APA's learner-centered psychological principles. In N. Lambert & B. L. McCombs (Eds.), *How students learn: Reforming schools through learner-centered education* (pp. 25–60). Washington, DC: American Psychological Association.

Alexander, P., & Riconscente, M. (2005). A matter of proof: Why achievement/learning. In J. Carlson & J. Levin (Eds.), *The No Child Left Behind legislation: Educational research and federal funding* (pp. 27–36). Charlotte, NC: Information Age Publishing.

Au, W. (2007). High-stakes testing and curricular control: A qualitative meta-synthesis. *Educational Researcher, 36,* 258–267.

Bailey, G., Shaw, E., & Hollifield, D. (2006). The devaluation of social studies in the elementary grades. *Journal of Social Studies Research, 30*(2), 18–29.

Balfanz, R. (2006). Closing the mathematics achievement gap in high-poverty middle schools: Enablers and constraints. *Journal of Education for Students Placed at Risk, 11*(2), 143–159.

Barr, R., & Dreeben, R. (1983). *How schools work.* Chicago: University of Chicago Press.

Bidwell, C. (2001). Analyzing schools as organizations: Long-term permanence and short-term change. *Sociology of Education, 74*(Extra Issue), 100–114.

Biesta, G. (2004). Education, accountability, and the ethical demand: Can the democratic potential of accountability be regained? *Educational Theory, 54*(3), 233–250.

Black, P., & Wiliam, D. (1998a). Assessment and classroom learning. *Assessment in Education, 5*(1), 7–74.

Black, P., & Wiliam, D. (1998b). Inside the black box: Raising standards through classroom assessment. *Phi Delta Kappan, 80*(2), 139–148.

Boardman, A. G., & Woodruff, A. (2004). Teacher change and "high-stakes" assessment: What happens to professional development? *Teaching and Teacher Education, 20*(6), 545–557.

Brabham, E. G., & Villaume, S. K. (2000). Questions and answers: Continuing conversations about literature circles. *The Reading Teacher, 54*(3), 278–280.

Bransford, J., Brown, L., & Cocking, R. (1999). *How people learn: Brain, mind, experience, and school.* Washington, DC: National Academy Press.

Bryk, A., & Schneider, B. (2002). *Trust in schools: A core resource for improvement.* New York: Russell Sage.

Cawelti, G. (2006). The side effects of NCLB. *Educational Leadership, 64*(3), 64–68.

Center on Education Policy. (2006, March). *From the capital to the classroom: Year 4 of the No Child Left Behind Act.* Washington, DC: Center on Education Policy.

Center on Education Policy. (2007a, May). *Answering the question that matters most: Has student achievement increased since No Child Left Behind?* Washington, DC: Center for Education Policy.

Center on Education Policy. (2007b, July). *Choices, changes, and challenges: Curriculum and instruction in the NCLB era.* Washington, DC: Center on Education Policy.

Center on Education Policy. (2007c, August). *Reauthorizing the Elementary and Secondary Education Act of 1965: Recommendations from the Center on Education Policy.* Washington, DC: Center on Education Policy.

Chall, J. S., & Jacobs, V. A. (2003, Spring). Poor children's fourth-grade slump. *American Educator, 27*(14–15), 44.

Chall, J. S., Jacobs, V. A., & Baldwin, L. E. (1991). *The reading crisis. Why poor children fall behind.* Cambridge, MA: Harvard University Press.

Choi, K., Seltzer, M., Herman, J., & Yamashiro, K. (2007). Children left behind in AYP and Non-AYP schools: Using student progress and the distribution of student gains to validate AYP. *Educational Measurement Issues and Practice, 26*(3), 21–32.

Coburn, C. (2006). Framing the problem of reading instruction: Using frame analysis to uncover the microprocesses of policy implementation. *American Educational Research Journal, 43*(3), 343–379.

Coburn, C., & Talbert, J. (2006). Conceptions of evidence use in school districts: Mapping the Terrain. *American Journal of Education, 112*(4), 469–495.

Cohen, D. K., & Hill, H. (2000). Instructional policy and classroom performance: The mathematics reform in California. *Teachers College Record, 102*(2), 294–343.

Cohen, D. K., & Spillane, J. P. (1992). Policy and practice: The relations between governance and instruction. In L. Darling-Hammond (Ed.), *Review of Research in Education* (Vol. 18, pp. 3–49). Washington, DC: American Educational Research Association.

Cohen, M., & Kottkamp, R. (1993). *Teachers: The missing voice in education.* Albany: State University of New York Press.

Croninger, R. G., & Valli, L. (Eds.). (Forthcoming). The challenges of studying teaching in schools (Special issue). *Teachers College Record.*

Croninger, R. G., Valli, L., & Price, J. (2003, April). Mapping the policy environment for high-quality teaching. Can we get there from here? In S. Dalton (Chair), *High-stakes accountability and high-quality teaching: Reconcilable or irreconcilable differences?* Symposium conducted at the meeting of the American Educational Research Association, Chicago, IL.

Darling-Hammond, L. (1997). *The right to learn: A blueprint for creating schools that work.* San Francisco: Jossey-Bass.

Darling-Hammond, L. (2004). From "separate but equal" to "no child left behind": The collision of new standards and old inequalities. In D. Meier & G. Wood (Eds.), *Many children left behind* (pp. 3–32). Boston: Beacon Press.

Darling-Hammond, L. (2007). Standards, accountability, and school reform. In C. Sleeter (Ed.), *Facing accountability in education: Democracy and equity at risk* (pp. 78–111). New York: Teachers College Press.

Deal, T., & Peterson, K. (2003). *Shaping school culture: The heart of leadership*. San Francisco: Jossey-Bass.

Desimone, L., Porter, A. C., Birman, B. F., Garet, M. S., & Yoon, K. S. (2002). How do district management and implementation strategies relate to the quality of professional development that districts provide to teachers? *Teachers College Record, 104*(7), 1265–1312.

Dilworth, M., & Brown, C. (2001). Consider the difference. Teaching and learning in culturally rich schools. In V. Richardson (Ed.), *Handbook of research on teaching* (pp. 643–667). Washington, DC: American Educational Research Association.

Elmore, R. F. (2005). Agency, reciprocity, and accountability in democratic education. In S. Fuhrman & M. Lazerson (Eds.), *American institutions of democracy: The public schools* (pp. 277–301). Oxford, England: Oxford University Press.

Fenstermacher, G. (1979). Educational accountability: Features of a concept. *Theory into Practice, 18*(5), 330–335.

Fenstermacher, G. D., & Richardson, V. (2005). On making determinations of quality in teaching. *Teachers College Record, 107*(1), 186–213.

Firestone, W. A., Mayrowetz, D., & Fairman, J. (1998). Performance-based assessment and instructional change: The effects of testing in Maine and Maryland. *Educational Evaluation and Policy Analysis, 20*(2), 95–114.

Firestone, W., Monfils, L., Hayes, M., Polovsky, T., Martinez, M. C., & Hicks, J. (2004). The principal, test preparation, and educational reform. In W. Firestone, R. Schorr, & L. Monfils (Eds.), *The ambiguity of teaching to the test: Standards, assessment, and educational reform* (pp. 91–112). Mahwah, NJ: Lawrence Erlbaum.

Firestone, W., Monfils, L., Schorr, R., Hicks, J., & Martinez, M. C. (2004). Pressure and support. In W. Firestone, R. Schorr, & L. Monfils (Eds.), *The ambiguity of teaching to the test: Standards, assessment, and educational reform* (pp. 63–89). Mahwah, NJ: Lawrence Erlbaum.

Firestone, W. A., Schorr, R. Y., & Monfils, L. F. (Eds.) (2004). *The ambiguity of teaching to the test: Standards, assessment, and educational reform*. Mahwah, New Jersey: Lawrence Erlbaum Associates.

Fountas, I. C., & Pinnell, G. S. (2001). *Guiding readers and writers: Teaching comprehension, genre, and content literacy*. Portsmouth, NH: Heinemann.

Fuller, B., Wright, J., Gesicki, K., & Kang, E. (2007). Gauging growth: How to judge No Child Left Behind? *Educational Researcher, 36*(5), 268–278.

Fulton, M. (2007, September). *ECS Briefing Report: Who says what about NCLB reauthorization. ECLS NCLB reauthorization database*. Denver, CO: Education Commission of the States.

Gamoran, A., Secada, W., & Marrett, C. (2000). The organizational context of teaching and learning: Changing theoretical perspectives. In M. Hallinan (Ed.), *Handbook of the sociology of education* (pp. 37–63). New York: Springer.

Gersten, R., Baker, S., & Pugach, M. (with Scanlon, D., & Chard, D.). (2001). Contemporary research on special education teaching. In V. Richardson (Ed.), *Handbook of research on teaching* (pp. 695–722). Washington, DC: American Educational Research Association.

Goetz, M. E. (2001, September). Redefining government roles in an era of standards-based reform. *Phi Delta Kappan, 83,* 62–66.

Goodlad, J. (1984). *A place called school: Prospects for the future.* New York: McGraw Hill.

Gorski, P. (2006, February 9). The classist underpinnings of Ruby Payne's framework [Post]. *Teachers College Record.* Retrieved September 9, 2007, from http://www.tcrecord.org

Graham, P. (1993). What America has expected of its schools over the past century. *American Journal of Education, 101*(2), 83–98.

Graham, S., & Harris, K. (2000). Helping children who experience reading difficulties: Prevention and intervention. In L. Baker, M. J. Dreher, & J. T. Guthrie (Eds.), *Engaging young readers: Promoting achievement and motivation* (pp. 44–67). New York: Guilford.

Greene, M. (1978). *Landscapes of learning.* New York: Teachers College Press.

Guthrie, J., Cox, K., Knowles, K., Buehl, M., Mazzoni, S., & Fasulo, L. (2000). Building toward coherent instruction. In L. Baker, M. J. Dreher, & J. Guthrie (Eds.), *Engaging young readers: Promoting achievement and motivation* (pp. 209–236). New York: Guilford Press.

Hamilton, M. L., & Richardson, V. (1995). Effects of the culture in two schools on the process and outcomes of staff development. *Elementary School Journal, 95*(4), 367–385.

Hargreaves, A. (1994). *Changing teachers, changing times: Teachers' work and culture in the postmodern age.* New York: Teachers College Press.

Hawley, W., & Valli, L. (1999). The essentials of effective professional development: A new consensus. In L. Darling-Hammond & G. Sykes (Eds.), *Teaching as the learning profession: Handbook of policy and practice* (pp. 127–150). San Francisco: Jossey-Bass.

Hawley, W., & Valli, L. (2007). Design principles for learner-centered professional development. In W. Hawley (Ed.), *The keys to effective schools* (2nd ed.). Thousand Oaks, CA: Corwin Press.

Huberman, A. M. (1993). *The lives of teachers.* New York: Teachers College Press.

Ingram, D., Louis, K. S., & Schroeder, R. (2004). Accountability policies and teacher decision making: Barriers to the use of data to improve practice. *Teachers College Record, 106*(6), 1258–1287.

International Reading Association & National Council of Teachers of English. (1996). *Standards for the English language arts: A project of International Reading Association and National Council of Teachers of English.* Newark, DE & Urbana, IL: Author.

Jackson, P. W. (1986). *The practice of teaching.* New York: Teachers College Press.

James, J. (2006). *Care in the lives of women teachers.* University of Maryland: Unpublished dissertation.

Jones, R., & Thomas, T. (2006). Leave no discipline behind. *Reading Teacher, 60*(1), 58–64.

Kerr, K. A., Marsh, J. A., Ikemoto, G. S., Darilek, H., & Barney, H. (2006). Strategies to promote data use for instructional improvement: Actions, outcomes, and lessons from three urban districts. *American Journal of Education, 112*(4), 496–520.

Kilpatrick, J., Swafford, J., & Findell, B. (Eds.). (2001). *Adding it up: Helping children learn mathematics*. Washington, DC: National Academy Press.

Lortie, D. (1975). *Schoolteacher: A sociological study*. Chicago: University of Chicago Press.

Malen, B., & Rice, J. K. (2004). Framework for assessing the impact of educational reforms on school capacity: Insights from studies of high-stakes accountability initiatives. *Educational Policy, 18*(5), 631–660.

McDonnell, L. (2005). No Child Left Behind and the federal role in education: Evolution or revolution? *Peabody Journal of Education, 80*(2), 19–38.

McGuinn, P. J. (2006). *No Child Left Behind and the transformation of federal education policy, 1965–2005*. Lawrence: University Press of Kansas.

Mercado, C. (2001). The learning: "Race," "ethnicity," and linguistic difference. In V. Richardson (Ed.), *Handbook of research on teaching* (pp. 668–694). Washington, DC: American Educational Research Association.

Mintrop, H. (2004). High-stakes accountability, state oversight, and educational equity. *Teachers College Record, 106*(11), 2128–2145.

National Council of Teachers of Mathematics. (2000). *Principles and standards for school mathematics*. Reston, VA: National Council of Teachers of Mathematics.

National Council of Teachers of Mathematics. (2006). *Curriculum focal points for prekindergarten through grade 8 mathematics: A quest for coherence*. Reston, VA: National Council of Teachers of Mathematics.

Newmann, F., King, M. B., & Youngs, P. (2000). Professional development that addresses school capacity: Lessons from urban elementary schools. *American Journal of Education, 108*, 259–299.

Newmann, F., Smith, B., Allensworth, E., & Byrk, A. (2001). Instructional program coherence: What it is and why it should guide school improvement policy. *Educational Evaluation and Policy Analysis, 23*, 297–321.

Nichols, S. L., & Berliner, D. C. (2007). *Collateral damage: How high-stakes testing corrupts America's schools*. Cambridge, MA: Harvard Education Press.

No Child Left Behind Act. (2001). Public Law 107-110.

Noddings, N. (2007). *When school reforms goes wrong*. New York: Teachers College Press.

Noe, K. S., & Johnson, N. J. (1999). *Getting started with literature circles*. Norwood, MA: Christopher-Gordon.

O'Day, J. (2002). Complexity, accountability, and school improvement. *Harvard Educational Review, 72*(3), 293–329.

O'Day, J., & Smith, M. (1993). Systemic school reform and educational opportunity. In S. Fuhrman (Ed.), *Designing coherent education policy: Improving the system* (pp. 250–311). San Francisco: Jossey-Bass.

Ogle, D. M. (1986). K-W-L: A teaching model that develops active reading of expository text. *Reading Teacher, 39,* 564–570.

Page, R. (1990). Cultures and curricula: Differences between and within schools. *Educational Foundations, 4*(1), 49–76.

Page, R. (1991). *Lower-track classrooms: A curricular and cultural perspective.* New York: Teachers College Press.

Patton, M. Q. (1990). *Qualitative evaluation and research methods* (2nd ed.). Newbury Park, CA: Sage.

Payne, R. (1996). *A framework for understanding poverty.* Highlands, TX: aha! Process, Inc.

Perlstein, L. (2007). *Tested: One American school struggles to make the grade.* New York: Henry Holt.

Popham, W. J. (2003). Preparing for the coming avalanche of accountability tests. In *Spotlight on high-stakes testing* (pp. 37–44). Boston: Harvard Education Press.

Porter, A. (1989). A curriculum out of balance: The case of elementary school mathematics. *Educational Researcher, 18*(5), 9–15.

Rinke, C., & Valli, L. (in press). Making adequate yearly progress: Teacher learning in school-based, accountability contexts. *Teachers College Record.*

Rosenholtz, S. (1991). *Teachers' workplace: The social organization of schools.* New York: Teachers College Press.

Rothstein, R. (2004). *Class and schools: Using social, economic, and educational reform to close the black-white achievement gap.* New York: Teachers College Press.

Rowan, B., & Miskel, C. (1999). Institutional theory and the study of educational organizations. In J. Murphy & K. S. Louis (Eds.), *Handbook of research on educational administration* (2nd ed., pp. 359–383). San Francisco: Jossey-Bass.

Rudalevige, A. (2003). No Child Left Behind: Forging a congressional compromise. In P. E. Peterson & M. R. Wes (Eds.), *No child left behind? The politics and practice of school accountability* (pp. 23–54). Washington, DC: Brookings.

Sarason, S. (1971). *The culture of the school and the problem of change.* Boston: Allyn and Bacon.

Schubert, W. (1986). *Curriculum: Perspective, paradigm, and possibility.* New York: MacMillan.

Scott, W. R. (2001). *Institutions and organizations.* Thousand Oaks, CA: Sage.

Sedlak, M. W., Wheeler, C. W., Pullin, D. C., & Cusick, P. A. (1986). *Selling students short: Classroom bargains and academic reform in the American high school.* New York: Teachers College Press.

Sharkey, N. S., & Murnane, R. J. (2006). Tough choices in designing a formative assessment system. *American Journal of Education, 112*(4), 572–588.

Shepard, L. (2001). The role of classroom assessment in teaching and learning. In V. Richardson (Ed.), *Handbook of research on teaching* (4th ed., pp. 1066–1101). Washington, DC: American Educational Research Association.

Sleeter, C. E., & Stillman, J. (2007). Navigating accountability pressures. In C. E. Sleeter (Ed.), *Facing accountability in education: Democracy and equity at risk* (pp. 13–29). New York: Teachers College Press.

Spellings, M. (2007, January). *Building on results: A blueprint for strengthening the No Child Left Behind Act.* Washington DC: U.S. Department of Education.

Spillane, J. P. (2002). Local theories of teacher change: The pedagogy of district policies and programs. *Teachers College Record, 104*(3), 377–420.

Spillane, J. P. (2005). Primary school leadership practice: How the subject matters. *School Leadership and Management, 25*(4), 383–397.

Spillane, J., & Jennings, N. (1997). Aligned instructional policy and ambitious pedagogy: Exploring instructional reform from the classroom perspective. *Teachers College Record, 98*(3), 449–481.

Sunderman, G., Kim, J., & Orfield, G. (2005). *NCLB meets school realities: Lessons from the field.* Thousand Oaks, CA: Corwin.

Sunderman, G., Tracey, C. A., Kim, J., & Orfield, G. (2004, September). *Listening to teachers: Classroom realities and No Child Left Behind.* Cambridge, MA: The Civil Rights Project at Harvard University.

Tom, A. (1984). *Teaching as a moral craft.* New York: Longman.

Valenzuela, A. (2005). *Leaving children behind: How "Texas-style" accountability fails Latino youth.* Albany, NY: SUNY Press.

Valli, L. (1986). *Becoming clerical workers.* London: Routledge & Kegan Paul.

Valli, L., & Buese, D. (2007). The changing roles of teachers in an era of high-stakes accountability. *American Educational Research Journal, 44*(3), 519–558.

Valli, L., & Chambliss, M. (2007). Creating classroom cultures: One teacher, two lessons, and a high-stakes test. *Anthropology and Education Quarterly, 38*(1), 42–60.

Valli, L., Croninger, R., & Walters, K. (2007). Who (else) is the teacher? A cautionary note on accountability systems. *American Journal of Education, 113*(4), 635–662.

Waller, W. (1932). *The sociology of teaching.* New York: Wiley & Sons.

Wayman, J., & Stringfield, S. (2006). Technology-supported involvement of entire faculties in examination of student data for instructional improvement. *American Journal of Education, 112*(4), 549–571.

Young, V. (2006). Teachers use of data: Loose coupling, agenda setting, and team norms. *American Journal of Education, 112*(4), 521–548.

About the Authors

LINDA VALLI is the inaugural Jeffrey and David Mullan Professor in Teacher Education–Professional Development at the University of Maryland, College Park. As a faculty member in the Department of Curriculum and Instruction, she works with preservice, inservice, and doctoral students, preparing them to study schooling practices as well as their own teaching. After receiving her PhD from the University of Wisconsin, Madison, she served as Director of Teacher Education at the Catholic University of America. Her other books include *Becoming Clerical Workers, Reflective Teacher Education: Cases and Critiques,* and (with Reba Page) *Curriculum Differentiation*; and her research articles have appeared in the *American Educational Research Journal, American Journal of Education, Teaching and Teacher Education, Anthropology and Education Quarterly,* and other refereed journals. Her research interests include teacher learning, teaching practices, school improvement, and cultural diversity.

ROBERT G. CRONINGER is an associate professor in education policy studies at the University of Maryland, College Park, where he also serves as the Director of the Center for Education Policy and Leadership. His scholarship focuses on the social context of schooling, research methods and policy analysis, school reform and policy implementation, teaching and teacher qualifications, and the distribution of educational opportunities. His research has appeared in the *Teachers College Record, Sociology of Education, Economics of Education Review, American Journal of Education, American Educational Research Journal,* and *Educational Evaluation and Policy Analysis.* Croninger received his PhD in education studies from the University of Michigan.

MARILYN J. CHAMBLISS is an associate professor in the Department of Curriculum and Instruction, University of Maryland, College Park. She graduated from Stanford University in 1990 and has had an abiding interest in studying effective instructional practices in reading instruction. She is the co-author (with Robert Calfee) of *Textbooks for Learning: Nurturing Children's Minds* and has published book chapters and articles in such journals as

Educational Psychologist, Reading Research Quarterly, Discourse Processes, and *Written Communication* on the relationships among writing quality, curricular integrity, and student learning.

ANNA O. GRAEBER is Associate Professor Emerita in the Department of Curriculum and Instruction at the University of Maryland, College Park. After receiving her EdD from Teachers College, Columbia University, she served as a writer, editor, and Associate Director of Basic Skills at Research for Better Schools in Philadelphia. Mathematics education is her specialty area, and her specific research interests include mathematics teacher education and (mis)conceptions in mathematics. Her research articles have appeared in the *Journal for Research in Mathematics Education, Educational Studies in Mathematics,* the *Journal of Mathematical Behavior,* and other refereed journals. Recently she has also written chapters (with Dina Tirosh) for the *Second International Handbook of Mathematics Education* and the *International Handbook of Mathematics Teacher Education.*

DARIA BUESE is an assistant professor and Coordinator for Curriculum and Instruction in Graduate and Professional Studies at McDaniel College in Westminster, Maryland. She received her PhD in education policy, planning, and administration from the University of Maryland, where she also held positions as research associate and lecturer. With research interests in education policy and its impact on classroom practices, she co-authored "The Changing Roles of Teachers in an Era of High-Stakes Accountability," which appeared in the *American Educational Research Journal* special issue on No Child Left Behind.

Index

Accountability: and becoming test managers, 49; benefits of, 159–60; and capacity, 160; concerns about, 157, 159, 160, 174; and creating a test-taking culture, 36, 41, 44, 46–47; and educational reform, 1; and erosion of quality teaching, 125, 128, 130, 131, 137, 138, 154, 155, 160; and expectations for American education, 23; and failure of American education, 2; findings concerning, 157–58, 161–69; forms of, 160–61, 169; impact of high-stakes testing on, 156–74; and NCLB, 2, 3, 24, 154, 158, 159; and professional development, 99, 103, 119, 121, 122; recommendations concerning, 160–61, 169–74; and state and federal policies, 172–74; support for high-stakes testing, 159; and teacher stress, 153–54; "unintended consequences" of, 174; weathering high-stakes testing, 157–74

Achievement: and creating a test-taking culture, 32, 36, 46; and erosion of quality teaching, 154; and expectations for American education, 23; findings concerning, 161, 162, 163; impact of high-stakes testing on, 158; individual, 173; and policy context, 9; recommendations concerning, 173; and support for NCLB, 158

Administrators, 17, 38–39, 74, 76, 95, 96, 102, 117. *See also* Principals; *specific person*

Alexander, P., 4, 25, 95, 141, 160

Allensworth, E., 73, 95

American Psychological Association, 4

Annual Measurable Objectives (AMO), 44–45

Assessment: alignment of curriculum and, 154; and alignment of state policies and NCLB, 8; alternative forms of, 173; and creating a test-taking culture, 35; and erosion of quality teaching, 125, 155; flexibility in, 159, 172; frequency of, 9; and impact of NCLB, 3; recommendations concerning, 171–72, 173; and research methodology, 7. *See also* High-stakes testing; State test; *type of assessment*

Attendance, 23, 44, 46

Au, W., 74, 158

Autonomy, 70, 71, 76–77, 110, 137–38

Bailey, G., 28, 74, 158

Baker, Chavaun, 149

Baker, S., 154

Baldrige system, 9–10, 37, 38, 42, 43, 100, 109, 117

Baldwin, L. E., 4

Balfanz, R., 4

Barnes, William, 8, 76

Barney, H., 50

Barr, R., 25

Batori, Melany, 89, 116, 119–20

Berliner, D. C., 158, 159

Bidwell, C., 13

Biesta, G., 46–47

Birman, B. F., 98

Black, P., 25, 48, 49, 71, 136–37, 164

Boardman, A. G., 119

Brabham, E. G., 103

Bransford, J., 4, 25, 95, 140

Breman, Lottie, 51, 64, 89, 109, 110, 111, 113, 115, 144

Tests (*continued*)
  teacher responses to, 53–56; volume
  of, 50. *See also type of test or specific test*
Thomas, T., 28
Time: and alignment of state tests and
  curriculum, 74, 83, 84, 86; and
  becoming test managers, 50, 52, 54,
  57–58, 61, 63, 64, 65, 72; and creating
  a test-taking culture, 25–31, 32, 41–43,
  47; and erosion of quality teaching,
  142–43, 146, 152; findings concerning,
  162; and functions of testing, 49; and
  professional development, 100, 118,
  122; recommendations concerning,
  170; repurposing, 41–43
Title I: and alignment of NCLB and state
  and district policies, 9; and becoming
  test managers, 59; and creating a test-
  taking culture, 26, 32, 34; and NCLB
  as expansion of federal control of
  schools, 2; and professional development, 99–100, 101, 115–16, 117, 122;
  and school profiles, 12, 19
Tom, A., 25–26
Tracey, C. A., 2, 158
"Trainer of trainers" model, 57, 72, 98,
  99, 100, 105, 117
Training: and alignment of state tests and
  curriculum, 87; and becoming test
  managers, 50, 51, 54, 56–62, 63, 72;
  cramming test-oriented, 105–8, 122,
  167–68; maximizing of test-oriented,
  119–21; transforming test-oriented,
  113–15, 122. *See also* Professional
  development
Turner, Nicky, 134, 135, 137

Unit tests, 52, 54, 55, 60–61, 63, 68, 82–
  83, 96, 135
U.S. Department of Education, 48

Valenzuela, A., 44
Valli, L., 1, 24, 25, 26, 41, 49, 66, 98, 106,
  114, 121, 140, 142, 146
Villaume, S. K., 103

"Walk-throughs," 39–41
Waller, W., 24
Walters, K., 66
Wayman, J., 62
Wheeler, C. W., 184
Wiliam, D., 25, 48, 49, 71, 136–37, 164
Wilson, Eddie, 79, 109, 140, 144, 146
Winchester, Vicky, 70–71, 91–92, 118,
  149–50
Wolfe, Sheila, 84
Woodruff, A., 119
Wright, J., 2, 173
Writing: and alignment of state tests and
  curriculum, 89, 93–94, 95–96; and
  creating a test-taking culture, 32, 33,
  34, 36, 43; and erosion of quality
  teaching, 142, 148–49, 152–53; and
  professional development, 109, 111–
  12, 113, 115, 123. *See also* Six Traits
  of Writing

Yamashiro, K., 173
Yoon, K. S., 98
Young, V., 72
Youngs, P., 13, 100, 171

Zwiller, Laura, 82, 132, 138